I07928833

IMAGES
of America

JEFFERSON COUNTY

On the Cover: The discovery of gold and other ore in Montana brought miners to Jefferson County with the hope that their fortunes would be found. The economy of Jefferson County depended on men who were willing to go down into the tunnels to find riches. (Courtesy of the Jefferson County Museum.)

IMAGES
of America

JEFFERSON COUNTY

Susanna M. Lindsay and the
Jefferson County Museum

ARCADIA
PUBLISHING

ISBN 978-0-7385-7035-8

Published by Arcadia Publishing
Charleston SC, Chicago IL, Portsmouth NH, San Francisco CA

Printed in the United States of America

Library of Congress Control Number: 2009920004

For all general information contact Arcadia Publishing at:
Telephone 843-853-2070
Fax 843-853-0044
E-mail sales@arcadiapublishing.com
For customer service and orders:
Toll-Free 1-888-313-2665

Visit us on the Internet at www.arcadiapublishing.com

To the late Paul E. Baum for sharing all those wonderful stories

Contents

Acknowledgments		6
Introduction		7
1.	Gold in the Hills	9
2.	The Silver Boom	21
3.	Riding the Rails	31
4.	Educational Opportunities	41
5.	Business and Commerce	55
6.	Stately Architecture	79
7.	Picnics and Parties	91
8.	Taking the Waters	107
Bibliography		127

ACKNOWLEDGMENTS

I would like to thank all of those donors who contributed to the Jefferson County Museum's photograph collection. Without those historic pictures, this book would not have been possible. I especially want to thank the late Olive Hagadone for keeping the history of Jefferson County alive through her writings.

In addition, I wish to thank Ellen Rae Thiel of the Jefferson County Genealogy and Heritage Center for sharing her knowledge of local history. She selflessly gave up her time to support this project. Also, I wish to thank the board members of the Jefferson County Genealogy and Heritage Center in Boulder for the use of their collection of photographs.

Finally, thanks to my family for their patience while I worked to complete this book.

INTRODUCTION

Jefferson County was one of the original counties created when the first Montana Territory Legislature met at Bannock in the winter of 1864–1865. Although the county boundaries have changed slightly since then, the development of the towns within the county changed significantly. Many early settlers came to Jefferson County in search of gold. Mining camps grew into more permanent towns that provided an array of services for Jefferson County residents. Soon the railroads brought the towns together. Boulder became the seat of government for Jefferson County, Elk Park prospered as a local dairy community, Whitehall shipped mining ore and supplies from its new Northern Pacific roundhouse, and the economic base of Jefferson County expanded when rich mineral deposits were discovered in Basin, Clancy, and Elkhorn.

Even before the first lawmakers convened in the new Montana Territory, settlers built a stage station on the Virginia City–to–Fort Benton road about 7 miles from Butte. They named the new stage station Whitehall. One early pioneer, Alexander Toponce, lived near Whitehall and operated a freighting business along the Virginia City–to–Fort Benton road. According to his autobiography, in just two years, he earned $100,000 transporting supplies from Salt Lake City to Virginia City and then to Fort Benton. The freight business was an important part of the economy of Montana. Without trains to bring fresh food, clothing, and mining supplies, the freight wagons ensured that people had the essentials. In 1899, the stage station closed when the Northern Pacific Railroad built a roundhouse in Whitehall. The new Northern Pacific line allowed Whitehall residents to receive goods and supplies easier than during the years when they relied on freighters traveling along the Virginia City–to–Fort Benton road. In addition, the easy access to rail travel ensured that mined products from the nearby Mayflower Mine were quickly transported across the United States.

While Whitehall grew as a center for railroad commerce, early Montana pioneer W. J. Ward settled in nearby Elk Park in 1879. Elk Park, located just north of Butte, was a wide valley flanked by mountains and blanketed with thick forests. By 1883, Ward and 170 other residents lived in the Elk Park area, and a post office, hotel, lumberyard, butcher, barber, and saloon were built. Logging and ice collection were some of the first industries in Elk Park. Later, families from Switzerland arrived, bringing with them dairy cattle. Soon the families in Elk Park provided fresh milk and sour cream to the Butte mines. According to author Joan Filpula in her book *Woodville—Trask and the Elk Park Valley*, Battista Strozzi left Switzerland in 1876 as a stowaway on a boat headed for America. He was just 14 years old. He hid in the boat's cargo hold with six dairy cows. Battista survived the journey on the cows' milk. In 1884, he moved to Elk Park and began a dairy. He owned 65 cows that were milked by hand every day. After milking, he hauled the fresh dairy products down to Butte with a team of horses. Soon his neighbors, the Parinis, also had a dairy farm with 100 Holsteins and 17 horses. Transportation of the milk by horse-drawn wagon was slow, but the dairy business provided a stable economy for the residents of Elk Park.

During the years when the southern portion of Jefferson County developed as a center for railroad commerce and dairy production, the area surrounding the town of Boulder developed into an agricultural community. The town of Boulder began as a main stop on the Virginia City–to–Fort Benton stagecoach line when early freighters settled in the Boulder Valley. Miners who initially moved into the area to try their hand at placer mining along the Boulder River gradually began using their land for cattle and sheep. Before long, ranches sprang up along the Boulder River Valley. In 1883, Boulder was chosen as the permanent location for the county government, and a courthouse was constructed in 1888. The establishment of the county seat for local government offered dependable employment to Boulder residents.

Historically, the Elkhorn mining district was connected to Boulder by a spur line of the Northern Pacific Railway constructed in 1887. The town of Elkhorn grew up around the Elkhorn Mine, which began producing silver ore in 1875. By 1891, seventy-six men worked in the mine. The U.S. Geological Survey Bulletin reported in 1900 that the Elkhorn Mining Company had produced 8,902,000 ounces of silver. The hardworking men who lived in Elkhorn brought their families to join them. The population of Elkhorn grew to around 2,500 by the late 1880s. Unfortunately, it was a hard life for families, especially children. When diphtheria swept through the town, most of the little children died. The cemetery reminded young families that life was short in Elkhorn.

In addition to Elkhorn, silver was discovered in the northern portion of Jefferson County in the little town of Clancy around 1865. The Legal Tender Mine was the most prolific of the silver mines in Clancy, producing around $1 million in total revenue until water filled the main shaft. In addition to the silver mines that dotted the Clancy hillsides, residents were able to work for the Montana Central Railway when a station was built in Clancy to store helper engines for use on the steep track between Clancy and Elk Park. After the silver market collapsed, many Clancy landowners turned to agriculture and ranching.

Although the mines in Elkhorn and Clancy primarily produced silver ore, the establishment of the town of Basin resulted from the large quantity of placer mines found nearby. Basin had its beginnings along the Virginia City–to–Fort Benton stagecoach line. Miners disembarking from the stage at Basin Creek built little cabins while searching the surrounding mountains for traces of gold. The area around Basin proved to be rich in gold mines, and Basin enjoyed a thriving economy. By 1905, Basin contained all the conveniences of a larger town. Two mines, the Katy and the Hope, contributed to the growth of Basin. By 1924, gold ore taken from the Hope, Katy, and White Elephant Mines produced $1.7 million in total revenues. However, as smelter costs escalated, the profitability of the mining industry in Basin fell.

The development of Jefferson County depended on the establishment of the mining industries, ranching, and the railroads. While some towns grew quickly from gold, silver, and other ores, other communities developed a strong agricultural economy. The railroad connected each of the diverse towns together. As a result, families grew, children were educated, and Jefferson County residents prospered.

One

Gold in the Hills

In 1880, John Allport discovered gold deposits near the tiny mining community of Basin. The area proved rich in placer mines. By 1905, the town contained a butcher shop, a millinery shop, a bowling alley, three hotels, three grocery stores, and one bathhouse. Two mines developed by the Glass brothers, the Katy and the Hope, contributed to the growth of Basin. While both the original Katy and Hope Mines were destroyed by fire, gold ore taken from them and the White Elephant Mine produced nearly $1.7 million in total revenue. Although mining establishments in Basin continued to work mine tailings, by 1924, mining revenues began to decline. In addition to Basin, gold discovered 4 miles west of Cardwell in 1895 at the Mayflower Mine determined that the southern end of Jefferson County would experience a mining boom as well. Butte mine owner William A. Clark quickly bought the Mayflower claim from the prospector who discovered the vein. Soon W. A. Clark authorized the construction of a smelter a few miles away from the Mayflower to smelt the ore. The new smelter, which became known as the Parrot, would smelt gold, silver, lead, and copper ores. A powerhouse was built to provide energy for the smelter. However, when the smelter chimney was nearly finished, W. A. Clark and partner Samuel T. Hauser cancelled further construction. The gold ore taken from the Mayflower Mine turned out to be a localized vein, and by 1905, the mine began to fill with water. While the development of the Mayflower shaft was short lived and the high smelting costs contributed to the decline of the Basin mines, the mining establishments greatly improved the economy of Jefferson County and produced a high standard of living for its residents. In more modern times, mines like the Golden Sunlight Mine, located 8 miles from Whitehall, and the Montana Tunnels Mine near Jefferson City continued to add to the prosperity of Jefferson County. The development of mining camps within Jefferson County ensured that future residents enjoyed all the benefits of a thriving economy.

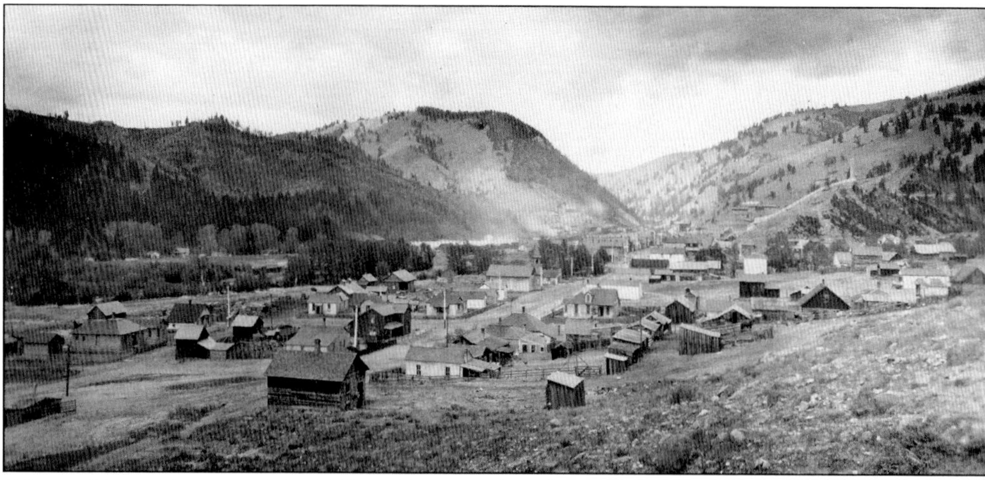

After gold was discovered in 1862 at Cataract Creek, miners began to steadily move into the area. The town of Basin was soon established and grew as a result of rich placer mines. By 1924, when the Jib Consolidated Mining Company employed 175 miners, the population of Basin had grown to nearly 1,000 residents. (Courtesy of the Jefferson County Museum.)

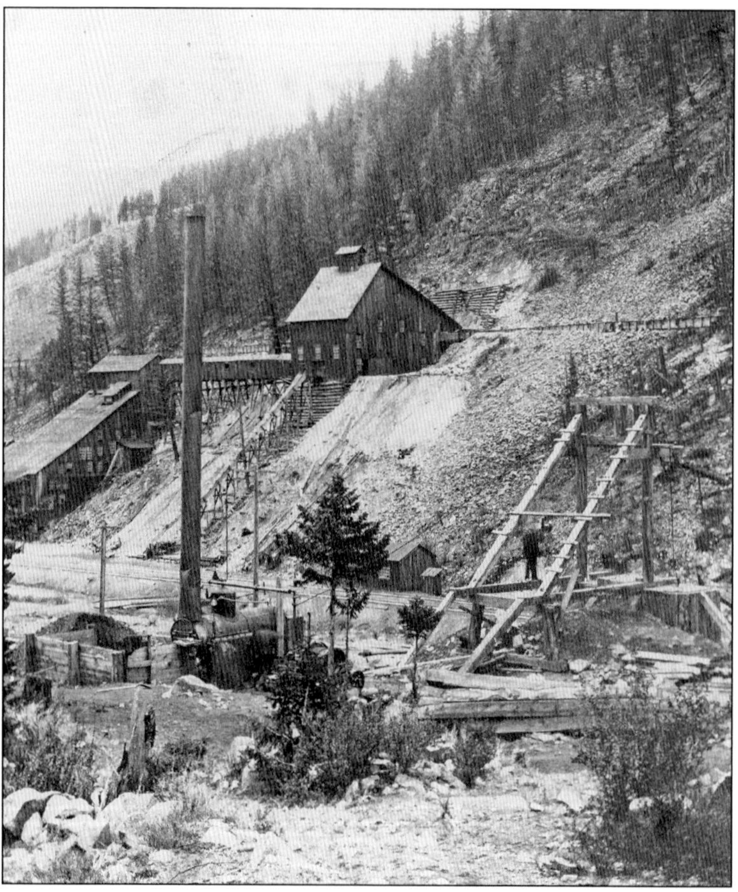

This photograph depicts the Hope Mine, which adjoined the Katy Mine in Basin. Unfortunately, its concentrator caught fire in April 1896, and seven miners died in the catastrophe. (Courtesy of the Jefferson County Museum.)

This photograph of the Hope Mine in Basin was taken prior to the devastating fire. (Courtesy of the Jefferson County Museum.)

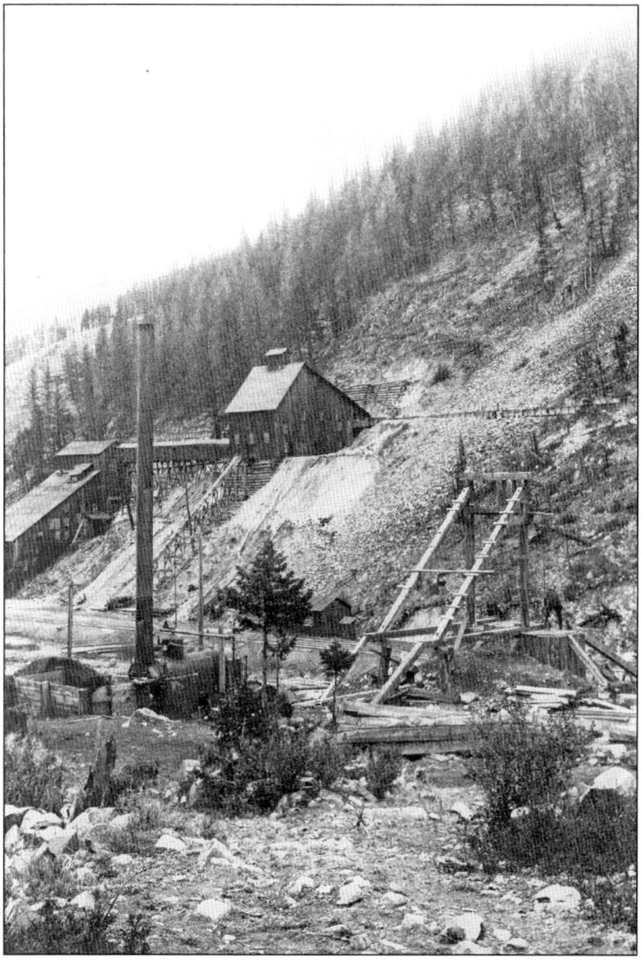

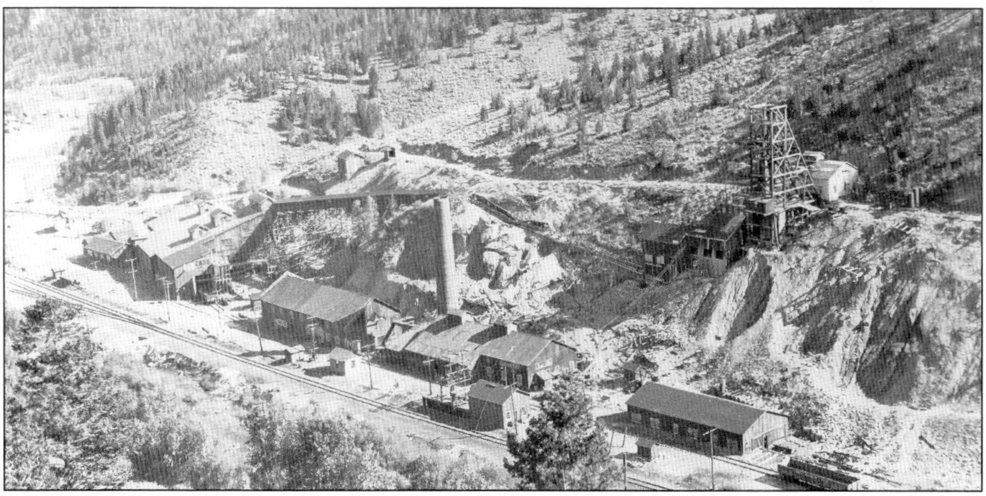

The Katy Mine in Basin was one of two mines owned by the Glass brothers until a fire destroyed the hoisting plant and shaft in 1895. A new mine was rebuilt over the site of the Katy, but flooding in the main shafts was difficult to control. (Courtesy of the Jefferson County Museum.)

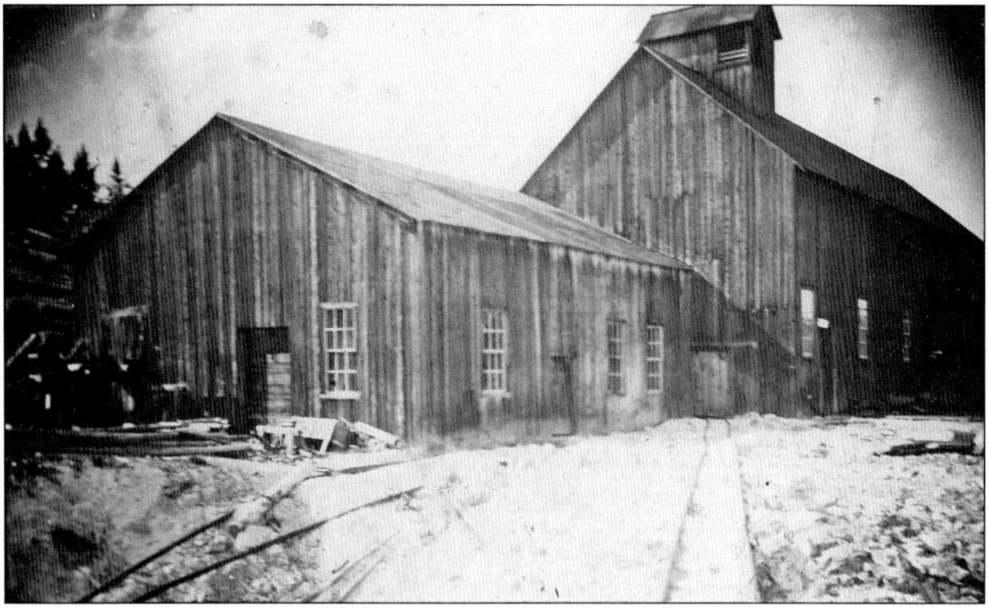

Mines, like this one in Basin, often changed ownership several times before the ore was completely extracted or production costs escalated. (Courtesy of the Jefferson County Museum.)

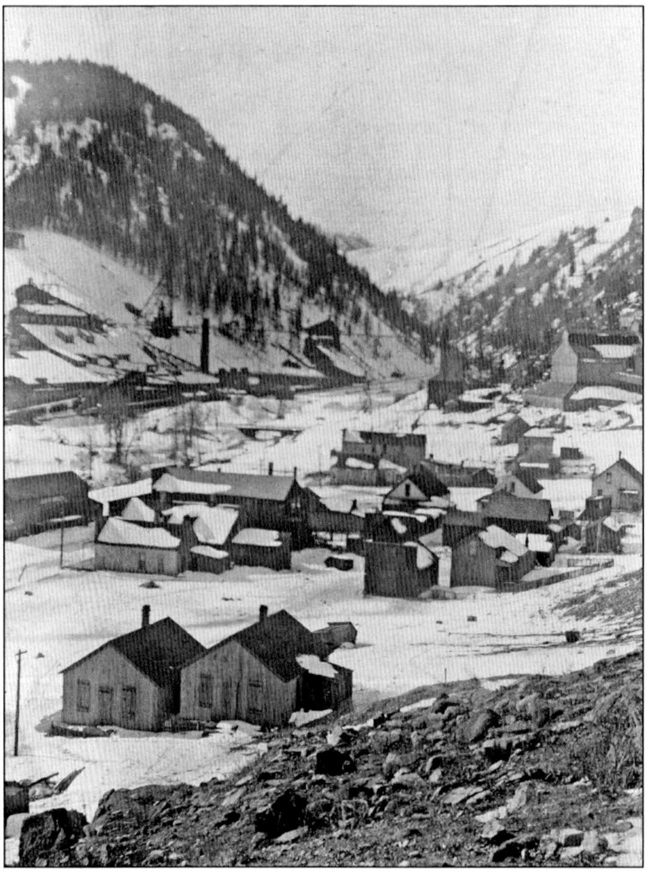

This photograph of the town of Basin was taken before the original Katy Mine, seen in the background, was destroyed by fire in 1895. (Courtesy of the Jefferson County Museum.)

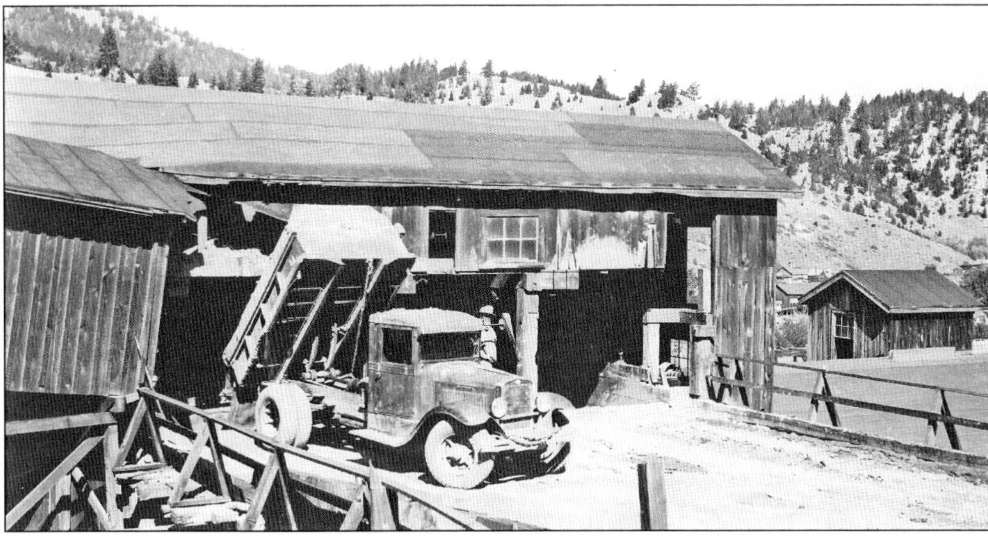

Basin residents unload mine tailings from the Katy Mine in Basin in 1932. By the time this photograph was taken, the original Katy Mine had been replaced by the Jib Consolidated Mine Company. The old tailings provided enough revenue for the Jib to continue operations. (Courtesy of the Jefferson County Museum.)

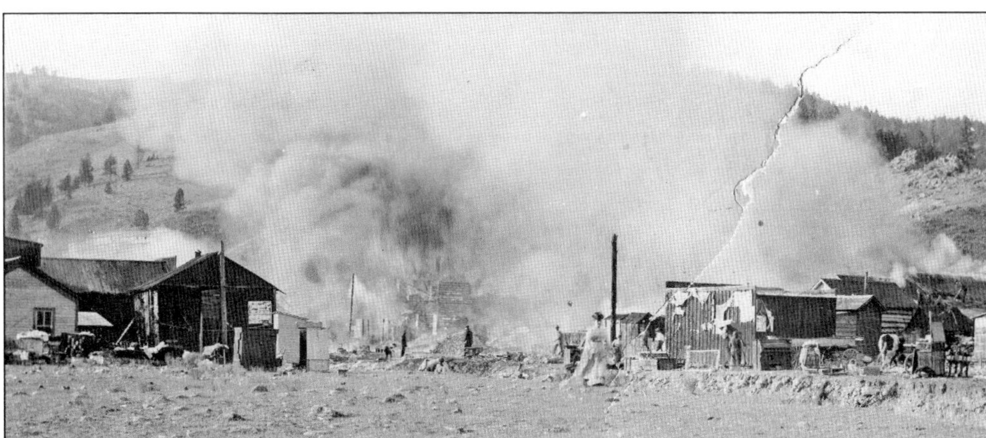

A woman hurries away from a fire that rages in the town of Basin. Unfortunately, fire was an all-too-common occurrence in mining communities, and the townspeople of Basin endured devastating fires in 1895 and 1896. (Courtesy of the Jefferson County Museum.)

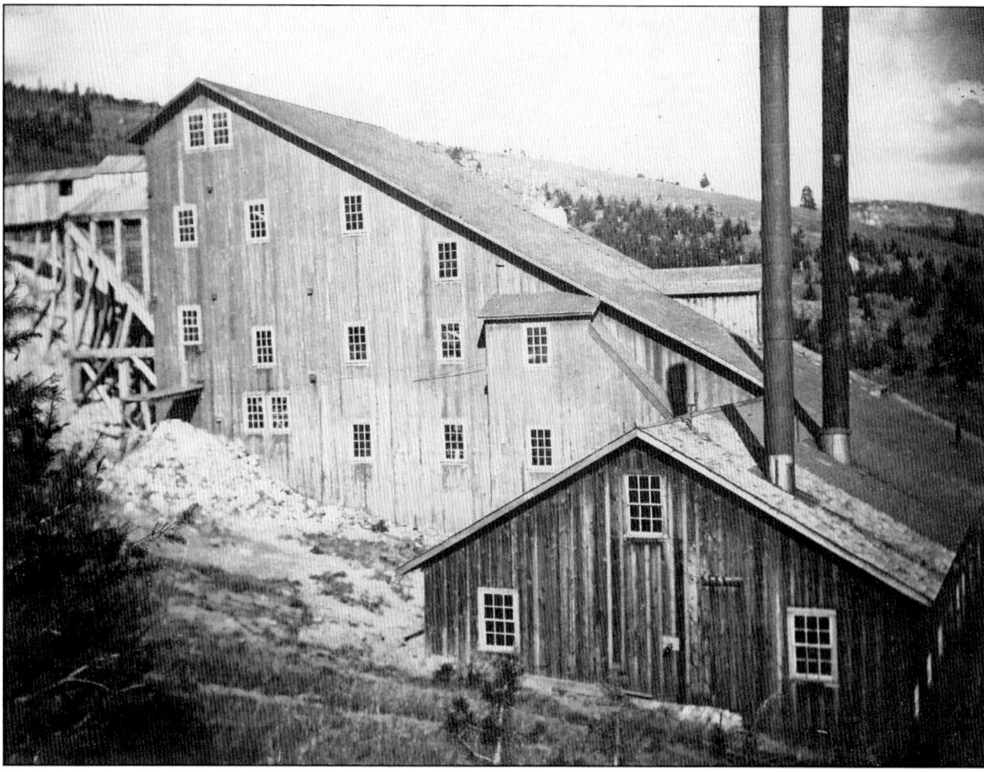

Taken from the back of the Basin Mill, this photograph chronicles a quiet day. (Courtesy of the Jefferson County Museum.)

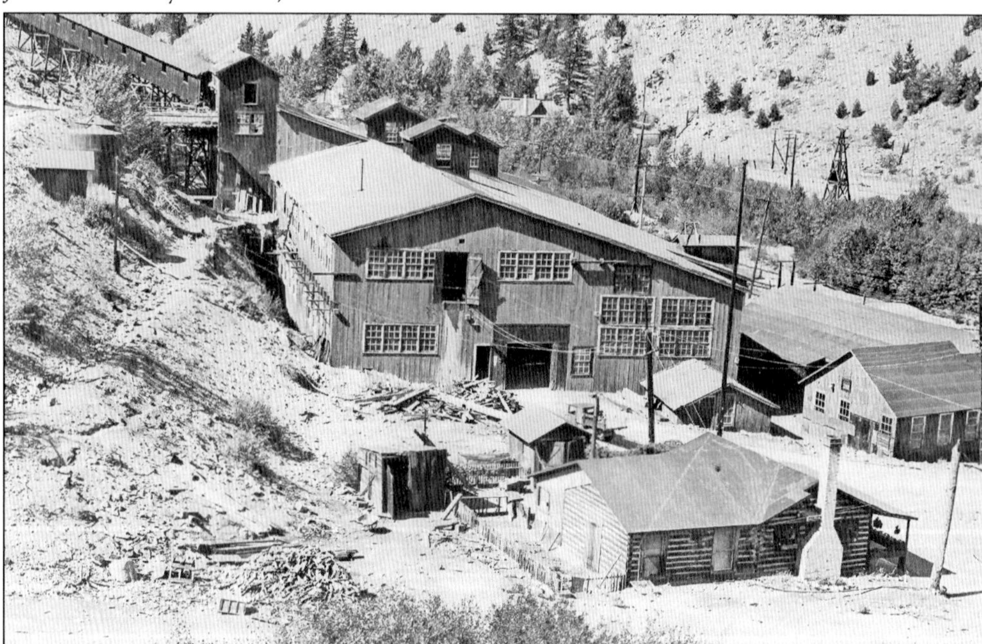

This photograph of the Basin Mill was taken about 1932. (Courtesy of the Jefferson County Museum.)

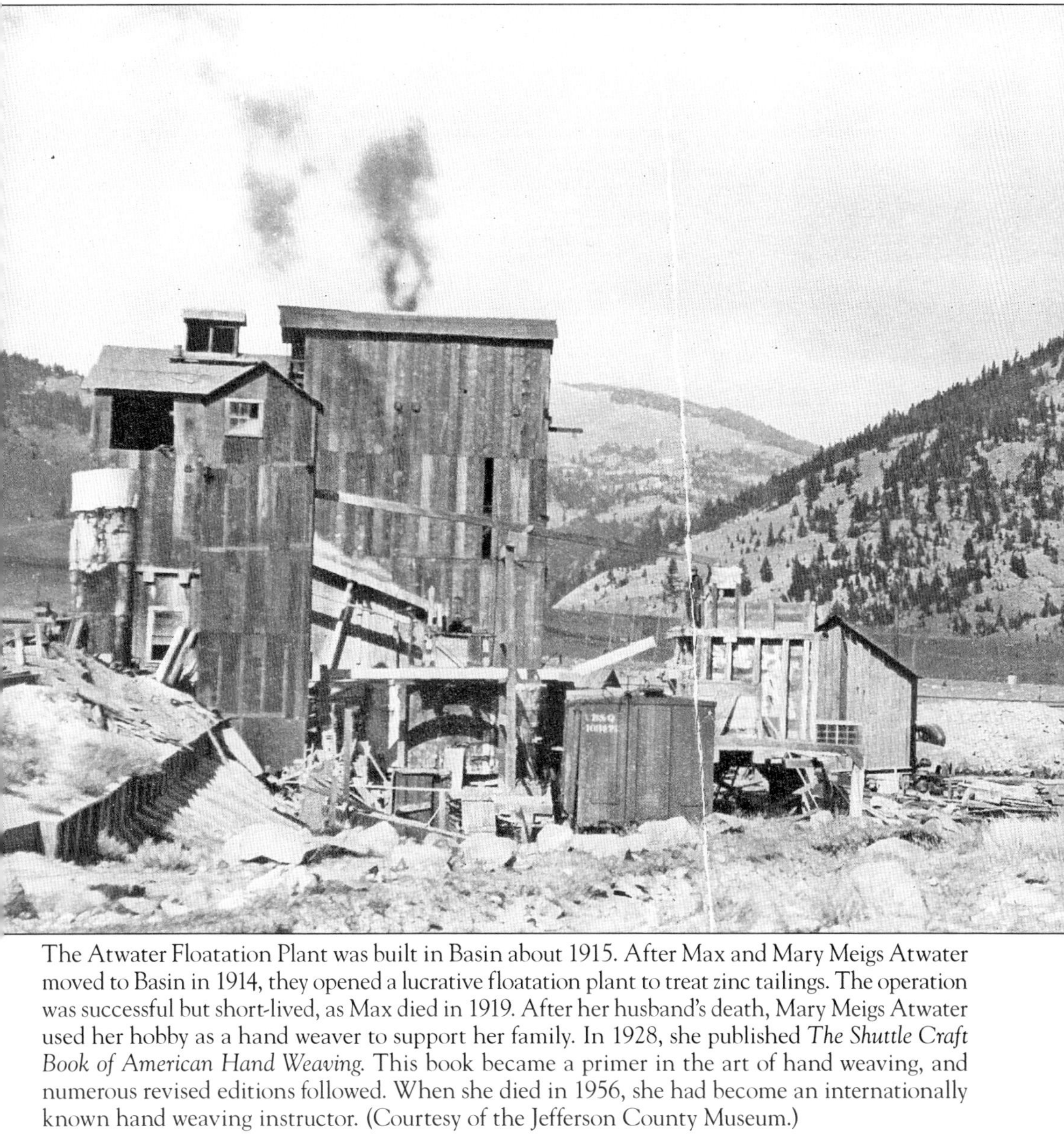

The Atwater Floatation Plant was built in Basin about 1915. After Max and Mary Meigs Atwater moved to Basin in 1914, they opened a lucrative floatation plant to treat zinc tailings. The operation was successful but short-lived, as Max died in 1919. After her husband's death, Mary Meigs Atwater used her hobby as a hand weaver to support her family. In 1928, she published *The Shuttle Craft Book of American Hand Weaving*. This book became a primer in the art of hand weaving, and numerous revised editions followed. When she died in 1956, she had become an internationally known hand weaving instructor. (Courtesy of the Jefferson County Museum.)

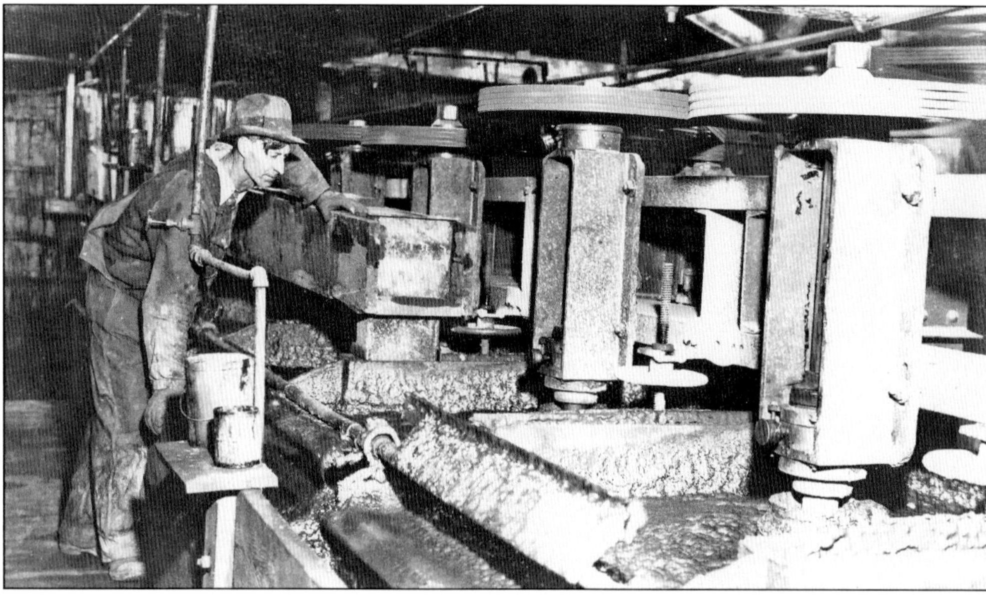

Miner Earl Williams monitors the floatation cells while he works in Basin in 1933. (Courtesy of the Jefferson County Museum.)

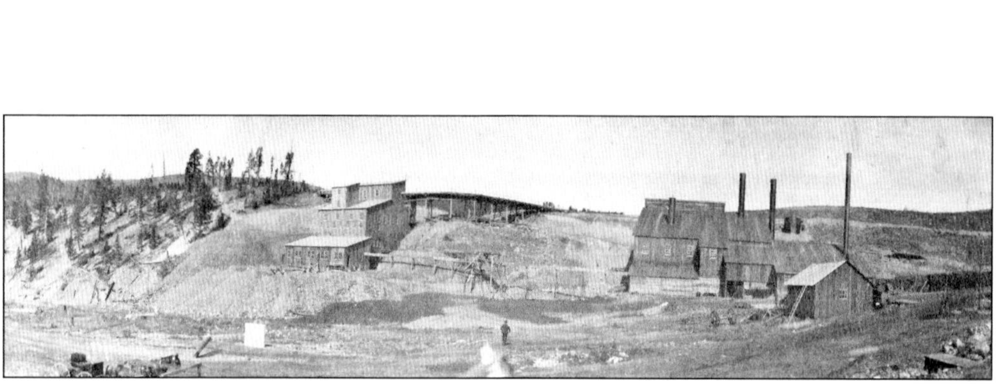

This photograph of an early Basin mining establishment shows a vast network of chutes. (Courtesy of the Jefferson County Museum.)

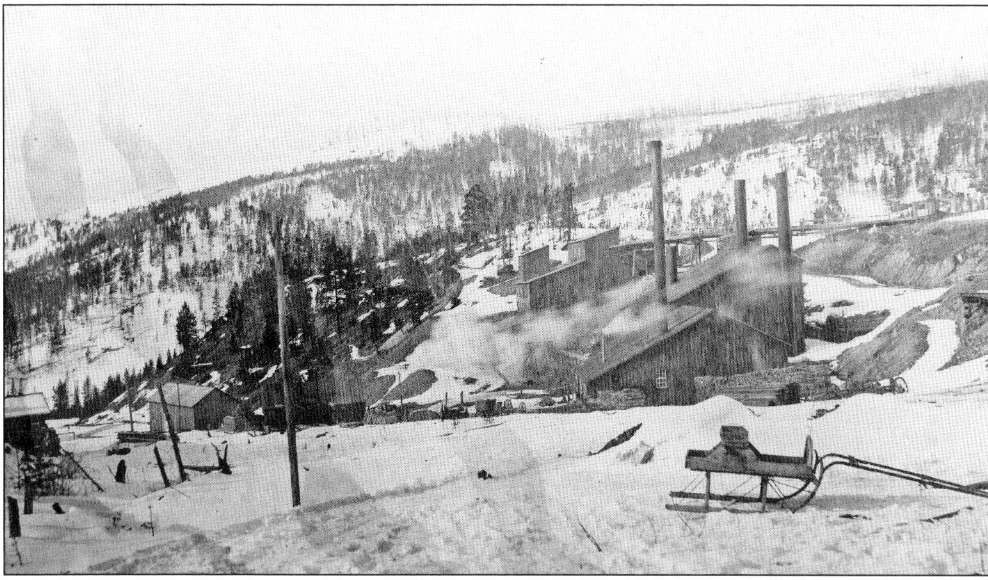

An abandoned sled waits for a team of horses to pull it through the town of Basin. One of Basin's numerous mining establishments stands in the background. (Courtesy of the Jefferson County Museum.)

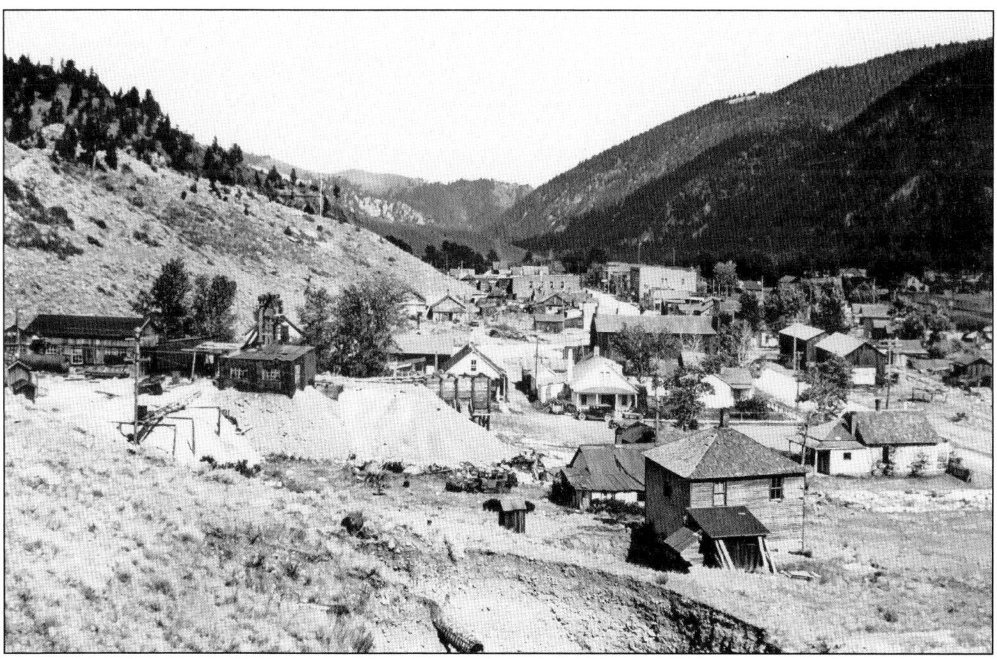

The White Elephant Mine in Basin is photographed in 1932. This mine produced a significant amount of income for its owners. (Courtesy of the Jefferson County Museum.)

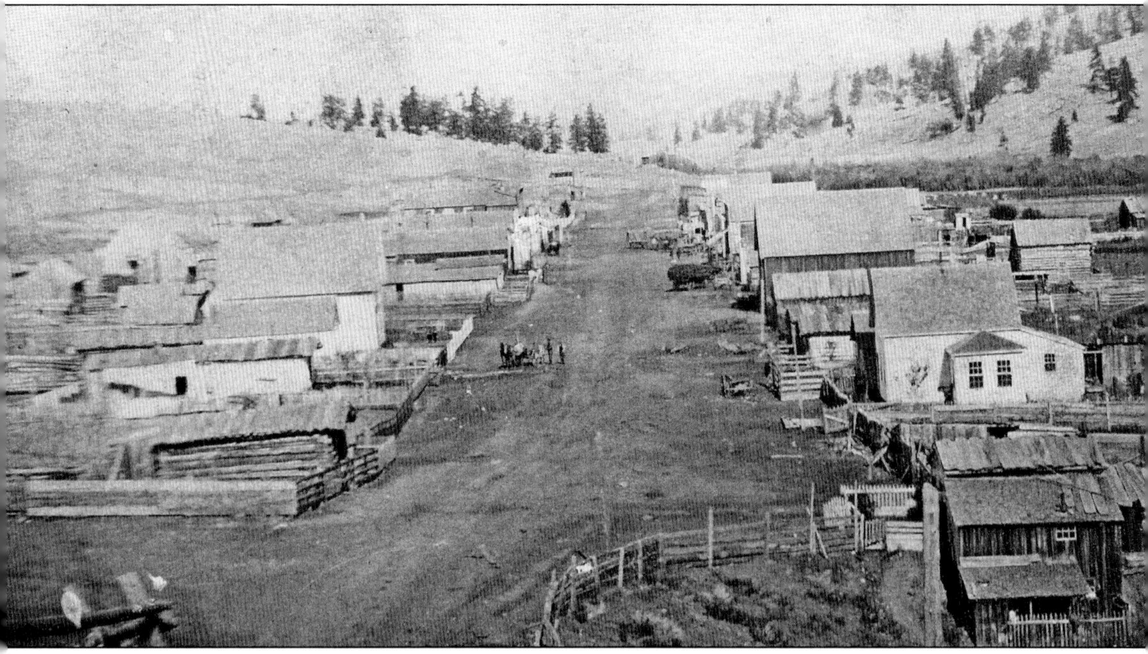

This early photograph of the town of Jefferson City, Montana, was taken around 1885. The little community of Jefferson City began in 1864 as a stage stop on the Virginia City–to–Fort Benton stage route. When gold was discovered along the Golconda Gulch and Prickly Pear Creek, miners settled in the area, raising the population to around 500 people by 1879. (Courtesy of the Jefferson County Genealogy and Heritage Center, Boulder, Montana.)

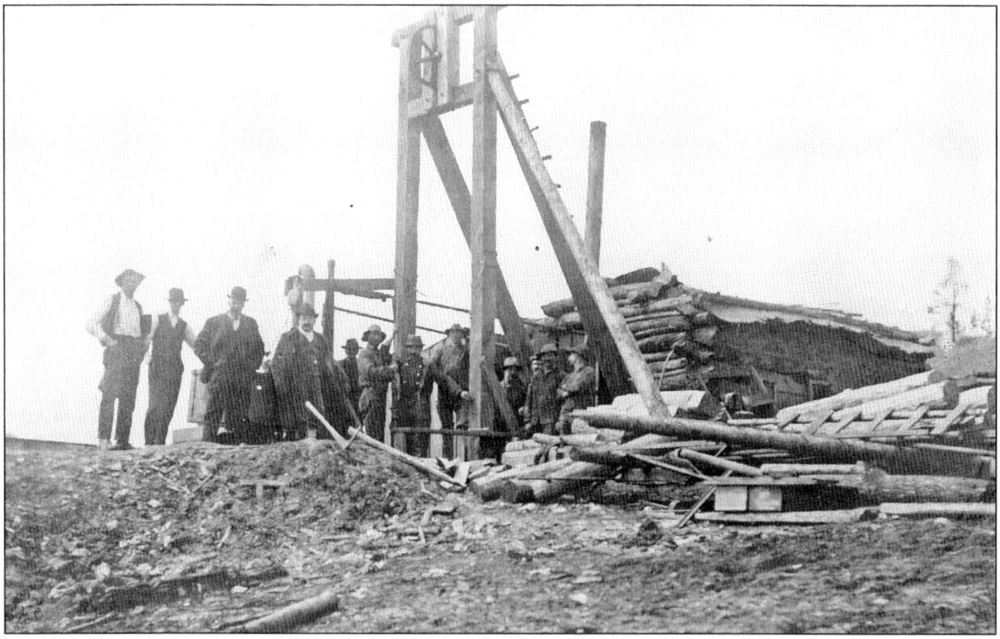

While working in the mining industry was always dusty, hard work, many men chose to endure in the hopes of striking it rich. (Courtesy of the Jefferson County Museum.)

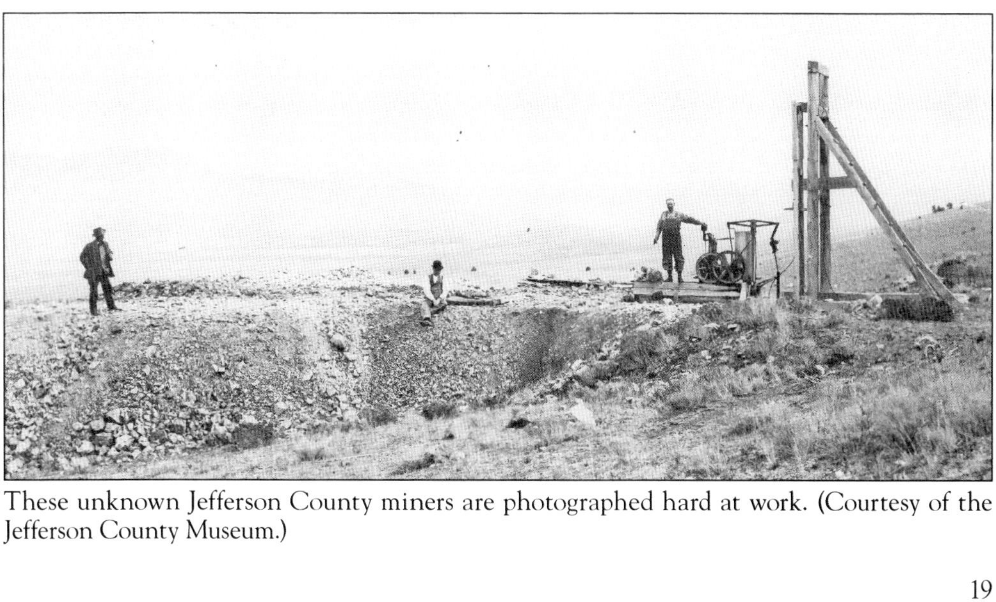

These unknown Jefferson County miners are photographed hard at work. (Courtesy of the Jefferson County Museum.)

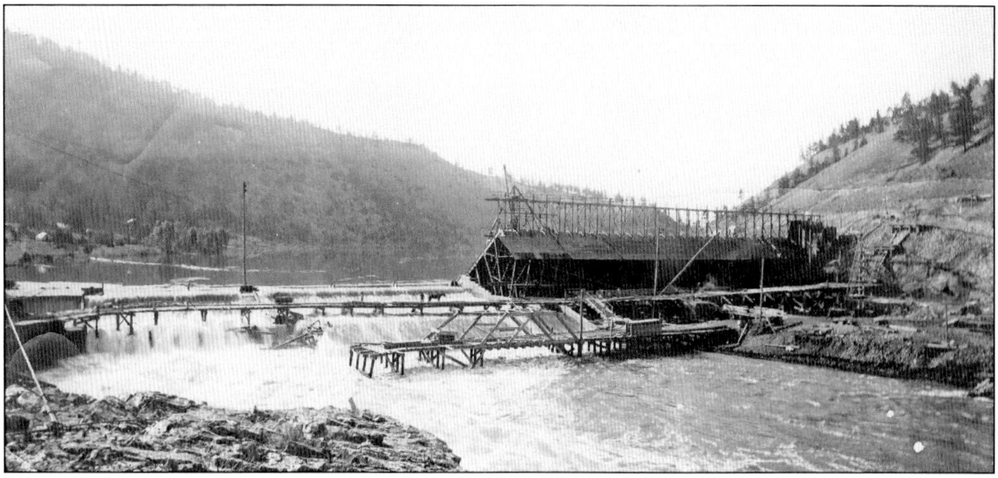

The dam at Basin spread across a wide section of the Boulder River. The mines in Basin required large quantities of water for mining operations. (Courtesy of the Jefferson County Museum.)

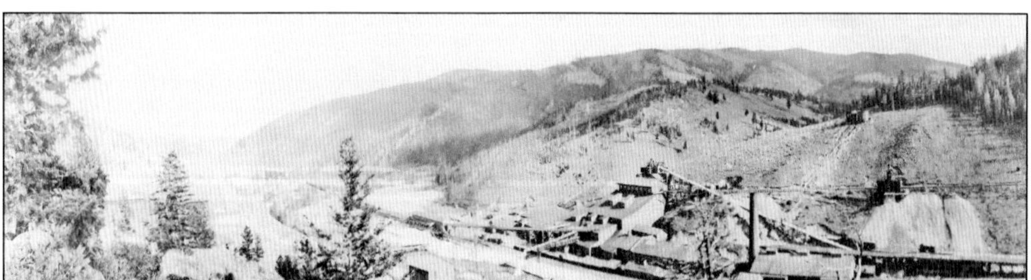

In this photograph, water, most likely mixed with mine pollutants, pours out of a chute from the mill directly into the Basin River. (Courtesy of the Jefferson County Museum.)

Two

THE SILVER BOOM

The lure of rich mineral deposits tempted many miners to move to Jefferson County in the 19th century. One adventurer, Thomas G. Merrill, settled in the Lump Gulch area just northwest of the present town of Clancy. In 1894, he saw a small amount of silver ore sticking out above the surface. The high-grade silver and zinc sulfide yielded 100 to 300 ounces of silver per ton. Merrill named his property the Liverpool Mine. Men working the mine brought the ore to the surface using a steam hoist, then sorted the ore and broke the larger pieces with hammers, casting aside rock that did not contain enough metal to be smelted. Employees of the mine brought their families and named the little town Lump City. By 1895, a quarter of a million dollars' worth of high-grade silver had been mined by Merrill. Meanwhile, silver had been discovered in the mining town of Elkhorn in the center of Jefferson County. The town of Elkhorn grew up around the Elkhorn Mine, which began producing silver ore in 1875. An early owner of the Elkhorn Mine, A. M. Holter, constructed a crushing plant and organized the Elkhorn Mining Company. He sold the mine in 1888. The London-based company that purchased the mine remodeled the mill and vigorously developed ore leads. By 1891, when 76 men were employed by the Elkhorn Mining Company, it produced around $1 million a year. With the sharp decline of silver prices as a result of the silver panic, the demand for silver ore plummeted. The Elkhorn Mining Company continued operation until the end of 1899, then sporadically until 1951, but it never produced as much as it had in 1891. By 1898, the silver market still had not recovered, and the residents of Lump City began to move away. A few years later, the Lump City School was closed, and the remaining children were sent to the nearby Clancy School. While some of the old town buildings remain in Elkhorn, most of the buildings in Lump City were torn down to make way for progress.

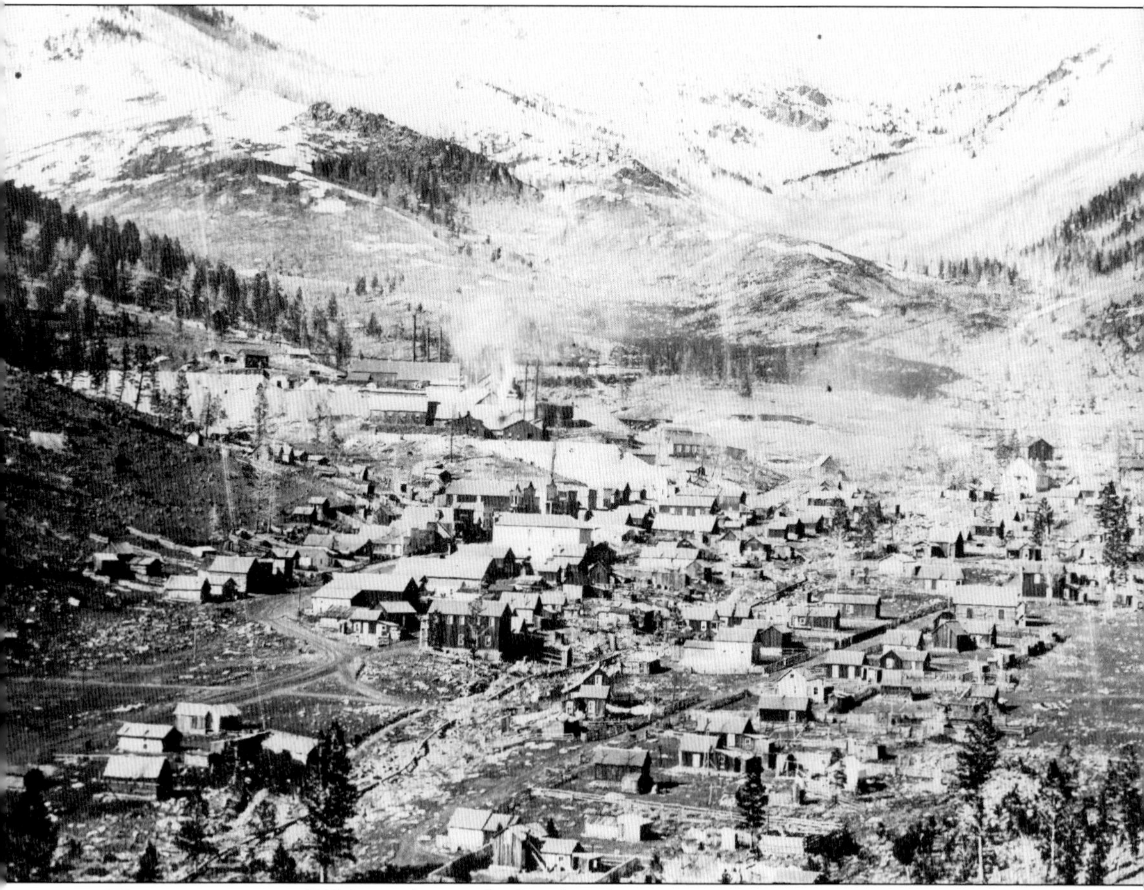

The mining town of Elkhorn during the height of mining operations offered residents a collection of businesses to fulfill their needs. By 1891, the Elkhorn Mining Company produced around $1 million a year, allowing the miners to enjoy prosperity as well. Elkhorn residents had a choice of restaurants, a shoemaker's shop, a barbershop for patrons to get a haircut and a bath, a candy store, a bowling alley, several boardinghouses, a blacksmith shop, a butcher shop, the stately Gillian Hall, which was used as a store and dance hall, and numerous saloons. (Courtesy of the Jefferson County Museum.)

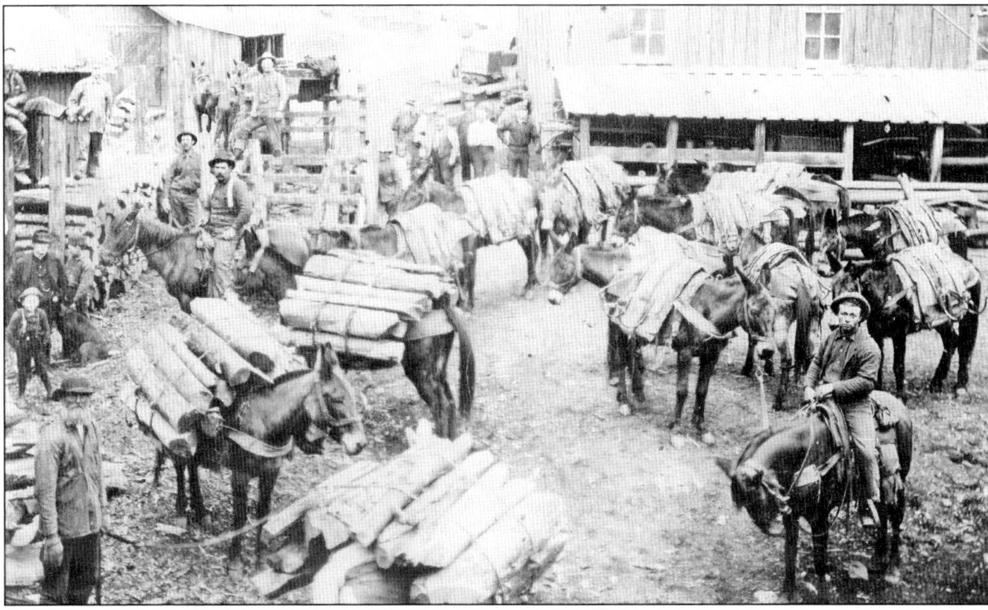

This photograph shows a group of miners with loaded mules full of timber for work in the mines. At one time in Elkhorn, 500 woodsmen and 1,500 mules worked the woods surrounding the town. (Courtesy of the Jefferson County Museum.)

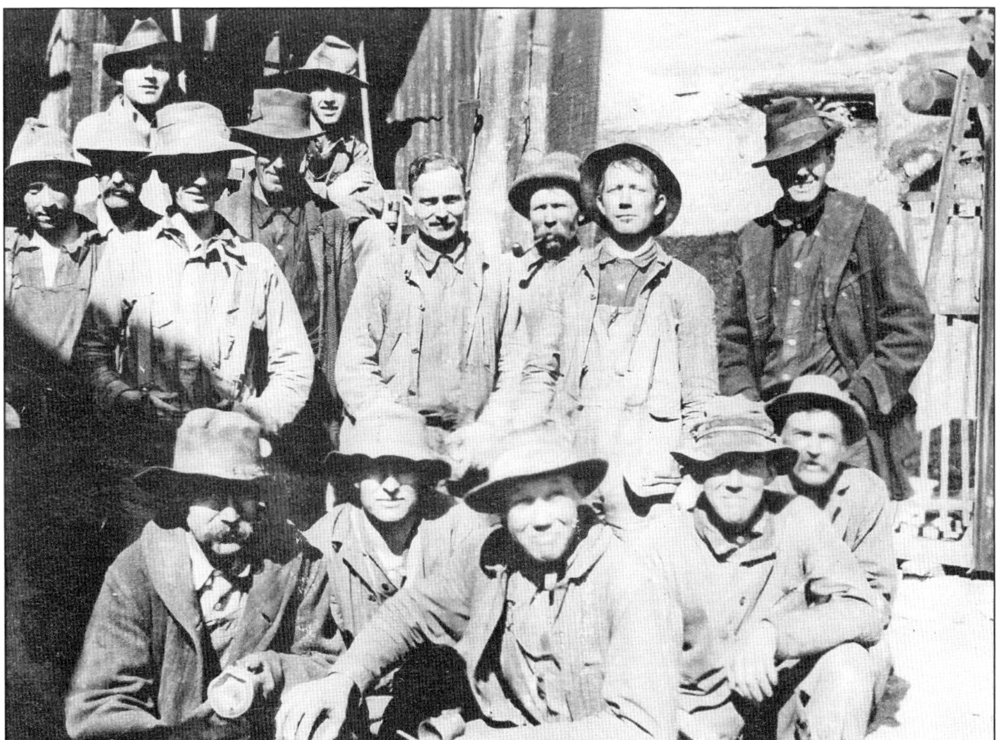

Miners in Comet enjoy a break in the sunshine before they descend into the inky darkness to work. The original Comet Mine was discovered by John W. Russell. The population peaked at around 300 people. (Courtesy of the Jefferson County Museum.)

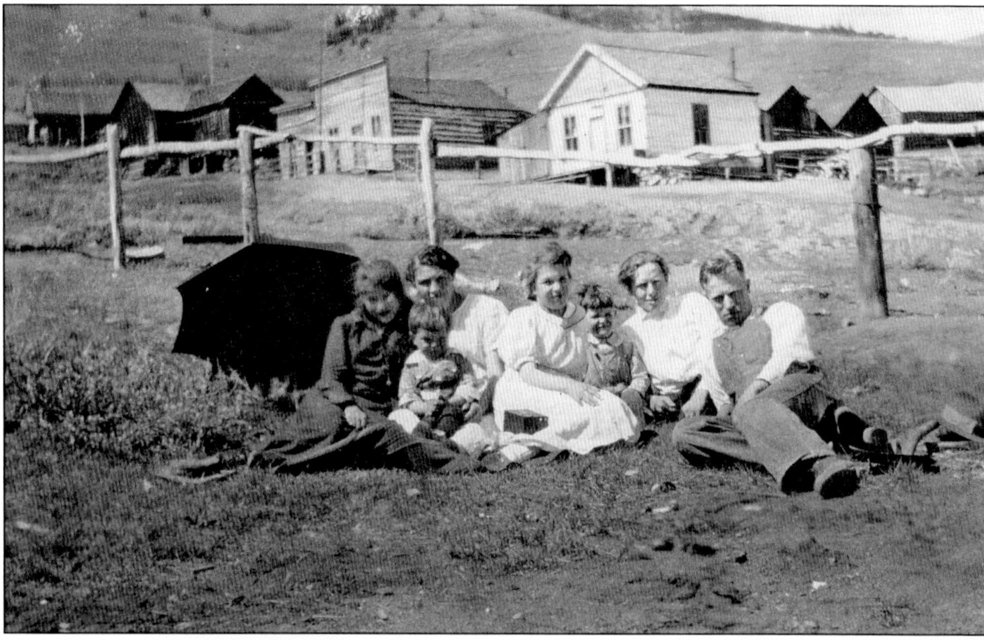

The Mattson family enjoys a day of sunshine in Comet. When mining operations in Comet were flourishing, Comet had a school with 20 students. (Courtesy of the Jefferson County Genealogy and Heritage Center, Boulder, Montana.)

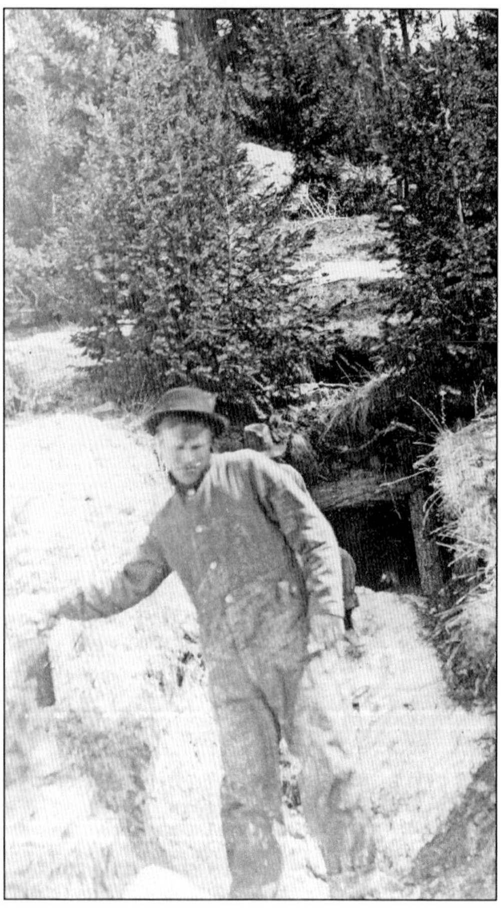

Arthur Mattson Sr. stands in front of a tunnel near Reed's Gulch in Comet to have his picture taken. (Courtesy of the Jefferson County Genealogy and Heritage Center, Boulder, Montana.)

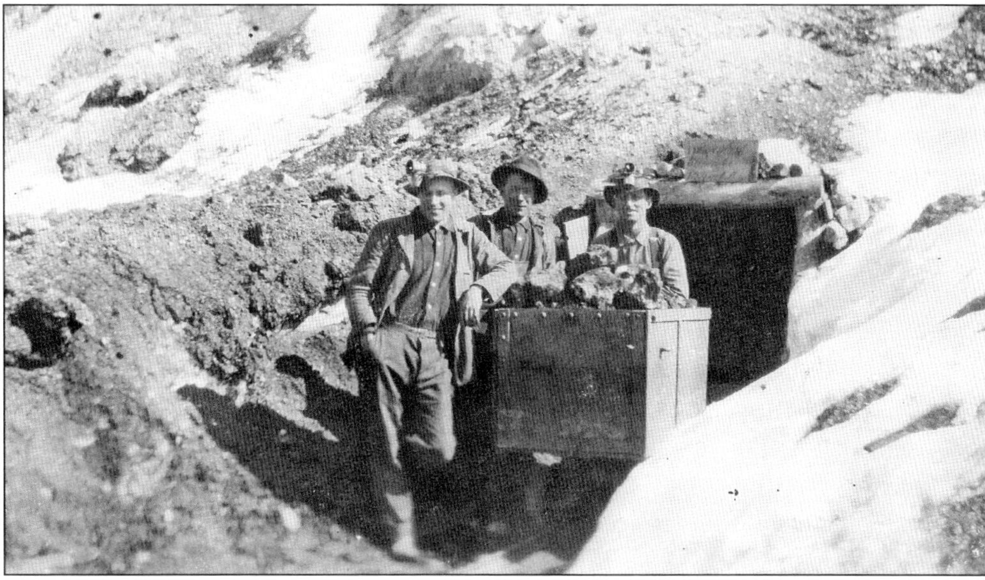

Comet miners stand next to a full ore cart at the entrance to Leasors Tunnel in Comet. The men wore carbide lamps on their hats to light the way in the dark tunnel. (Courtesy of the Jefferson County Museum.)

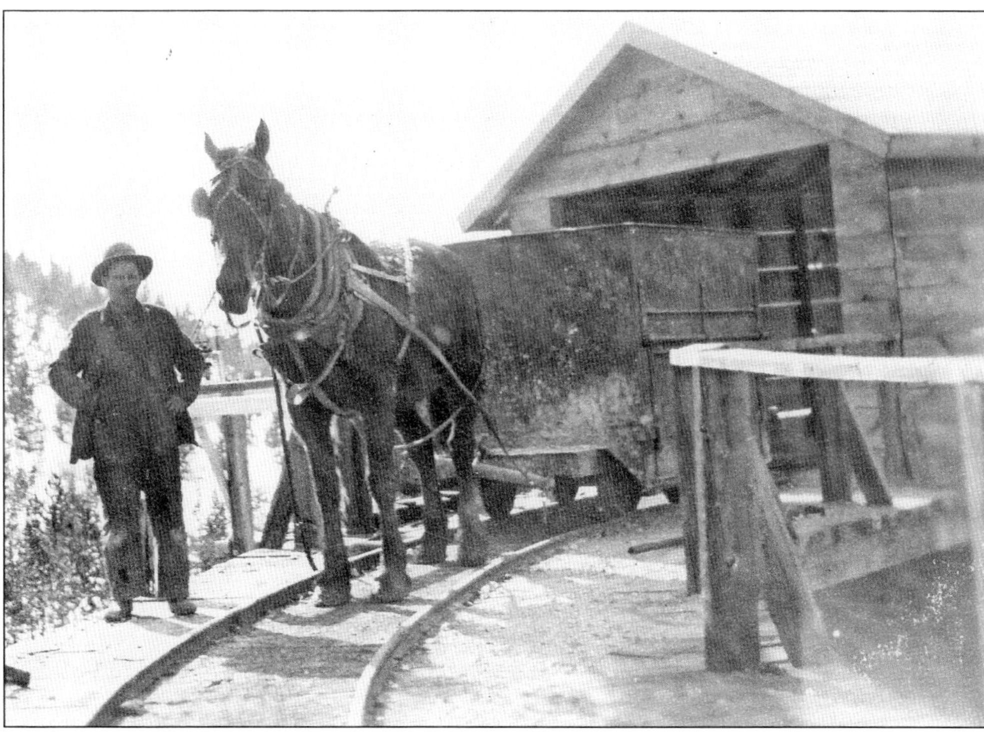

A horse-drawn tramcar was used to dump ore into the ore bins in Comet. (Courtesy of the Jefferson County Museum.)

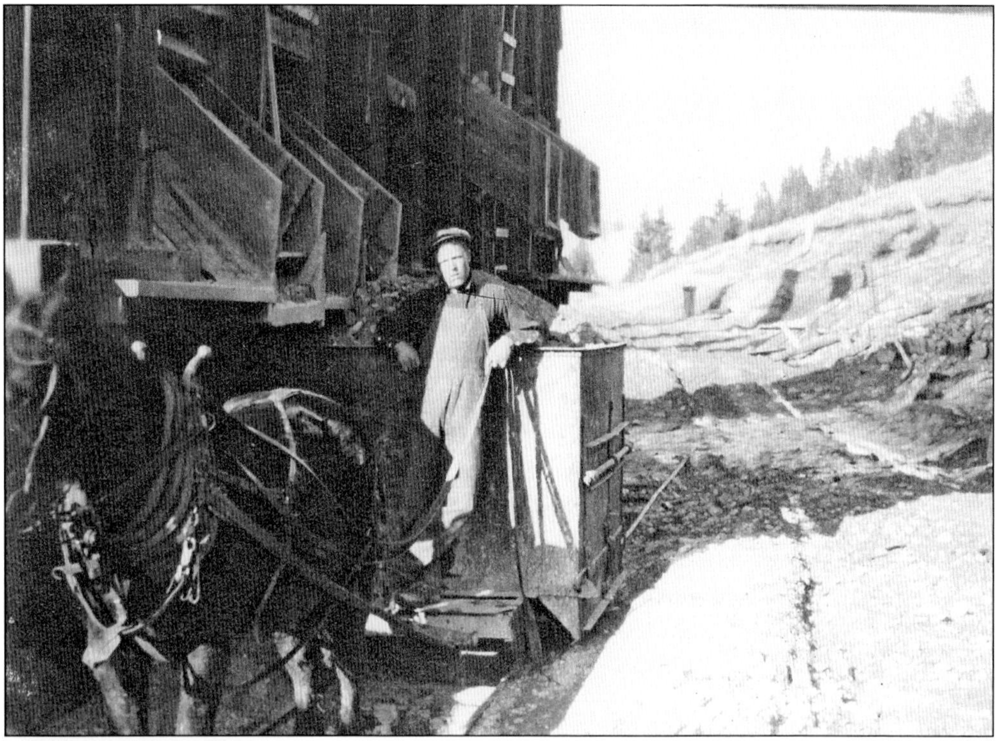

Jacob Mattson stands at the ore bins in Comet. (Courtesy of the Jefferson County Museum.)

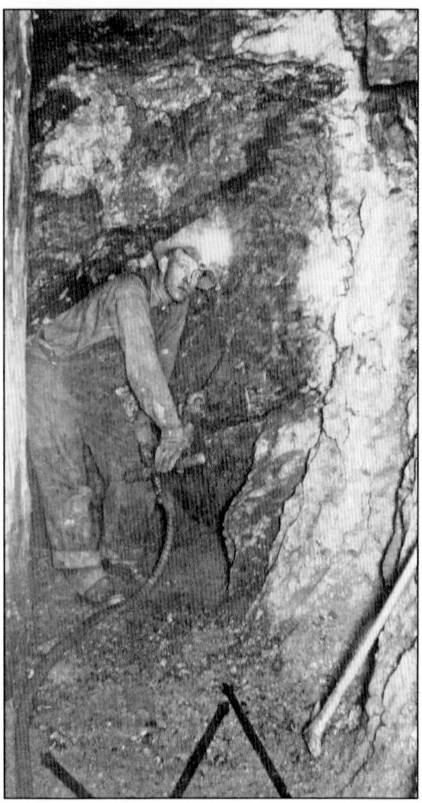

Matt Kosola stops drilling long enough to have his picture taken. Matt worked in the mines in Comet during the 1930s. He married Esther Louise Kyler in 1935. (Courtesy of the Jefferson County Museum.)

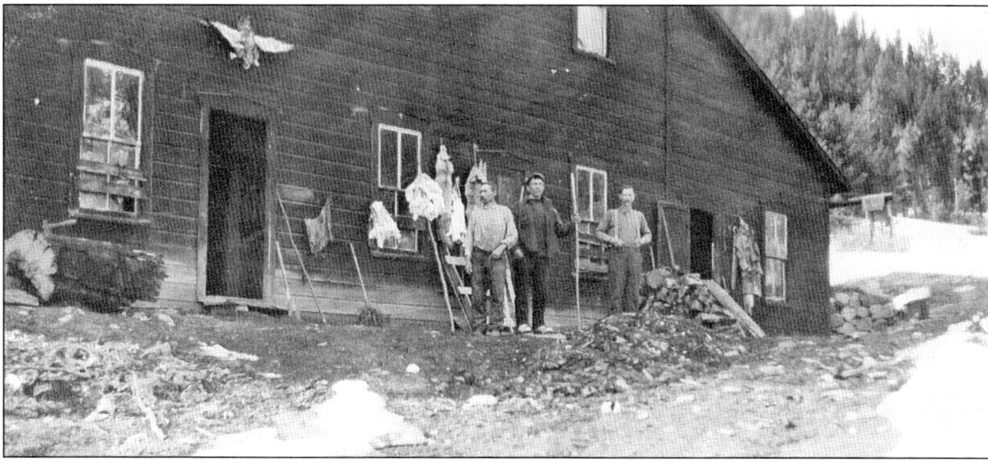

This bunkhouse was located at the Grey Eagle Mine shaft and served as a home for miners who needed a place to stay. From left to right, Comet residents John Hedquist, Jacob Mattson, and Charlie Larson stand in front of the bunkhouse. (Courtesy of the Jefferson County Genealogy and Heritage Center, Boulder, Montana.)

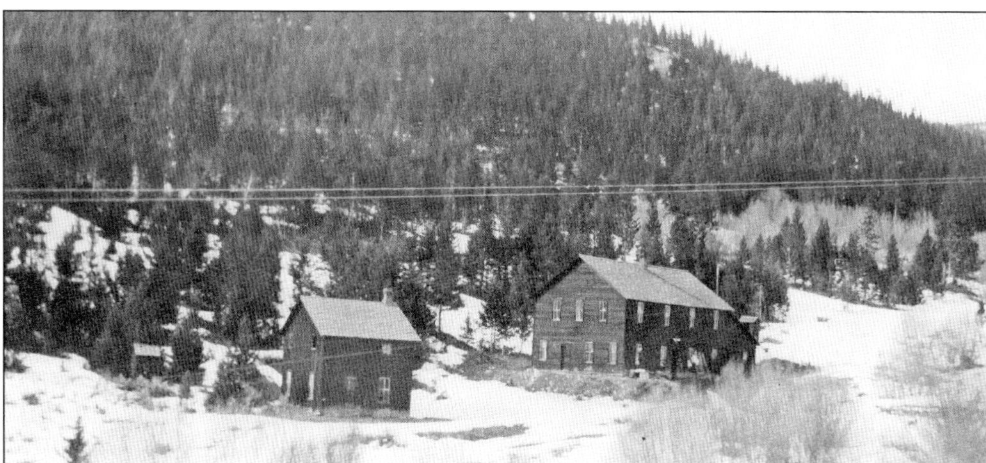

The Grey Eagle Bunkhouse was located just a short distance from Comet. (Courtesy of the Jefferson County Museum.)

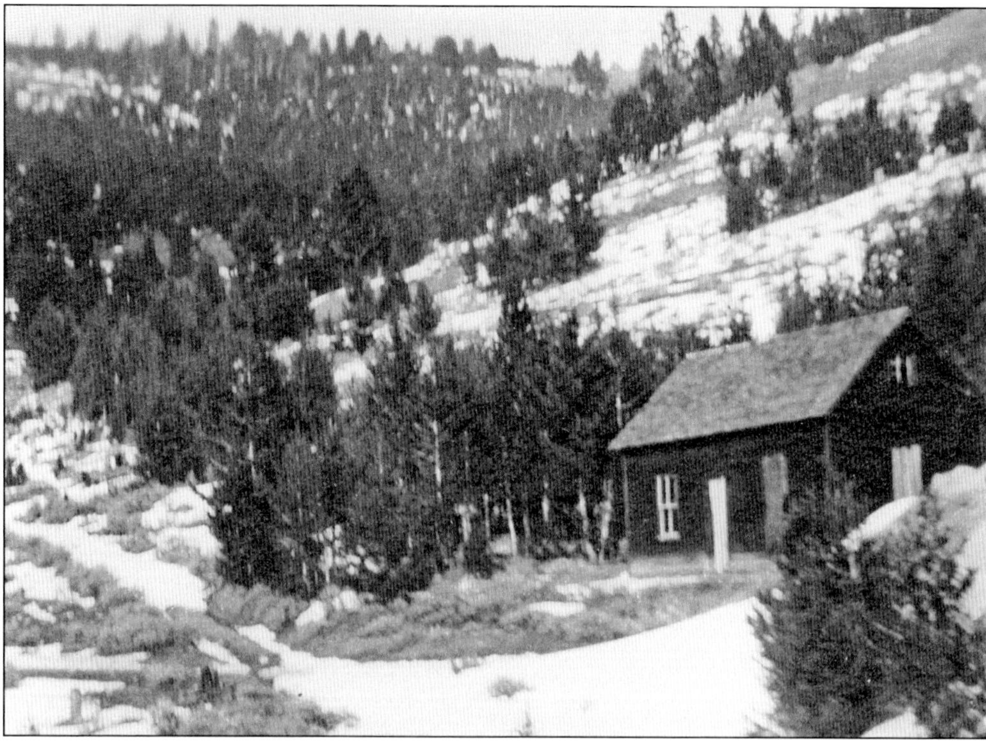

The Grey Eagle Mine was operated by owner and general manager Marcus Hewett from 1901 to 1904. He named his company the Cataract Copper Mining Company, and he owned the Grey Eagle Mine until smelting costs were too high to continue extracting ore. (Courtesy of the Jefferson County Museum.)

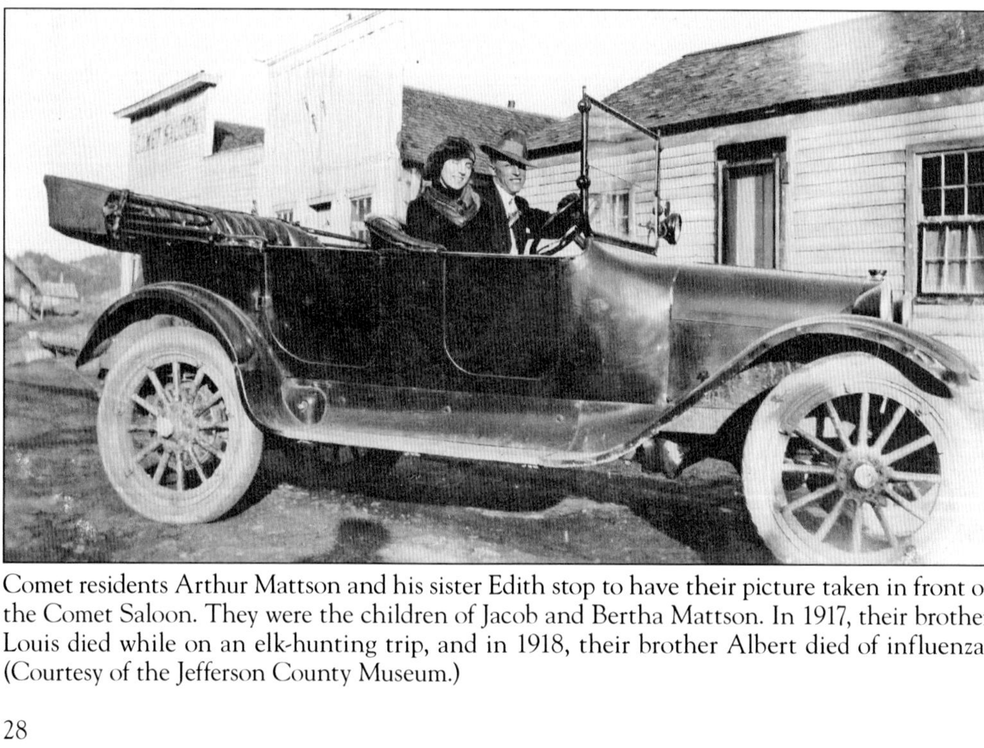

Comet residents Arthur Mattson and his sister Edith stop to have their picture taken in front of the Comet Saloon. They were the children of Jacob and Bertha Mattson. In 1917, their brother Louis died while on an elk-hunting trip, and in 1918, their brother Albert died of influenza. (Courtesy of the Jefferson County Museum.)

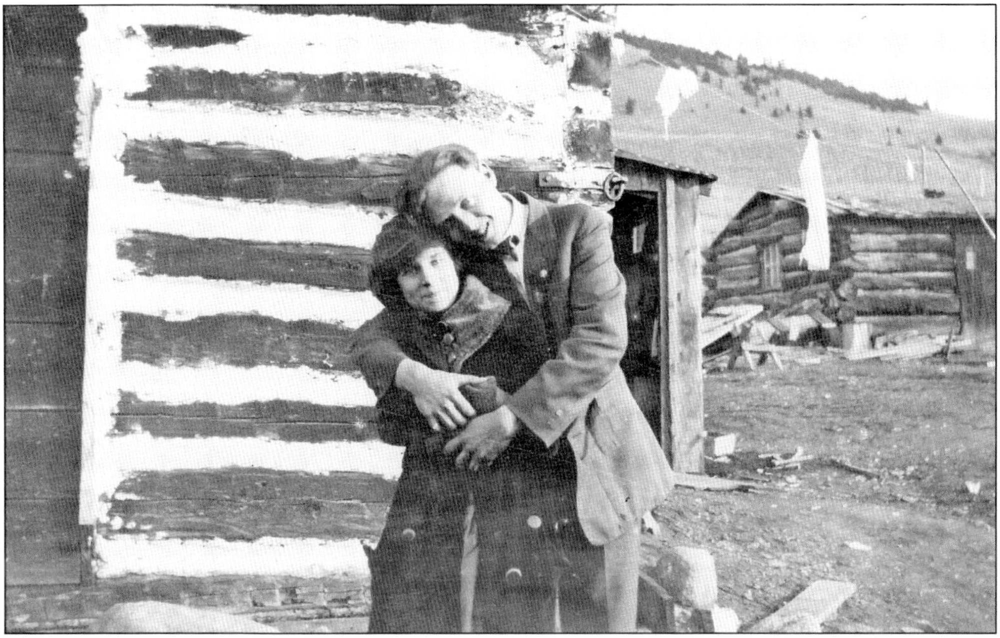

Comet resident Edith Mattson and an unidentified man enjoy a hug outside the Mattson family home. (Courtesy of the Jefferson County Genealogy and Heritage Center, Boulder, Montana.)

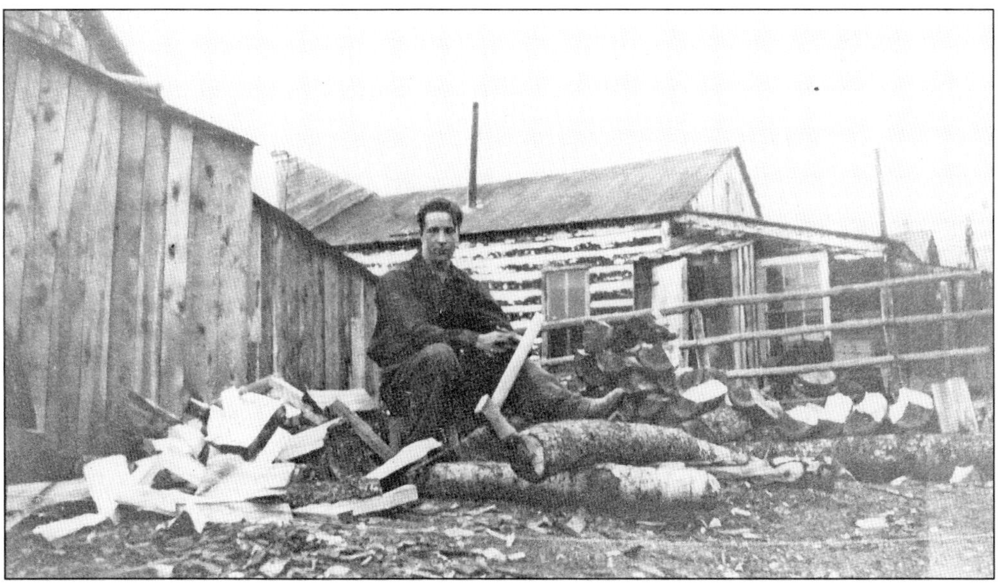

Many homes in Jefferson County were heated with wood at the time of this photograph. One of the Comet boys takes a break from his job of splitting wood to have his picture taken. (Courtesy of the Jefferson County Genealogy and Heritage Center, Boulder, Montana.)

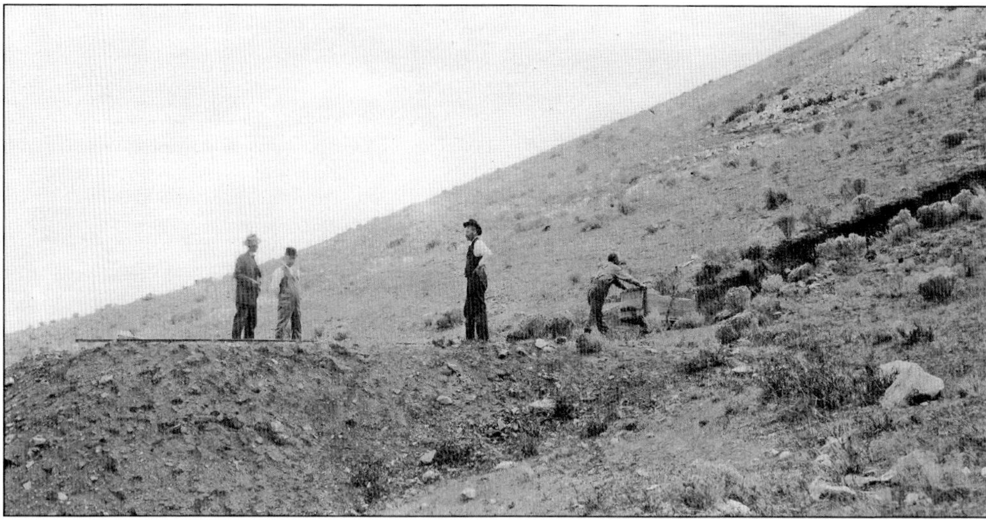

As this scene portrays, mining was often a lonely job. (Courtesy of the Jefferson County Museum.)

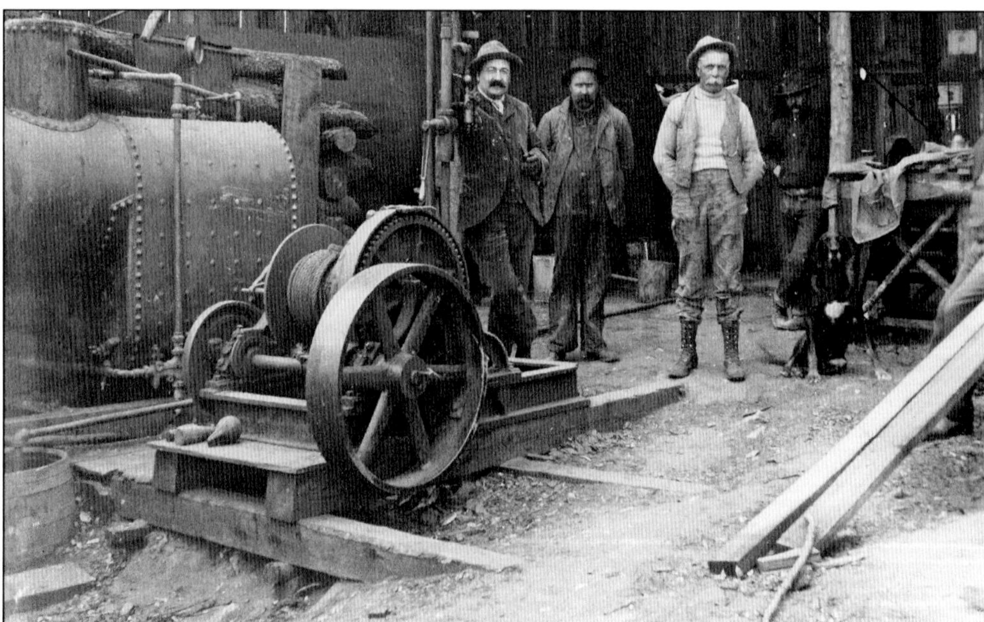

These men took a break from work to stand next to their heavy machinery for a photograph. Most likely the machinery pictured was a steam hoist used for bringing ore to the surface of a mine shaft. (Courtesy of the Jefferson County Museum.)

Three

Riding the Rails

The population of the western United States during the latter part of the 19th century depended on the railroad industry not only for transportation but for supply distribution as well. Miners delivered ore to the nearest railroad station for shipment to smelters. As mines were discovered and ranch land developed in Jefferson County, the railroad companies built additional track and stations to serve the growing population. Since towns were separated by vast distances, train travel replaced horses as a much faster mode of transportation. Although train travel was faster, it still had disadvantages. For example, the ride was slow when steep grades, narrow corners, or deep snow were encountered. Another drawback was the sometimes high cost of shipping and travel. The Northern Pacific Railroad arrived in Jefferson County in December 1883 with the first link from Helena to Wickes. Later Northern Pacific tracks continued through three tunnels to end at Calvin, between present-day Basin and Bernice. In 1889, the Northern Pacific finished the tracks from Garrison, Montana, through Whitehall to Logan, Utah. This branch firmly established Whitehall as a railroad town. In 1909, the Northern Pacific built a 90,000-gallon water tank to supply its trains in Whitehall. While Jefferson County residents appreciated the convenience of the Northern Pacific lines, high prices left many unable to use the services. Finally, on July 12, 1888, a competing company, the Montana Central Railway, completed 73 miles of track between Helena and Butte. The line traveled through the 6,145-foot Wickes Tunnel over Boulder Hill. The track climbed 2,300 feet, requiring the use of helper trains stationed at Clancy to push cars all the way up through the tunnel and down to Woodville at the extreme southern end of Jefferson County. With two train services linking the communities of Jefferson County, the cost of rail prices fell, and residents enjoyed a freedom of movement previously unknown to them.

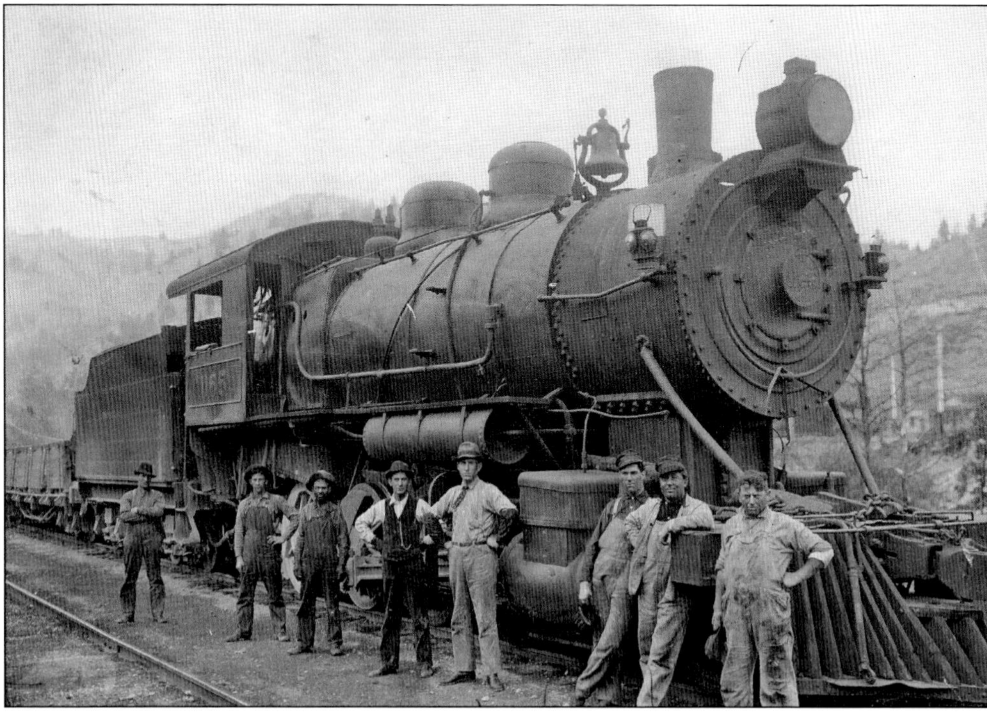

Employment with the railroad provided a steady income. For some railroad employees in Clancy, sturdy brick homes were provided as housing. These train employees proudly stand next to an engine. (Courtesy of the Jefferson County Museum.)

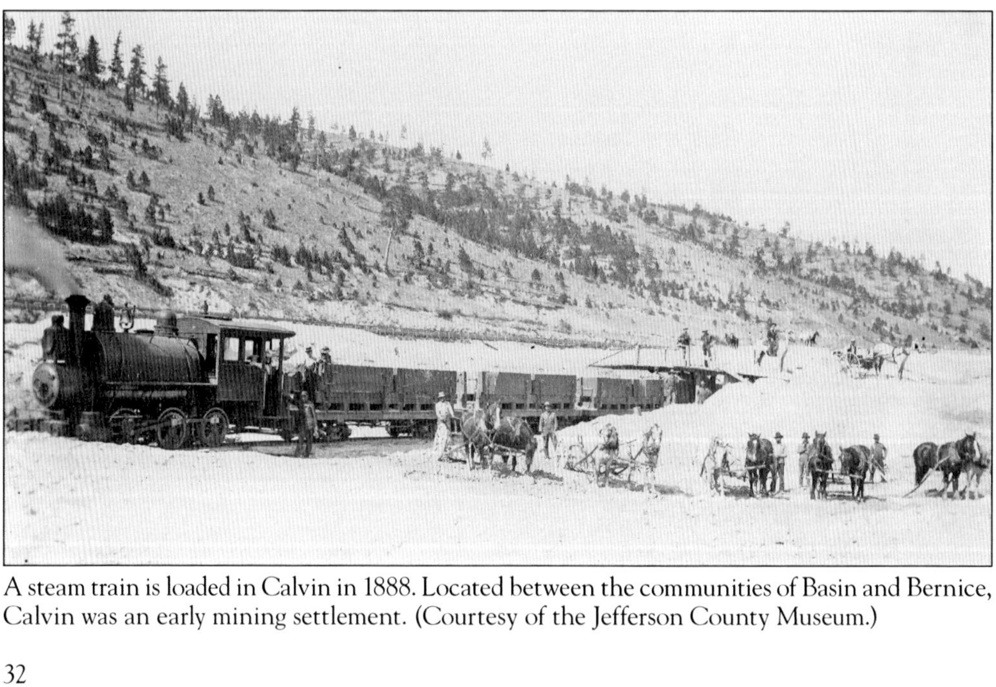

A steam train is loaded in Calvin in 1888. Located between the communities of Basin and Bernice, Calvin was an early mining settlement. (Courtesy of the Jefferson County Museum.)

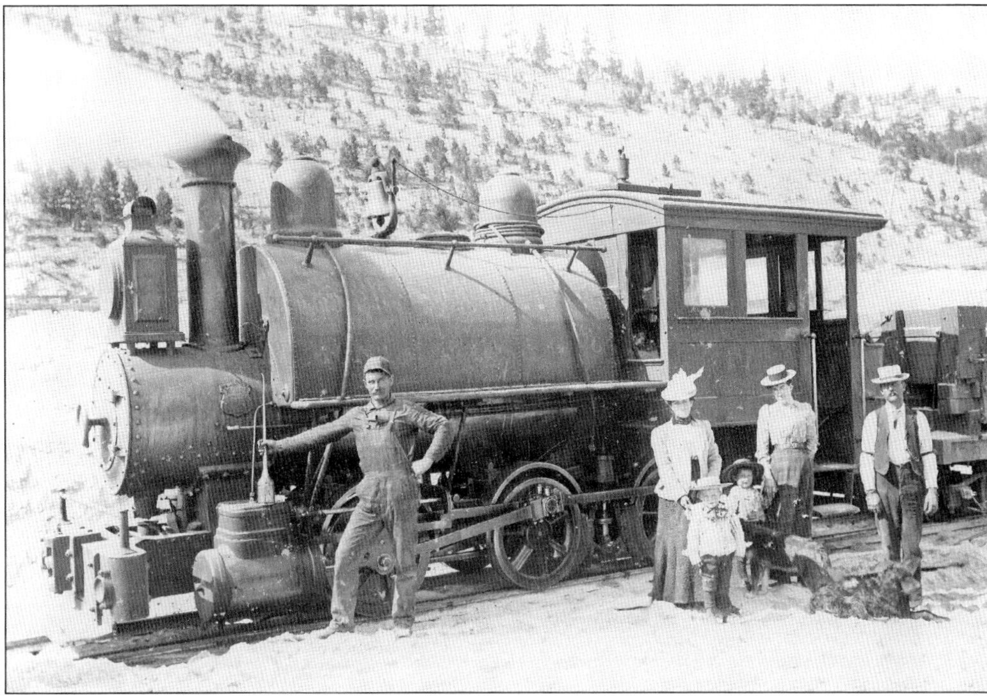

The train engineer stands next to a well-dressed family in Calvin in 1888. Although this family dressed in their finest clothing, riding a steam train often meant that clothing did not remain clean. After a day on a steam train, the black smoke usually left passengers covered in grime. (Courtesy of the Jefferson County Museum.)

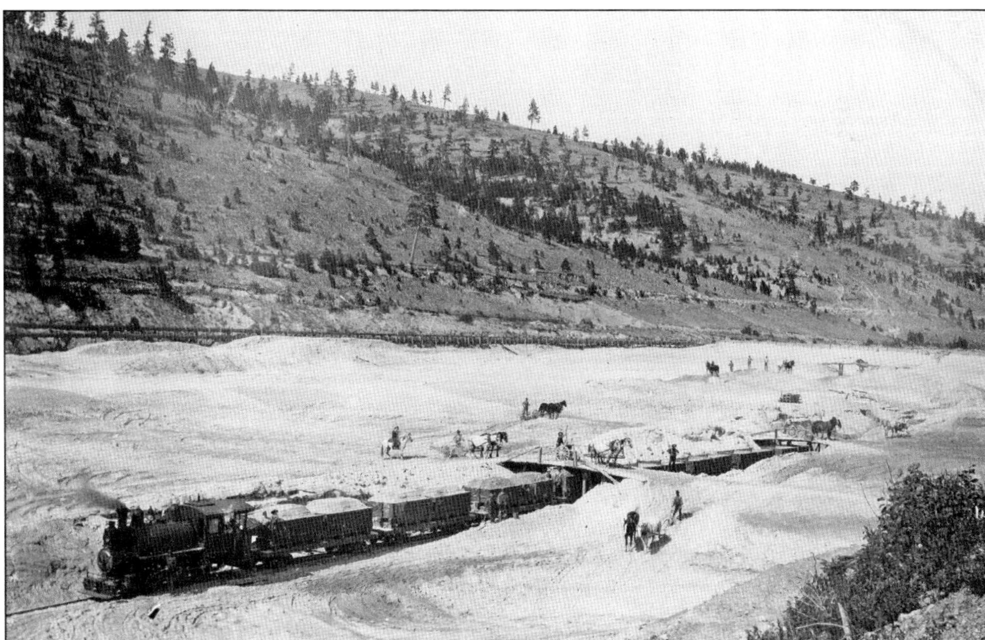

A Northern Pacific Railroad steam train stops for loading in Calvin in 1888. (Courtesy of the Jefferson County Museum.)

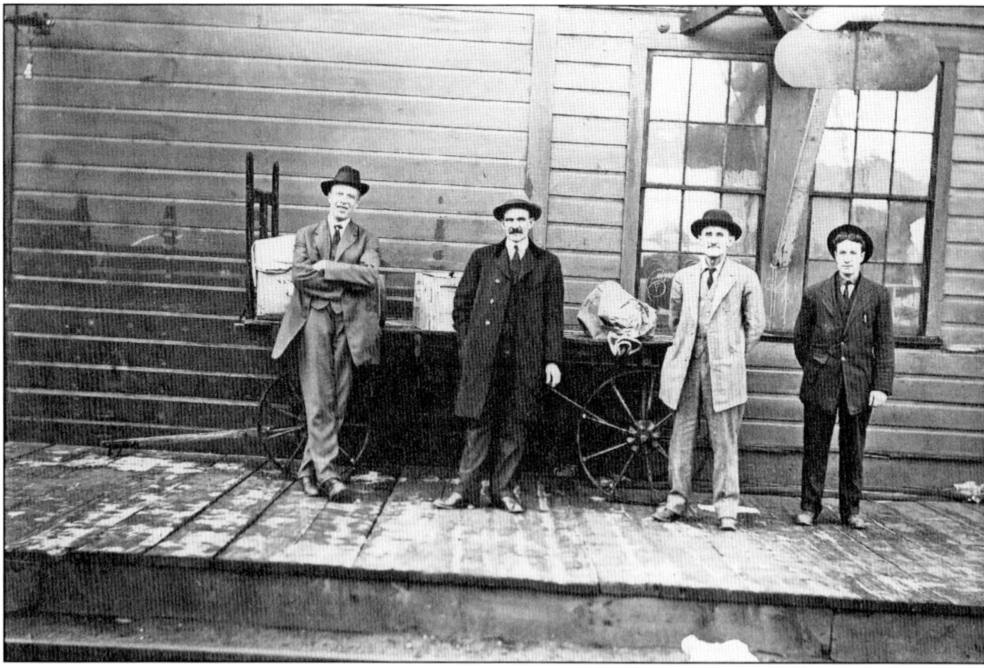

Men stand on the Basin railroad depot platform waiting for the next train to arrive. (Courtesy of the Jefferson County Museum.)

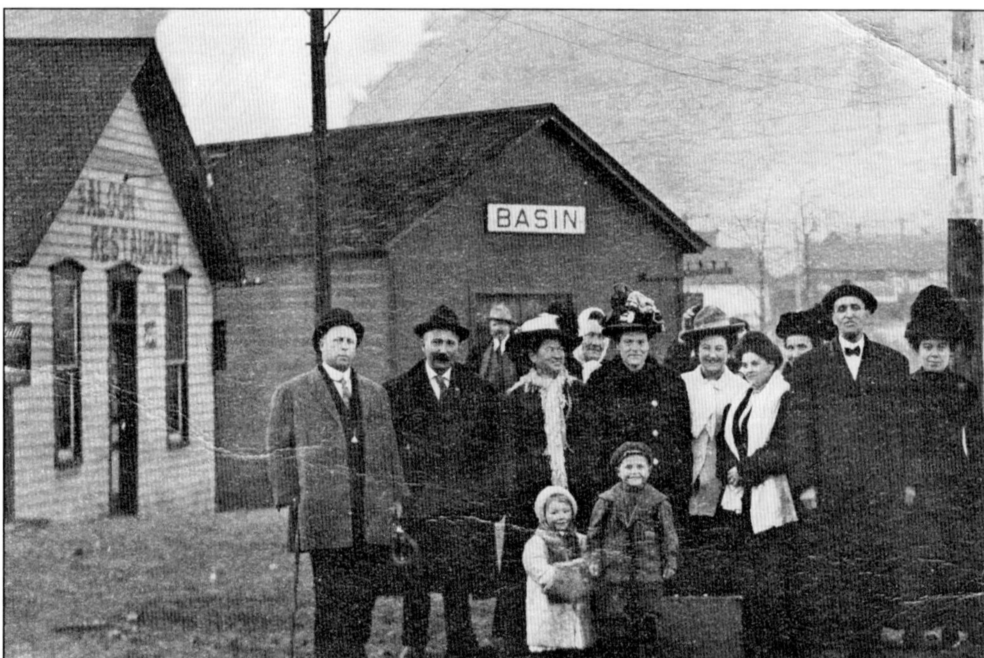

The Waldie and Sponheim families wait for the train at the Basin depot around 1910. The photograph depicts happy times as the families prepare for their journey. In 1917, tragedy struck when two of Clarence Waldie's children died in a horrible fire that burned their grandparents' home. (Courtesy of the Jefferson County Museum.)

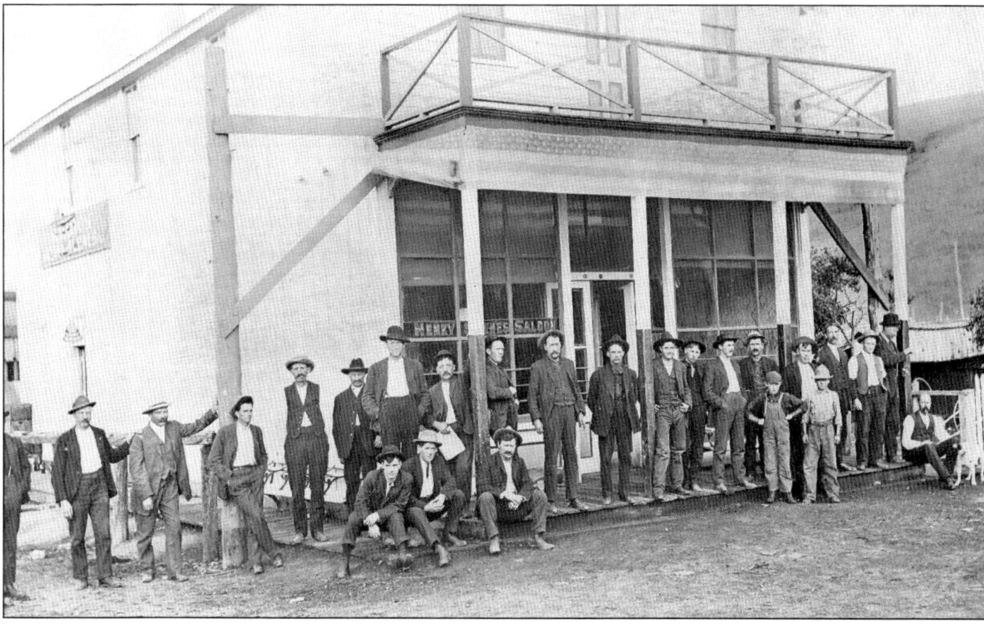

Men congregate outside Henry Slene's Saloon in Corbin. The mining community of Corbin contained several concentrators and a 711-foot railroad trestle used by the Montana Central Railway to transport mine tailings to the smelter in East Helena. (Courtesy of the Jefferson County Museum.)

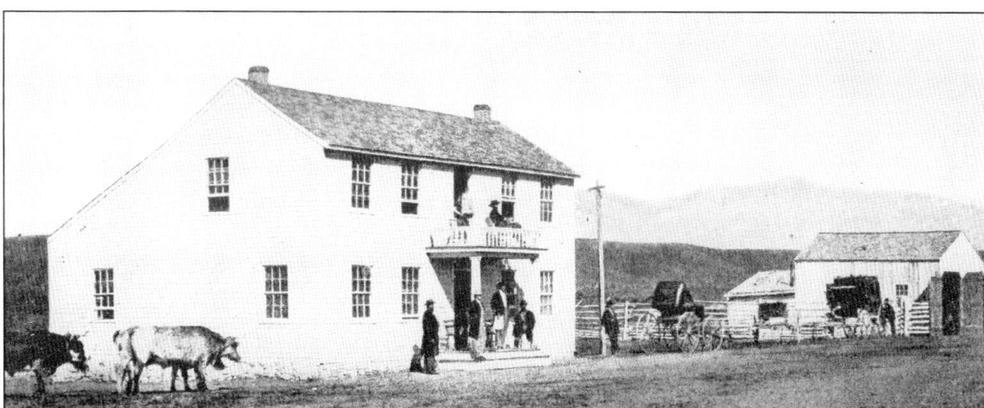

In the 1860s, Thomas Brooks built a stage station on the Virginia City–to–Fort Benton road 4 miles from present-day Whitehall. He named his station Whitehall. Freighters traveling on the road would stop for a hot meal and a place to rest for the night. In 1889, when the Northern Pacific completed laying track 4 miles from the station, the finished rail track made the stage station no longer necessary. (Courtesy of the Jefferson County Museum.)

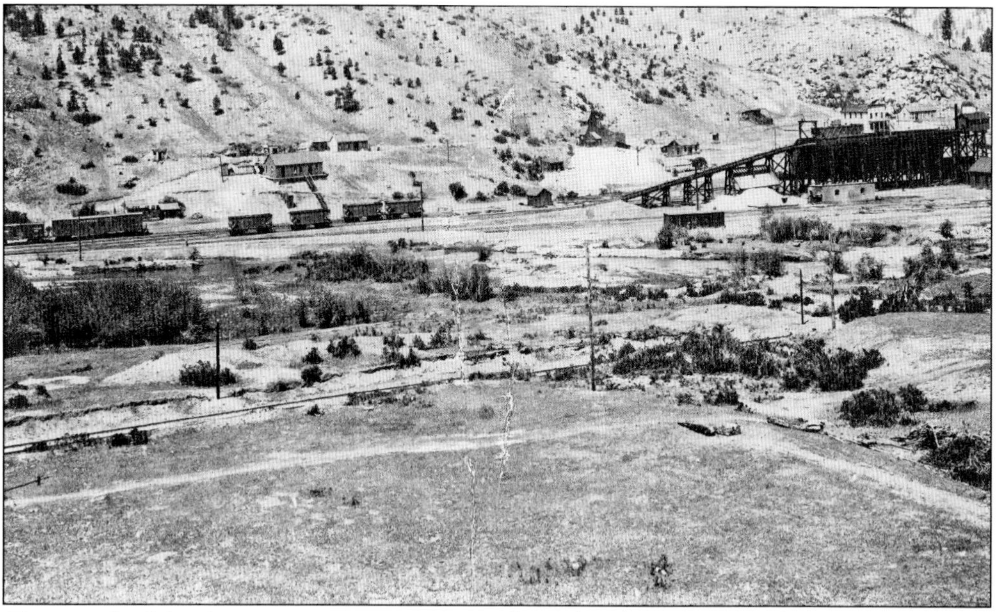

Chutes to load freight trains were important to the railroad community of Clancy. Goods like timber and mining ore were shipped all across the United States. (Courtesy of the Haab family of Clancy.)

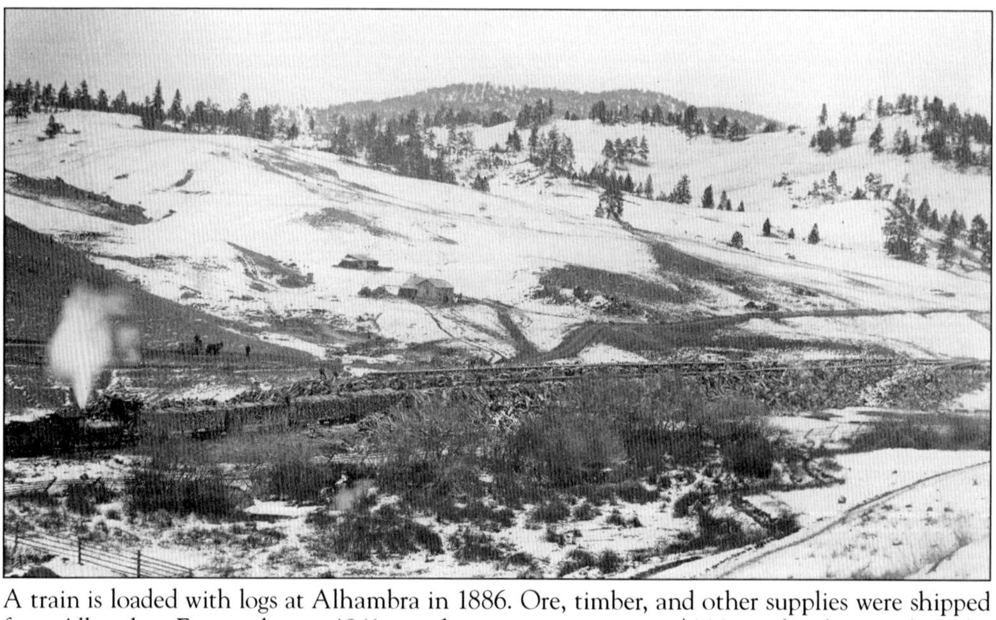

A train is loaded with logs at Alhambra in 1886. Ore, timber, and other supplies were shipped from Alhambra. Even as late as 1941, ore shipments were paying $800 per freight car when the White Pine Mine sent their load of silver, lead, and zinc ore to the Timber Butte Milling Company in Butte. (Courtesy of the Jefferson County Museum.)

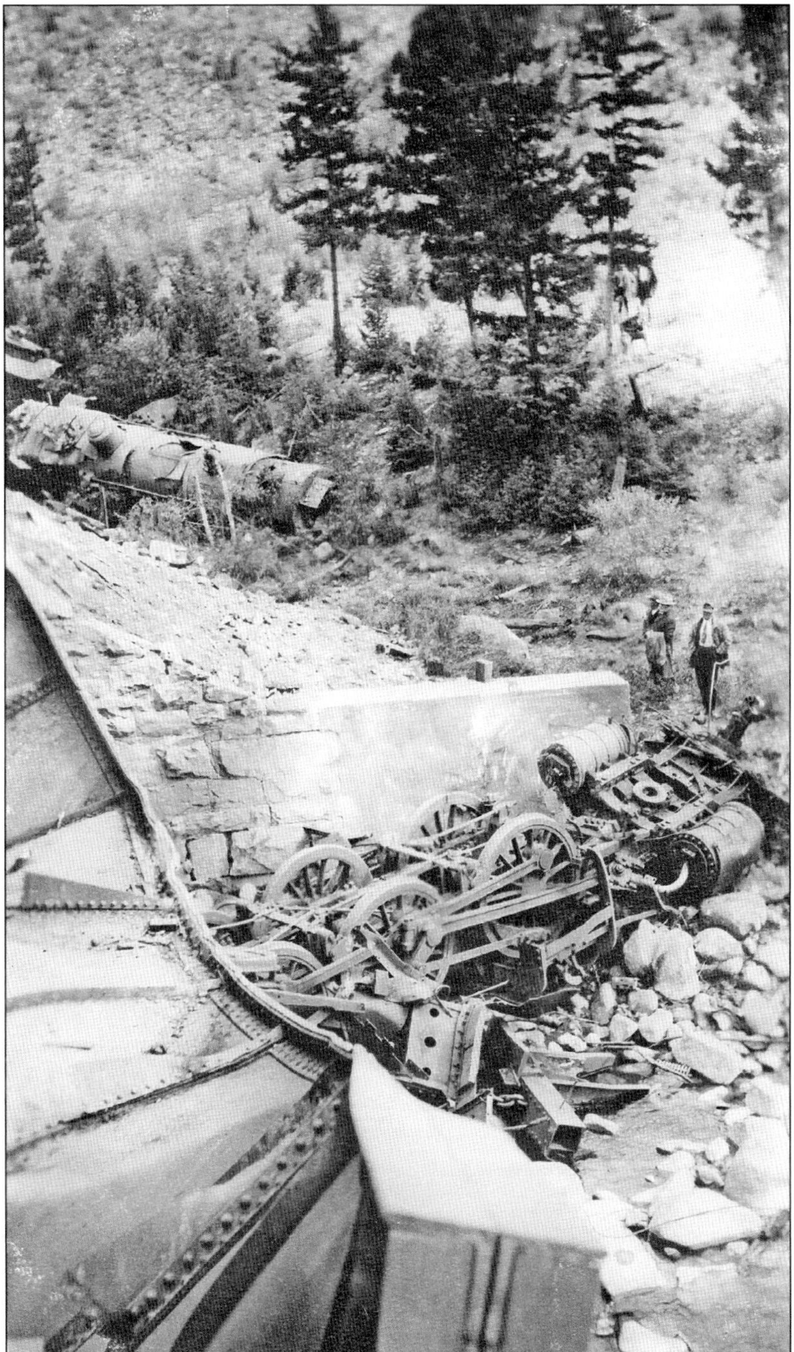

One of the worst Great Northern train accidents in Jefferson County occurred on the morning of September 14, 1917. Passenger train No. 238, due to arrive in Boulder at 9:30 a.m., was wrecked at about 9:00 a.m. at High Ore, about 6 miles west of Boulder. The wreck occurred on a sharp curve where a bridge crossed the Boulder River. The engine was completely smashed, the combination mail and baggage car was thrown across the river, and the smoker stood with one end on the bridge and the other end in the river. (Courtesy of the Jefferson County Museum.)

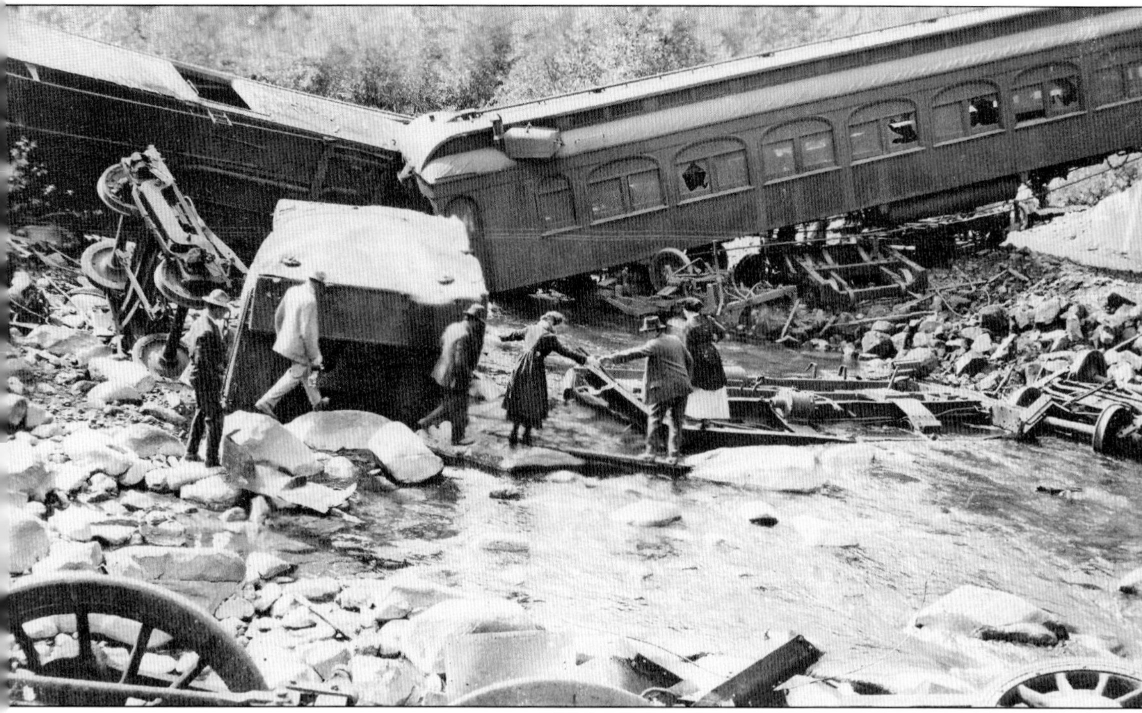

When the Great Northern passenger train No. 238 derailed on September 14, 1917, the engineer, Hiram "Nick" Carter, and the fireman, Earl Rutledge, were killed instantly. The cook, Henry Street, died later in the day of injuries sustained in the accident. In addition, four railroad attendants and two passengers were seriously injured but later recovered. The day had been Nick Carter's first time as an engineer. While this accident was tragic, it was unfortunately an all-too-common occurrence. Narrow canyons with multiple curves, frequent heavy snows, and steep grades all added to the hazards of train travel. (Courtesy of the Jefferson County Museum.)

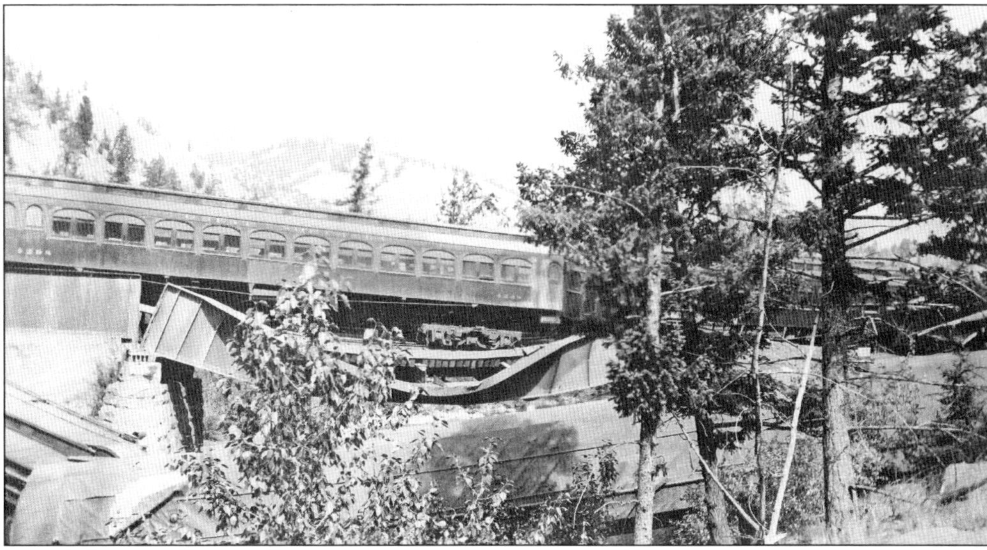

After Great Northern passenger train No. 238 wrecked in 1917, war rumors circulated that German sabotage had somehow been to blame. However, an investigation found excessive speed had been the reason for the derailment. (Courtesy of the Jefferson County Museum.)

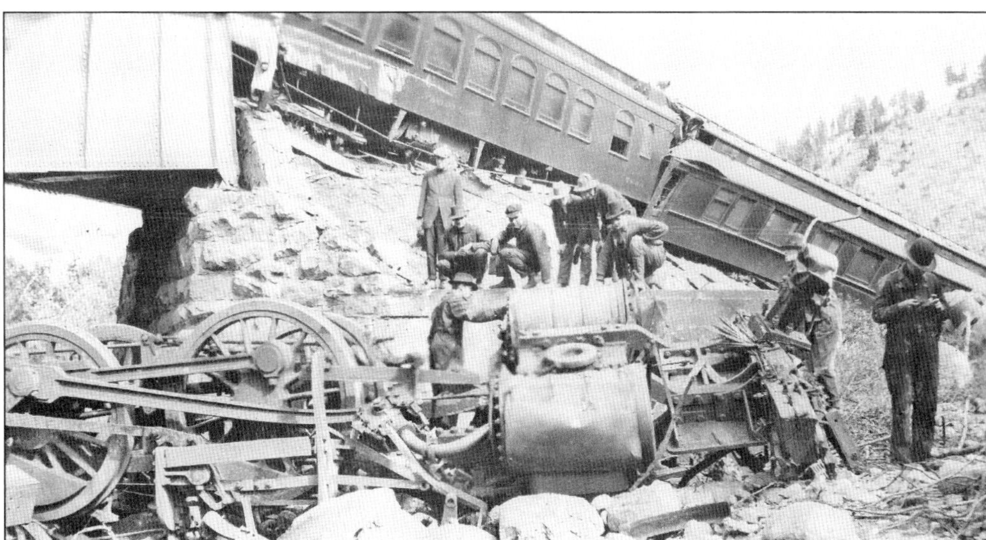

Curious residents of Jefferson County and a detachment of soldiers led by Corporal Thompson investigate the Great Northern passenger train wreck. (Courtesy of the Jefferson County Museum.)

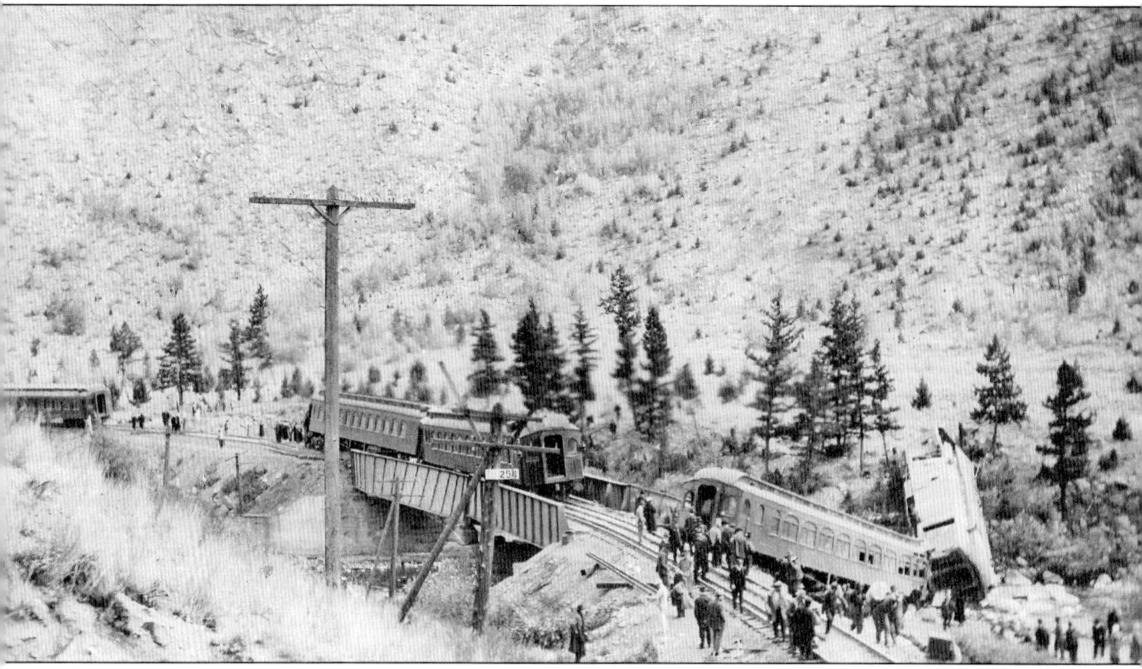

Great Northern passenger train No. 238 is pictured with its smoker car hanging off the bridge and the boilerplate nearly 100 feet away on the hillside. (Courtesy of the Jefferson County Museum.)

Four

EDUCATIONAL OPPORTUNITIES

Through hard work and determination, the early residents of Jefferson County provided a better life for their families. Eager to advance their children's education, taxpayers in Jefferson County funded new schools. In addition to schools, other educational opportunities were provided when neighbors shared their varied skills with each other. Aurilla Preston Elder Myers came to Boulder as a young schoolteacher from the Mount Carroll Seminary in Illinois. She was contracted to teach at the Muskrat School in the Boulder Valley. When the young, beautiful teacher arrived in Boulder, she was spotted by a highly respected bachelor named Alexander Elder. According to the *Jefferson County Sentinel* newspaper, Alexander James Elder was superintendent of common schools, undersheriff, justice of the peace, and judge for Jefferson County during the time he lived there. Aurilla and Alexander were married in Boulder on September 21, 1879. Although married women generally were not hired to teach, Aurilla continued to instruct the children of Jefferson County for many years. Some forms of education were not found in Jefferson County schools. Mary Atwater arrived in Basin in 1914 with her husband Max, a mining engineer. She soon grew restless in the tiny mining town. She wanted to learn hand weaving to keep busy. She purchased a loom from California and asked for a teacher to come to Basin to instruct her. A quick student, Mary was soon weaving her own blankets. She invited women in Basin to come to her house to learn the craft. Soon Basin women were enjoying this art and making lovely pieces for themselves. Mary began drawing her own weaving patterns and sending them out in newsletters, which she sold as *Shuttlecraft Bulletins*. Mary's art of hand weaving outgrew the town of Basin. She became well known throughout the United States and Europe for her skills. Children and adults of Jefferson County benefited from diverse educational opportunities. Whether they were children or bored housewives, the chance to learn new ideas abounded. The determination of residents in Jefferson County to have a better future endured.

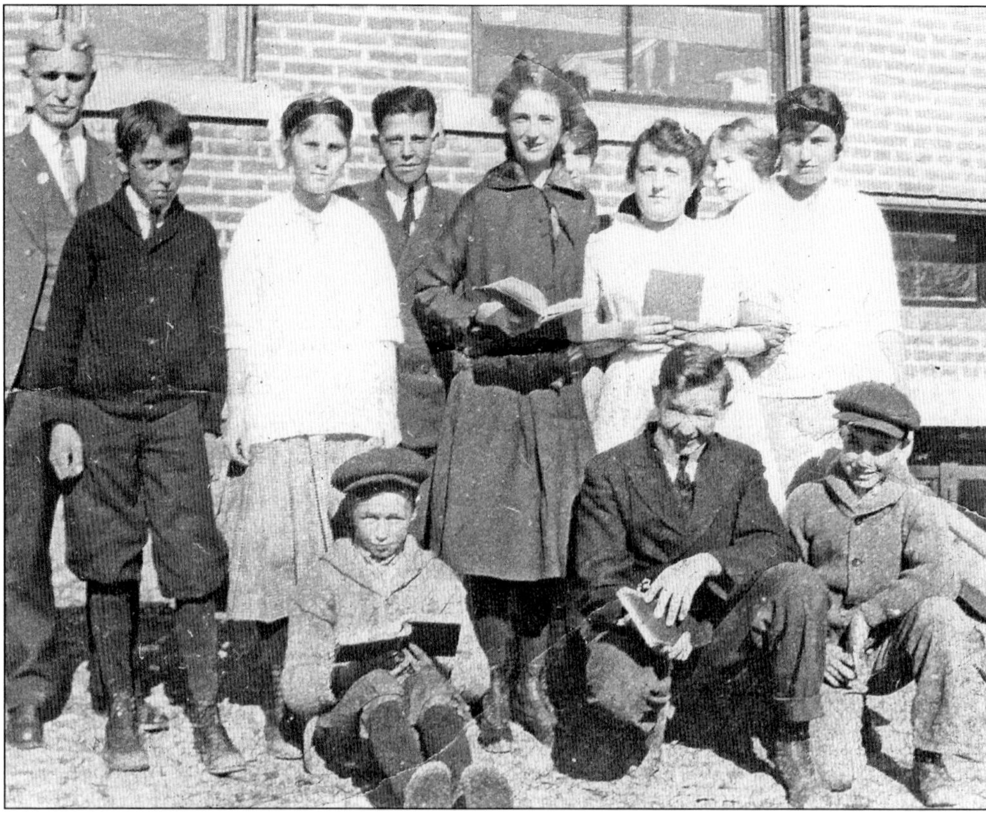

The Boulder Grade School seventh- and eighth-grade classes took their lesson books outside to pose for this photograph in front of their school in 1915. (Courtesy of the Jefferson County Museum.)

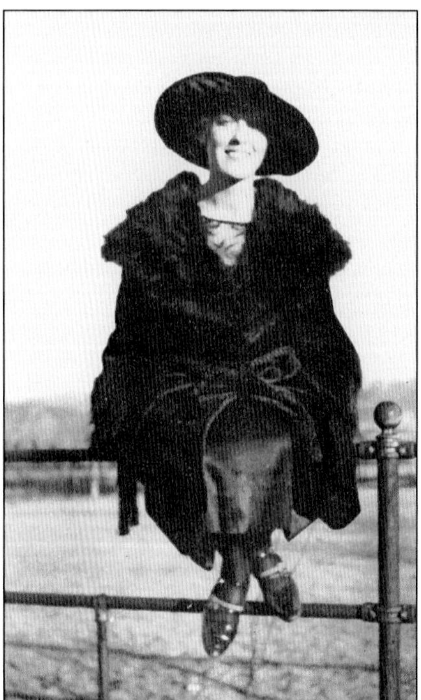

Maude Watkins, a second-grade teacher at the Boulder Grade School, relaxes on a fence. (Courtesy of the Jefferson County Museum.)

C. W. Tenny was the eighth-grade teacher at the Boulder Grade School in 1917, when he replaced J. R. Norville, who was ill. (Courtesy of the Jefferson County Museum.)

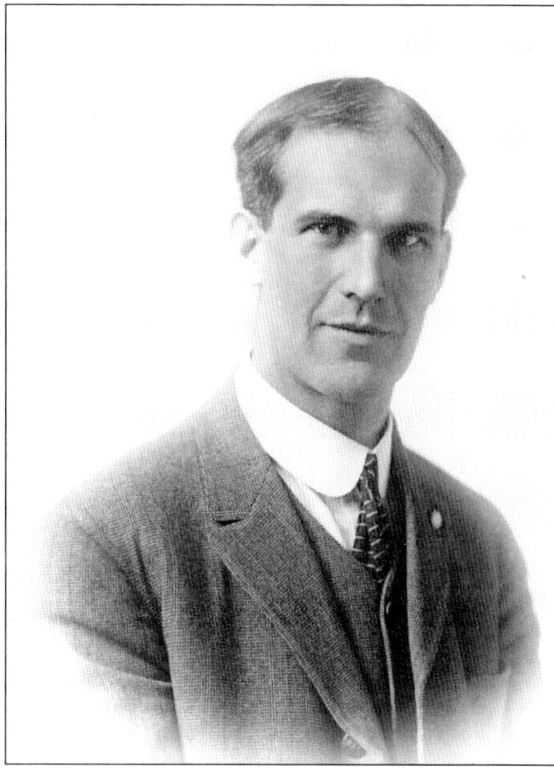

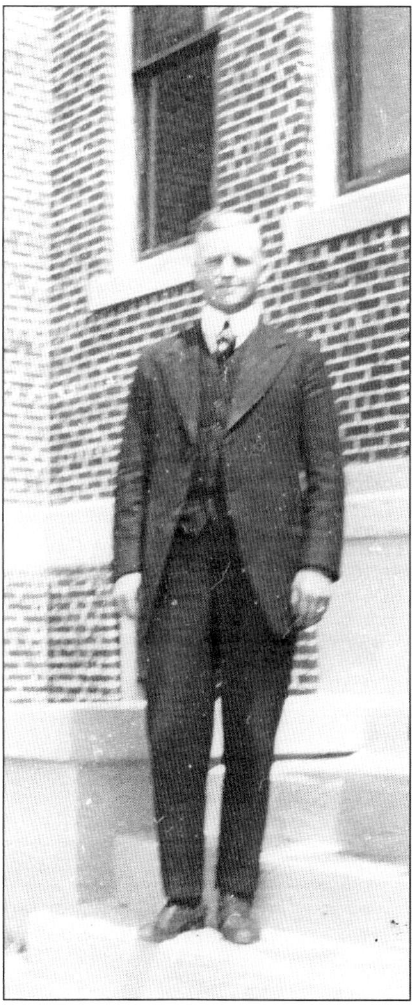

Jefferson County High School principal A. T. Peterson had his picture taken on the steps of the school. He served as superintendent of Jefferson County High School in 1914 and as principal in 1917. He left Jefferson County in 1920 to accept a job with Custer County High School. (Courtesy of the Jefferson County Museum.)

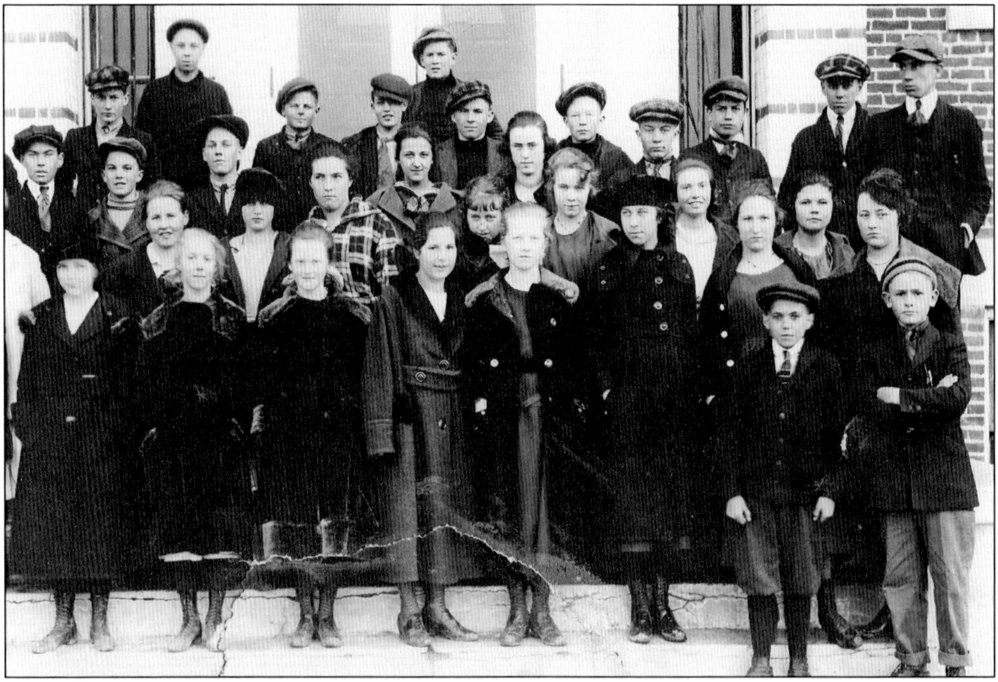

Jefferson County High School students pose in front of their school on February 3, 1920. (Courtesy of the Lindsay family, Clancy, Montana.)

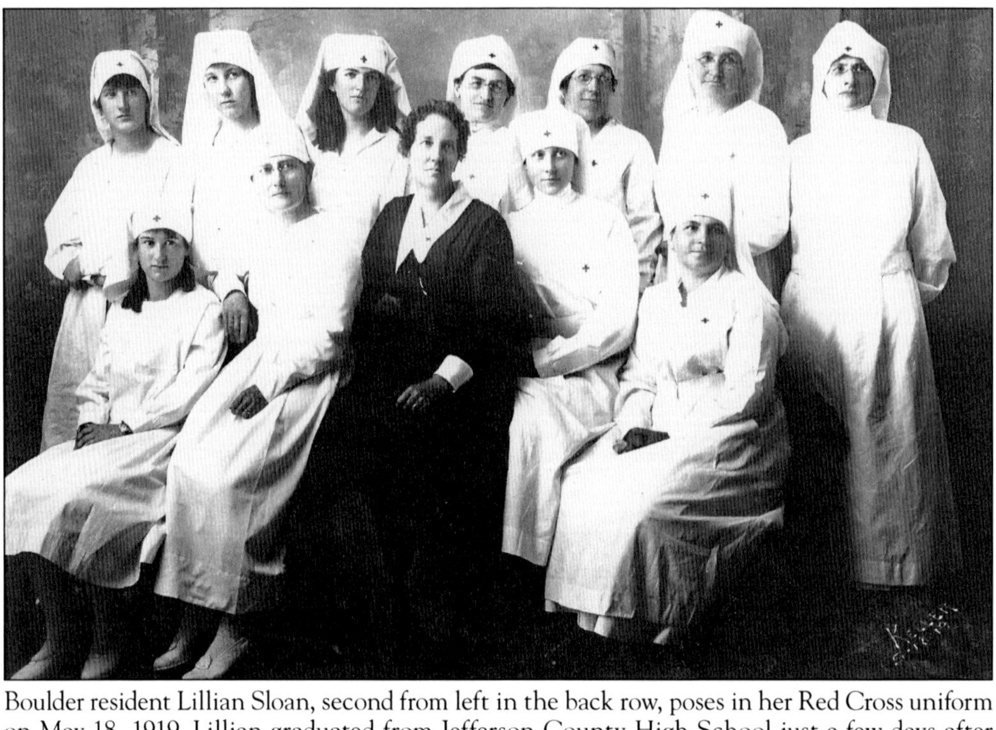

Boulder resident Lillian Sloan, second from left in the back row, poses in her Red Cross uniform on May 18, 1919. Lillian graduated from Jefferson County High School just a few days after this picture was taken. (Courtesy of the Jefferson County Genealogy and Heritage Center, Boulder, Montana.)

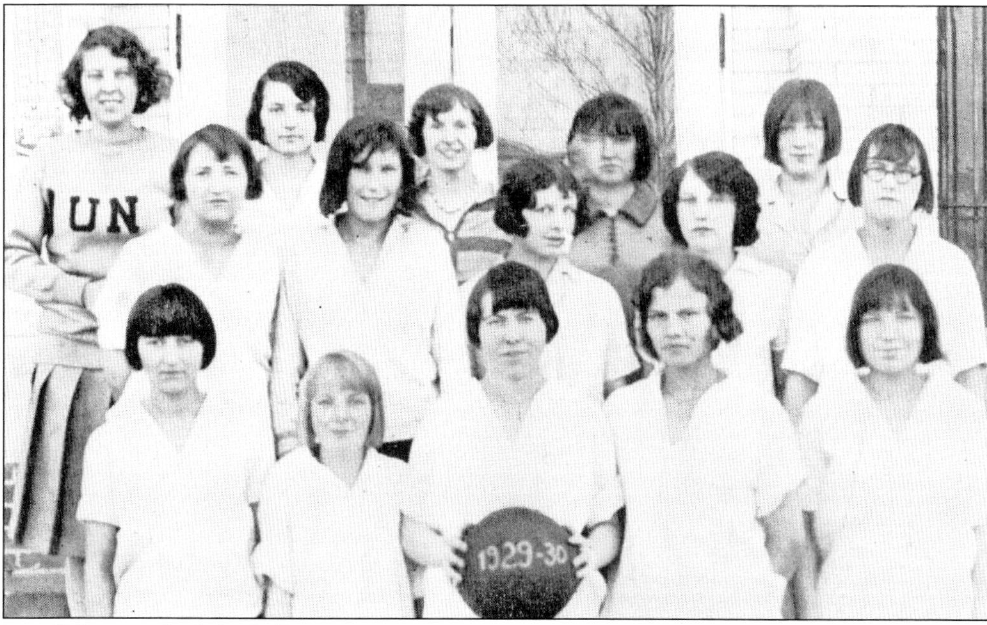

Inez Killer coached the Jefferson County High School girls' basketball team in 1929–1930. Basketball was the only sport available to the girls in those years at Jefferson County High School. The girls played only four games. (Courtesy of the Jefferson County Museum.)

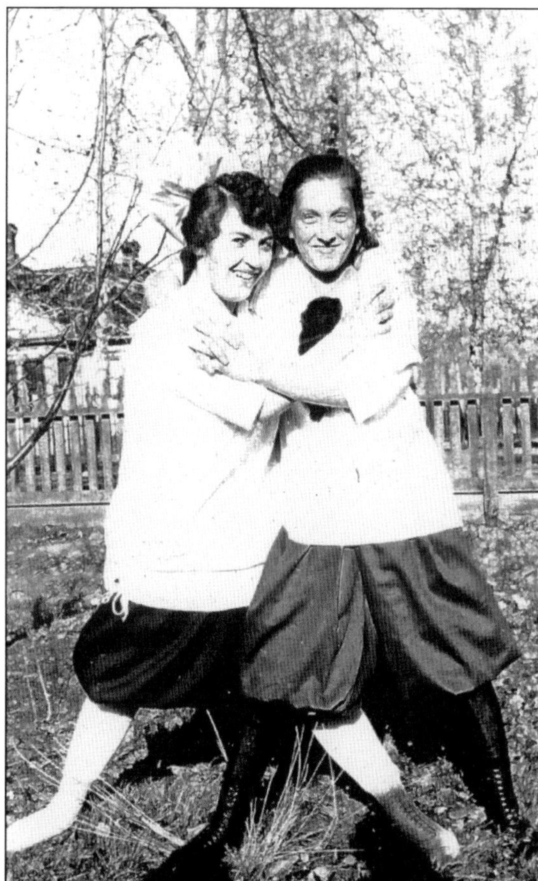

Ready for basketball, Jessie Steele (left) and a friend pose in their Jefferson County High School uniforms. (Courtesy of the Jefferson County Museum.)

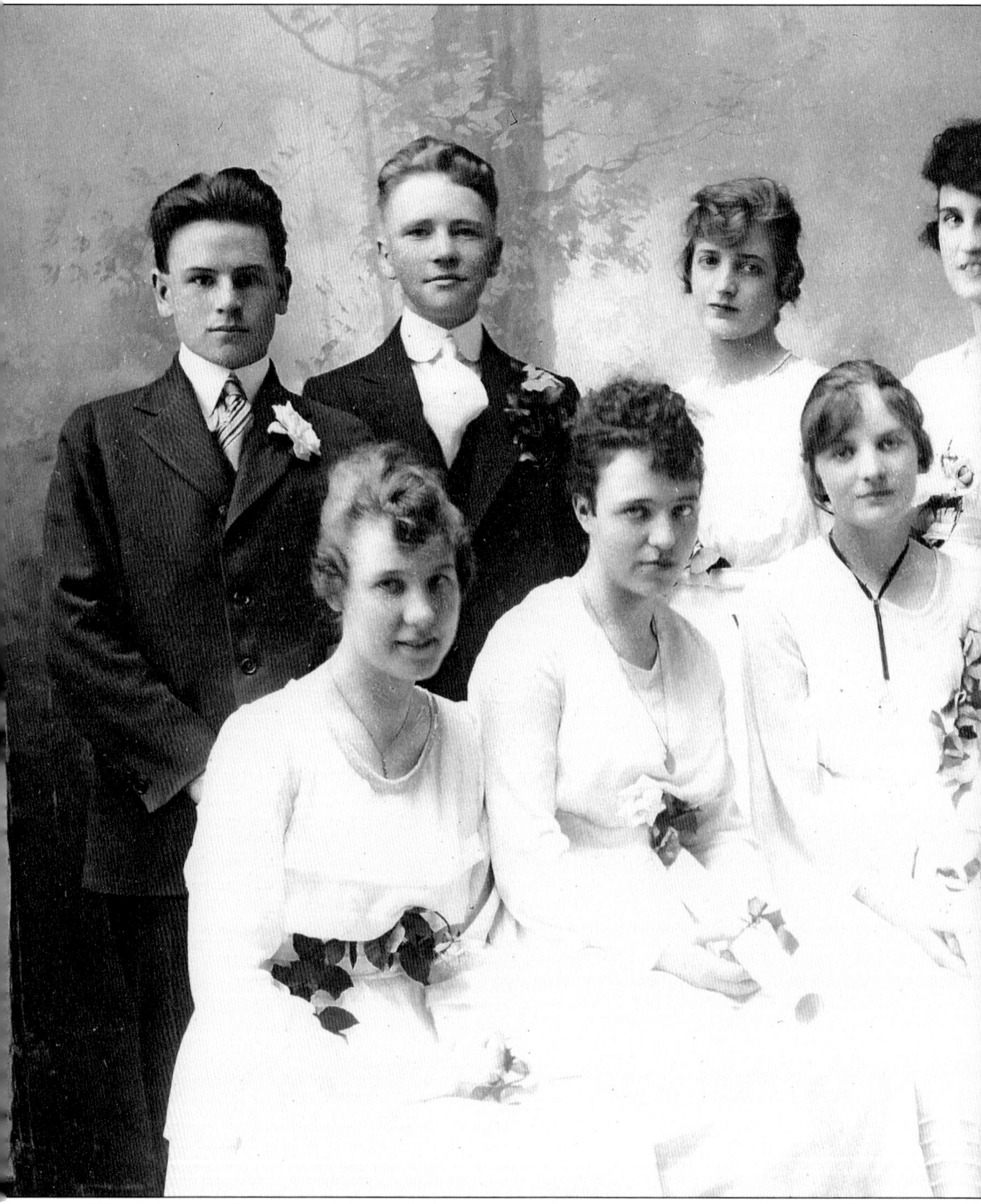

The Jefferson County High School class of 1919 dressed in their finest clothes to have their picture taken on May 24, 1919. From left to right are (first row) Lillian Sloan, Leila Dowling, Yvette Halford, Edna Dowling, Marguerite Hundley, and Anna O'Rourke; (second row) Grover Taylor, Lynn Falch, Lucy Buhrer, Alice Ramsey, Dwight Johnson, Albert Beck, and Ben Quinn. When sisters Edna and Leila Dowling graduated that year, their mother, Bessie, was not able to

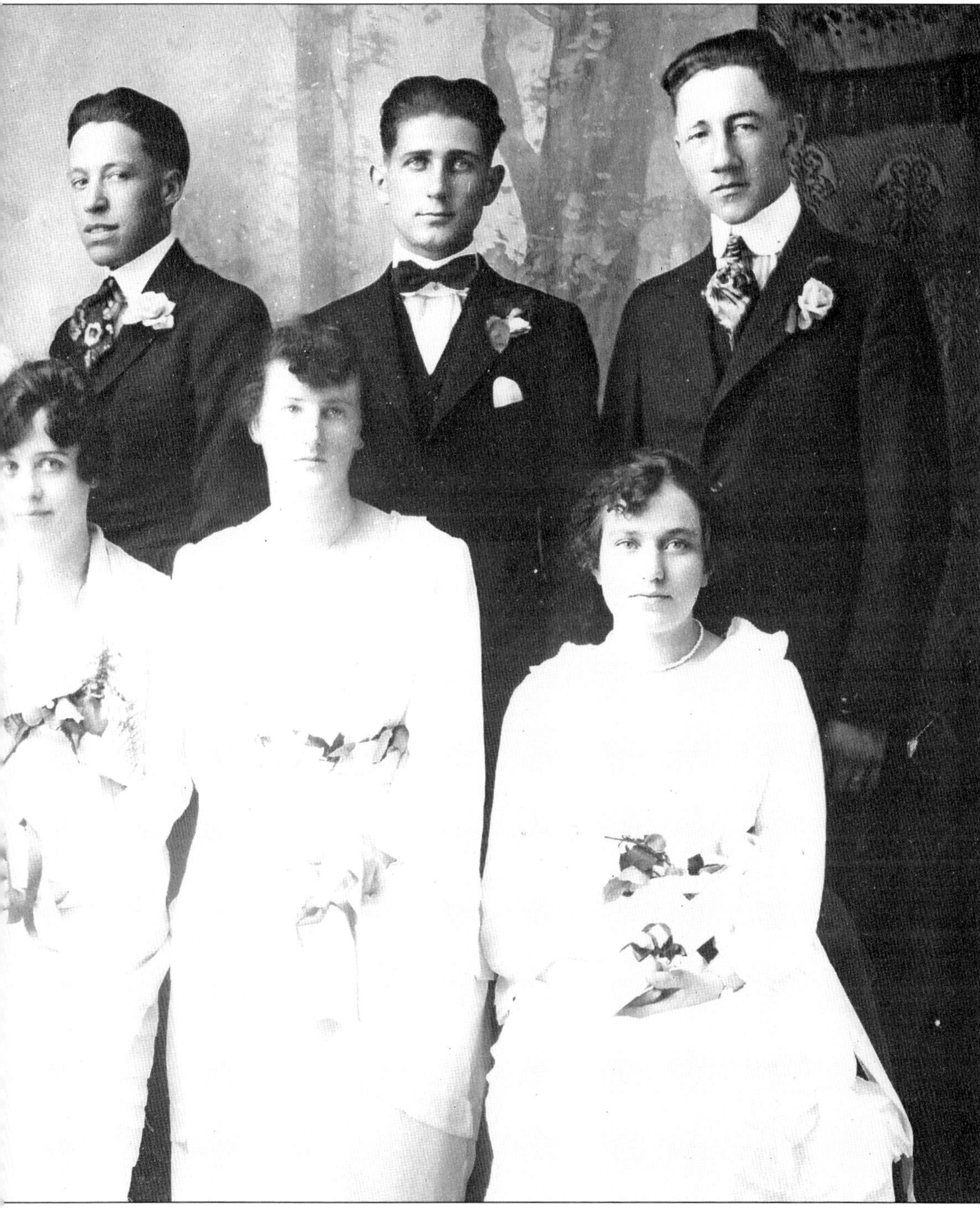

celebrate the milestone. Bessie had died the previous year. Grover Taylor became a butcher and worked for Helena Meat Company, Montana Meat Company, and Tom's Meat Market in Helena. Grover married Jessie Steele in 1926. (Courtesy of the Jefferson County Genealogy and Heritage Center, Boulder, Montana.)

Shall bonds be issued and sold to the amount of Five Thousand Dollars bearing not more than six per cent. interest, redeemable in one year, and payable in twenty years, for the purpose of purchasing a school lot, and building a school house thereon ?

BONDS YES.

BONDS NO.

In 1898, Clancy residents voted for a special school bond to fund the building of a new school. The measure passed, and students moved into their new school in January 1899. (Courtesy of the Jefferson County Museum.)

MONTHLY STATEMENT

HELENA, MONTANA, June 29, 1904

M Clancy School Dist.

IN ACCOUNT WITH

W. A. Moore Book & Stationery Co.

BOOKS, STATIONERY, OFFICE SUPPLIES

UNDERWOOD TYPEWRITERS

Special Agents for Spaulding and Victor's Athletic Goods

FISHING TACKLE
ENGRAVING

STATE DEPOSITORY
FOR SCHOOL BOOKS

50 North Main Street. Phone 150.

Acc't Rendered

Merchandise

W. A. MOORE BOOK PAID & STATIONERY CO.

	√History of England	.48
	√Little Smoke	1.20
	√Howell Story Book	.45
	√History of the U. S.	.72
	√Men Places and Things	1.20
	√With Robert's in Pretoria	1.08
	√Heart of the Rockies	1.20
	√Historic Boston	.45
	√Bow-Wow and Mew- Mew	.18
	√Plattime and Seedtime	.29
	√Earth and Sky	.26
	√True Bear Stories	1.00
	√Chesterfield's Letters	.22
	√Rab and his Friends	.23
	√Sara Crewe	1.00
√6	Lay of the Last Minstrel @ 22¢	1.32
√6	Lady of the Lake @ 32¢	1.92
	√Wings and Stings	.36
	√Folk Tales from the Russians	.36
	√Child Stories	.27
	√Lobo Rag and Vixen	.40
	Don Quixote	.40
	√Children's Stories	.90
	√Eugene Field Book	.40
	√Fanciful Tales	.40
	√Thrall of Lief the Lucky	1.13
		$17.82

A list of library books ordered by the Clancy School in June 1904 shows a few unusual choices. (Courtesy of the Jefferson County Museum.)

Members of the Jefferson County High School class of 1921 painted a large "21" on one of the many boulders located in Jefferson County. (Courtesy of the Jefferson County Museum.)

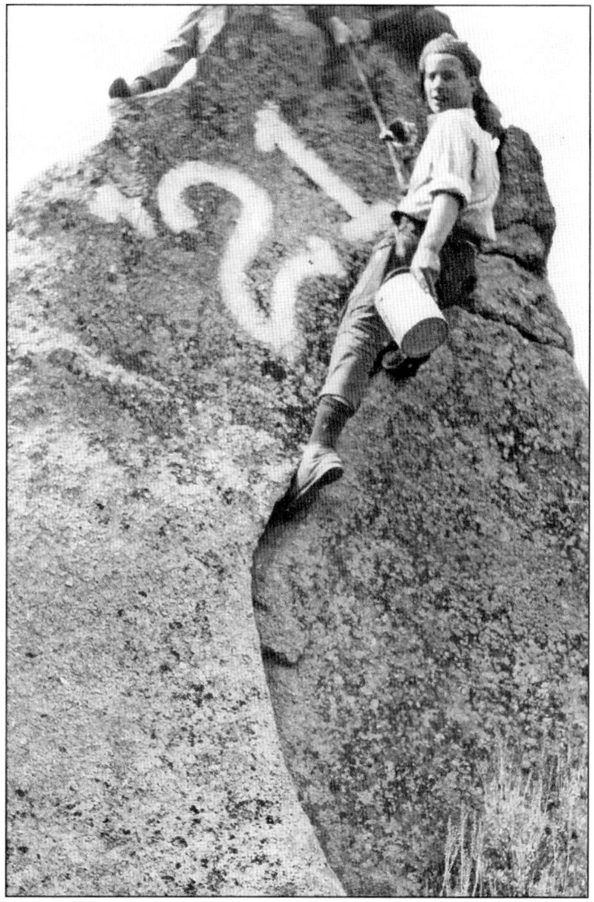

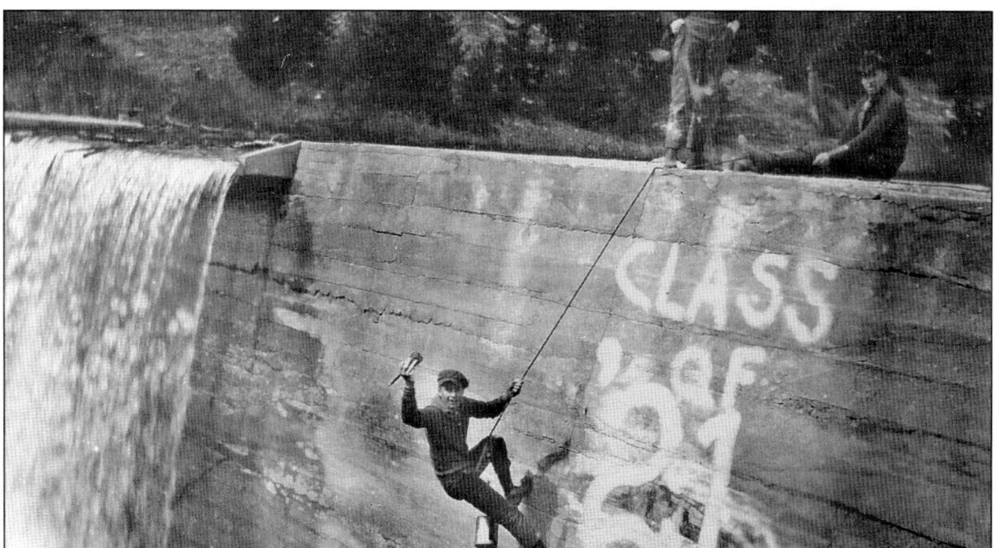

The Jefferson County High School class of 1921 used ropes to lower a fellow classmate down to paint a "21" on the Little Boulder River dam. (Courtesy of the Jefferson County Museum.)

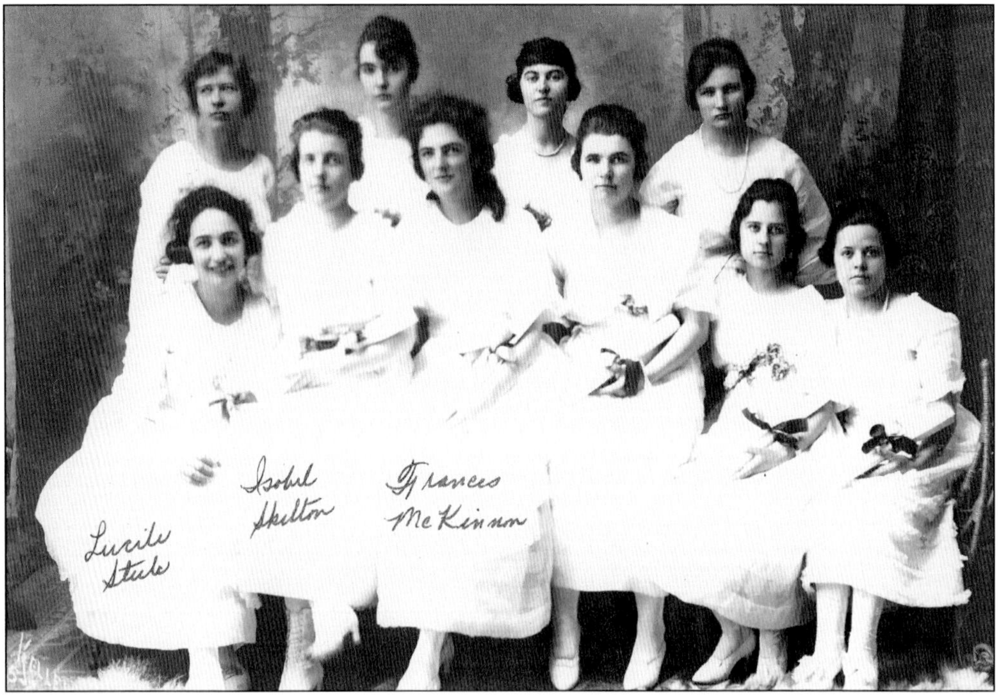

The Jefferson County High School graduating girls of 1920 are dressed in fancy white dresses in this photograph. In the front row, from left to right, sit Lucille Steele, Isabel Skelton, and Frances McKinnon. The other girls that graduated that year were Nellie McCauley, Edith Ahl, Shirley Williams, Florence Marks, Mildred Hersey, Alice Laramie, Lillian Wilson, and Alice Rand. (Courtesy of the Jefferson County Museum.)

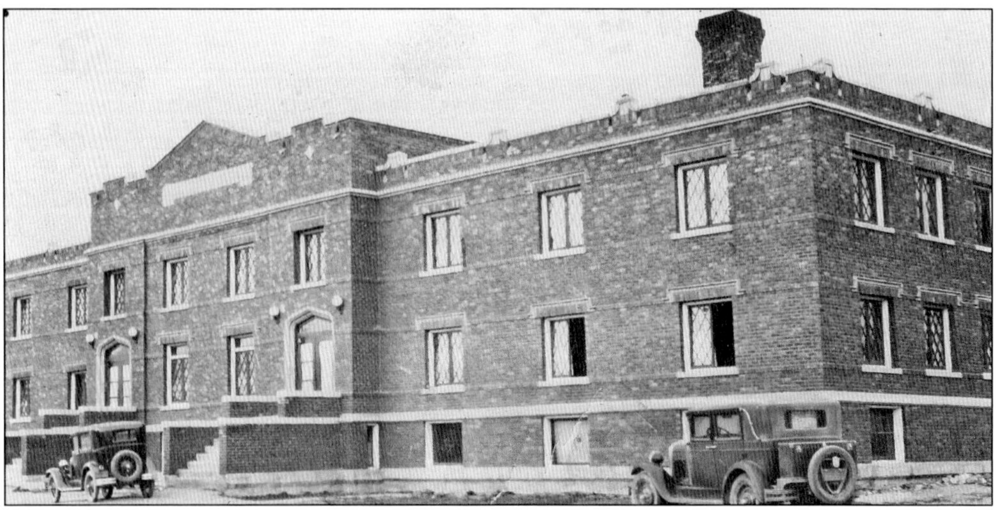

The Jefferson County High School dormitory housed students that lived too far away from the school to travel home each day. (Courtesy of the Jefferson County Genealogy and Heritage Center, Boulder, Montana.)

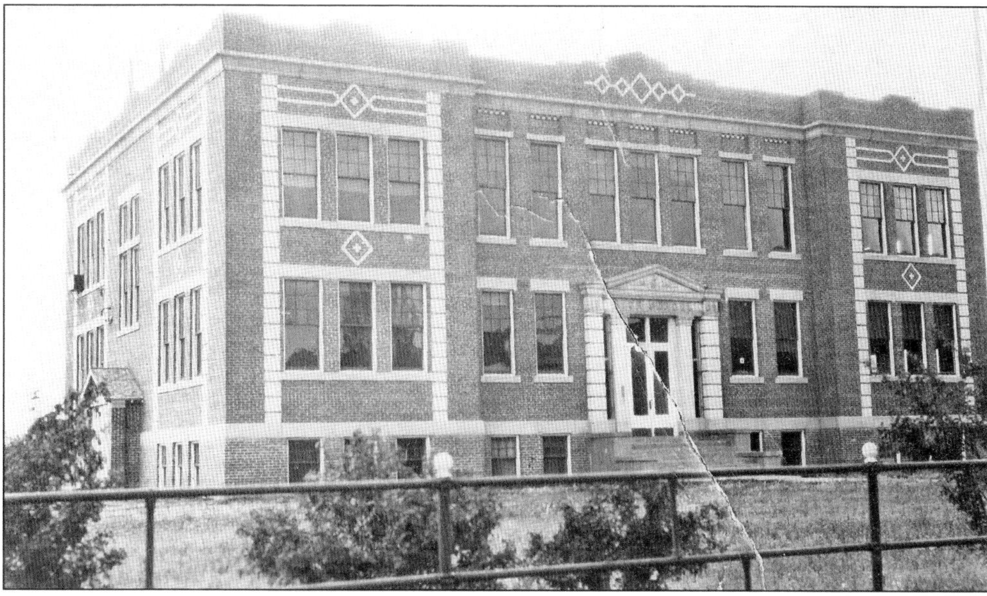

The original Jefferson County High School building was torn down in 1986 to make way for the new building. (Courtesy of the Jefferson County Genealogy and Heritage Center, Boulder, Montana.)

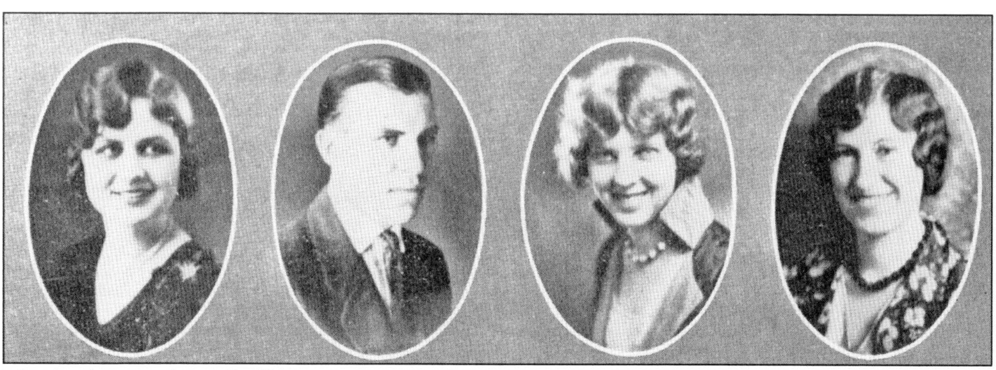

The faculty members of Jefferson County High School in 1930 are, from left to right, Evelyn Knutson, J. D. Fellows, Inez Killer, and Rosie Copenhaver. (Courtesy of the Jefferson County Museum.)

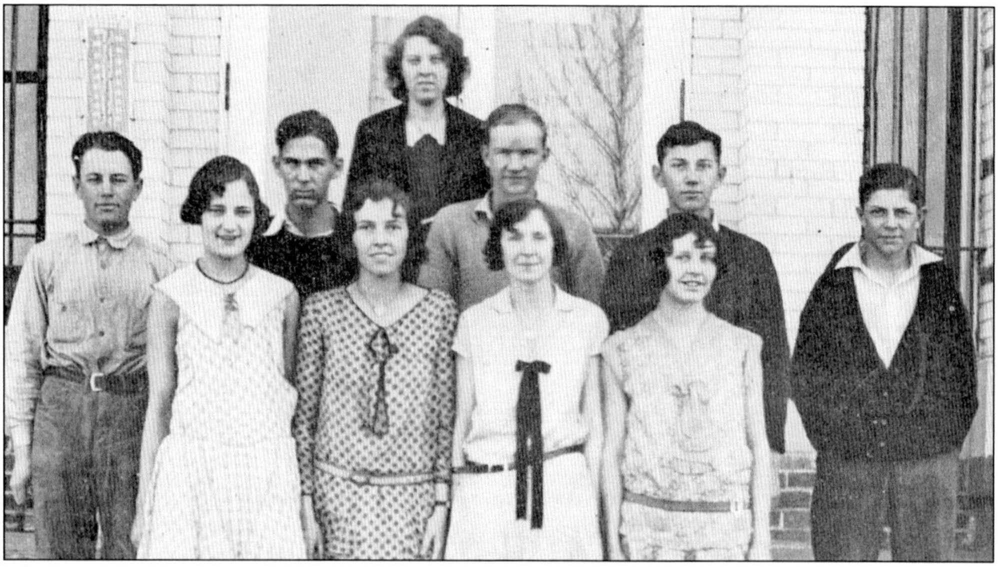

The 1931 class at the Jefferson County High School stands outside for their picture. (Courtesy of the Jefferson County Museum.)

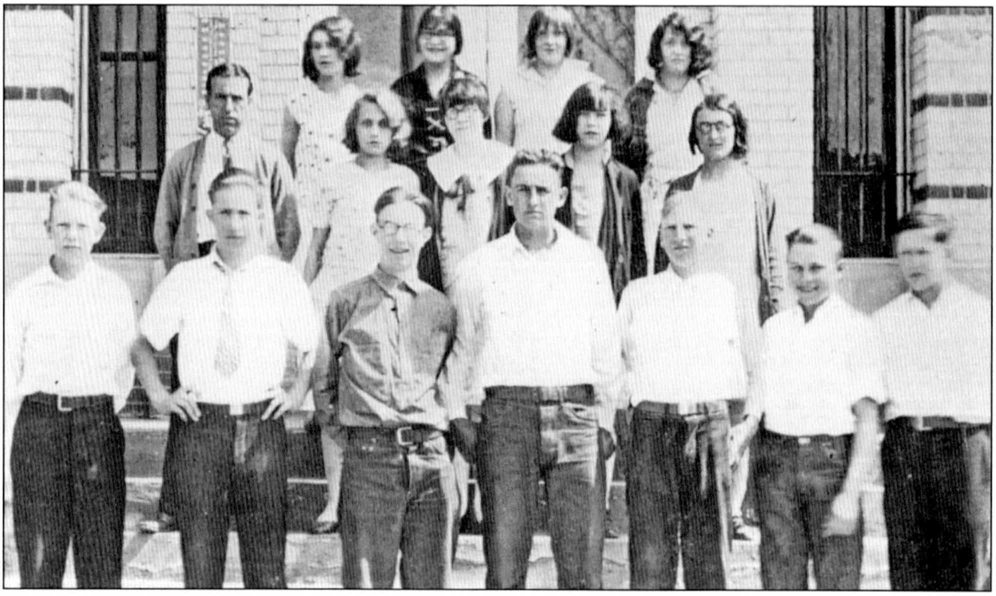

The 1932 class at the Jefferson County High School waits for the photographer to take their picture. (Courtesy of the Jefferson County Museum.)

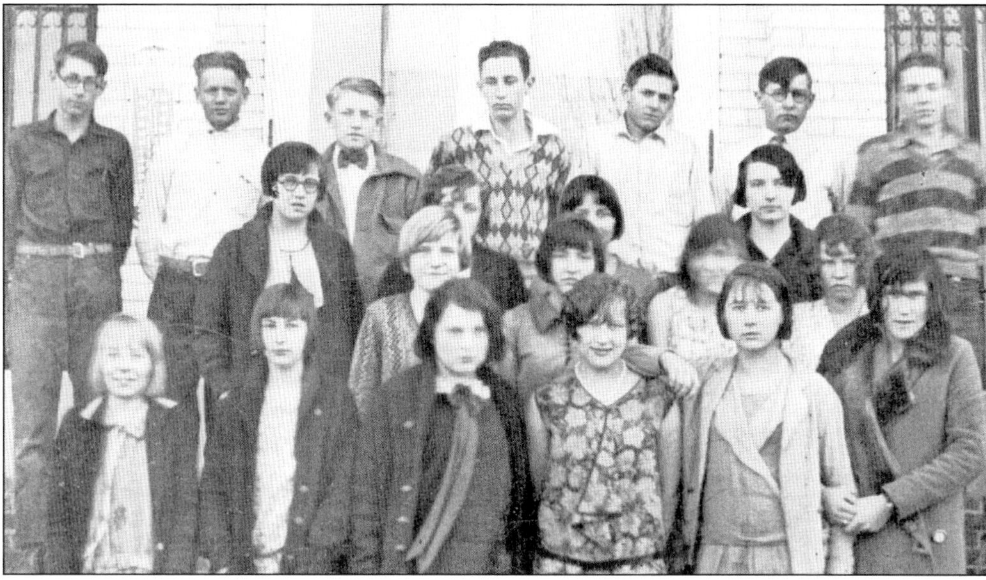

The 1933 class at the Jefferson County High School happily smiles for the camera. (Courtesy of the Jefferson County Museum.)

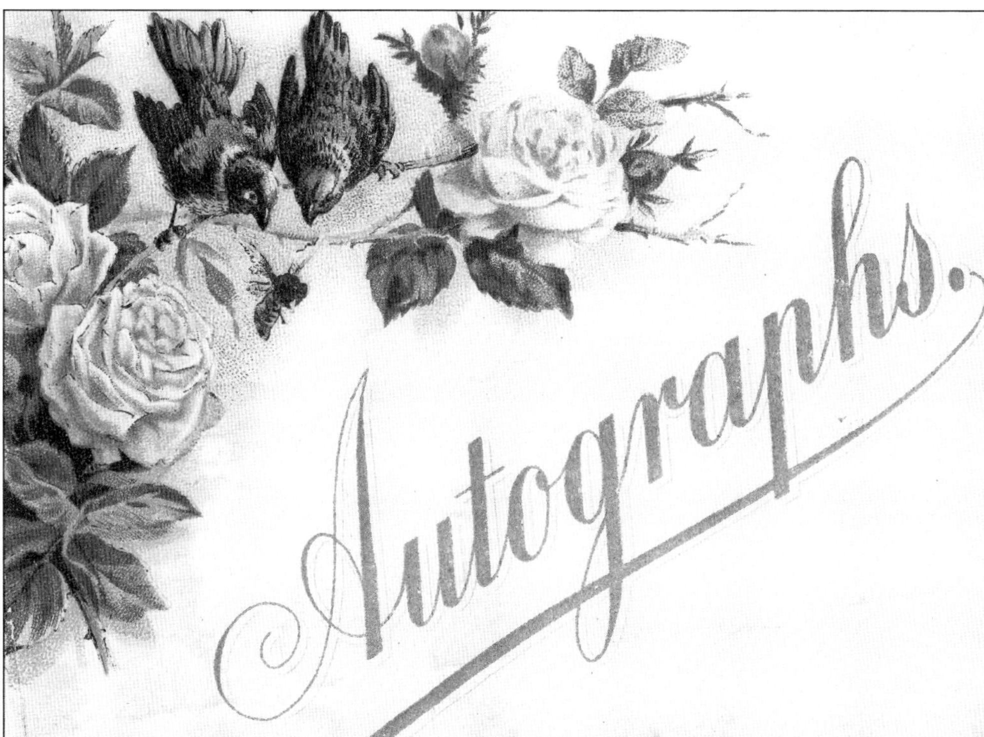

School autograph books were popular when Alhambra resident Ada Glass was a child attending school in 1888. Her classmate Nannie Bailey wrote a whimsical note to her. Another school friend, Laura Hutinson, admonished her to "remember your school mate." (Courtesy of the Lindsay family, Clancy, Montana.)

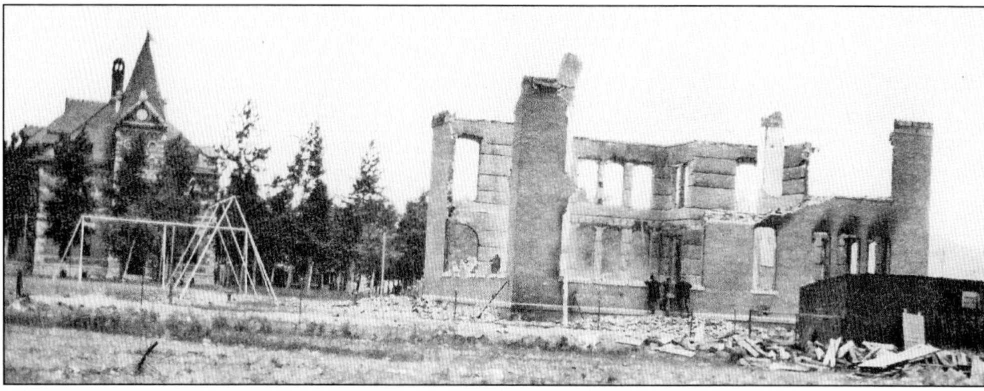

The charred remains of the original two-story Boulder Grade School are seen here. It was completely destroyed after a fire started in the basement. (Courtesy of the Jefferson County Museum.)

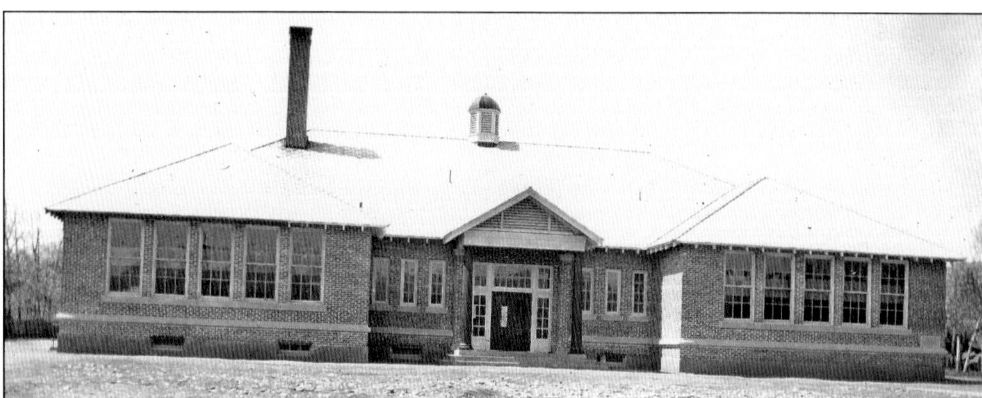

This picture, taken in 1925 of the newly constructed Boulder Grade School, shows the new school was ready for students. (Courtesy of the Jefferson County Museum.)

Five

Business and Commerce

Twenty-four year old Roy Walsh and 17-year-old accomplice Arthur Hughes planned and executed an armed robbery of the general store in Renova, 7 miles south of Whitehall. When storeowner Albert Johnson locked up on the evening of June 26, 1923, he did not know he was being watched. As he secured his store for the night, a bullet struck him in the throat. Roy Walsh had shot Albert Johnson. Mortally wounded, Johnson staggered to a neighbor's house, while his attackers got away. Jefferson County residents, enraged by the murder, started combing the surrounding area in the early morning of June 27. Sheriff John Mountjoy responded to a tip and tracked down Arthur Hughes in Butte and a few hours later picked up Roy Walsh hiding near Cardwell. Roy's trial was quickly set for July 21, 1923, and ended on July 27 with a guilty verdict and a sentence to hang. The sentence was carried out on February 14, 1925. While Albert Johnson died defending his business, his experience was the exception in Jefferson County. Business owners in the county more often than not experienced prosperous transactions. In 1909, Whitehall proprietors offered a variety of services, purchased arc lamps to light the streets, and maintained a secure banking establishment. Boulder storeowners like William and John Steele provided supplies to a growing agricultural community. One early rancher named Edward Ryan arrived in Montana in 1864 by wagon train. He spent a short time in Virginia City but soon searched for a place suitable for cattle. With his wife, Helen Lacey, he homesteaded 160 acres in the Boulder Valley and had eight children. Ed Ryan served as the vice president of the Boulder Bank and was a Jefferson County commissioner.

Business and commerce in Jefferson County played an important part in the development of southwestern Montana. Early businessmen like Johnson, Ryan, and the Steeles provided employment and reliable income for the residents of the county.

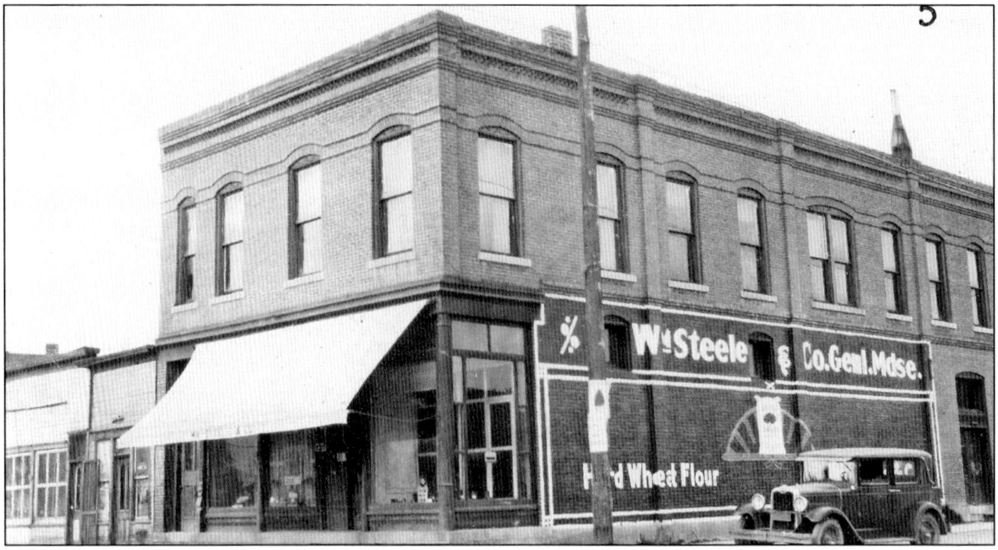

Brothers William and John Steele owned the general mercantile store on Main Street in Boulder. The store provided a stable income for the Steele family and their employees Jess Ripley and Ann McGonigle. (Courtesy of the Jefferson County Genealogy and Heritage Center, Boulder, Montana.)

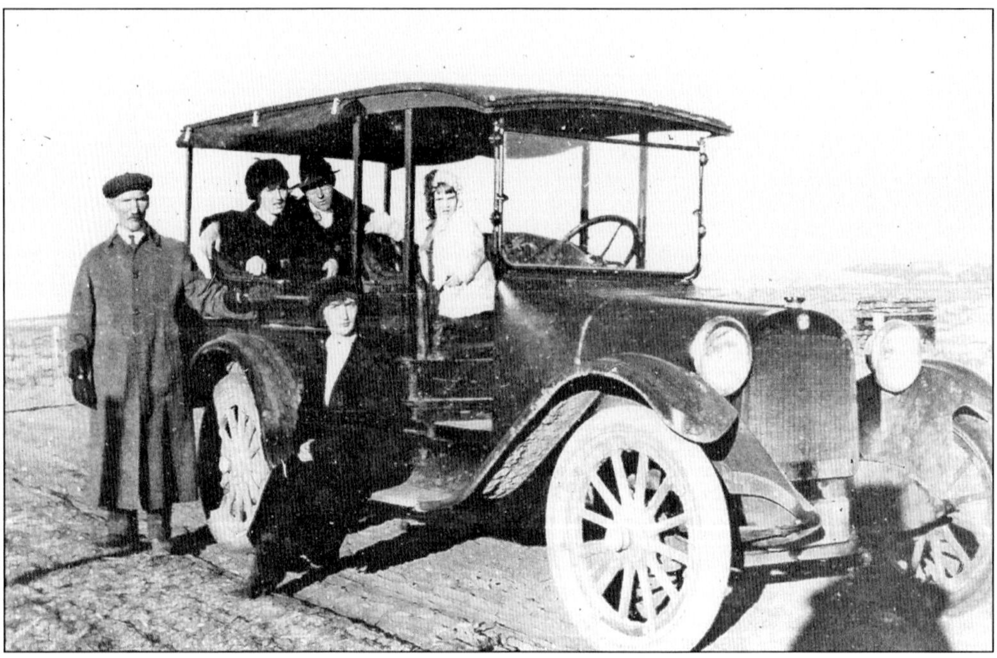

The Steele family poses next to their delivery truck, used for the mercantile store operations in Boulder. (Courtesy of the Jefferson County Museum.)

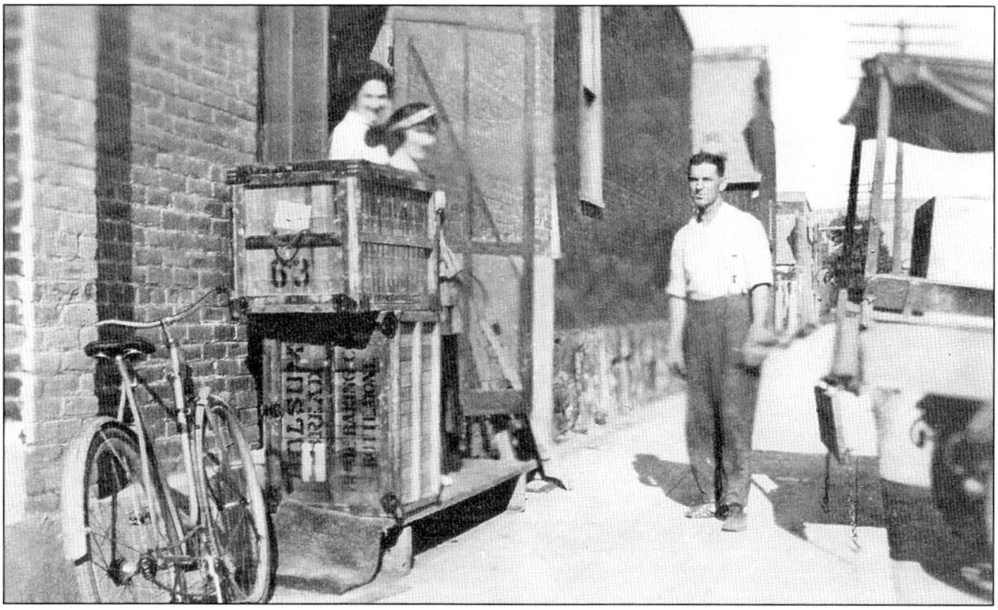

Lucille Steele stands in the doorway with Margaret Steele in front of her as they watch Jess Ripley unload dry goods for the Steele Mercantile Store in Boulder. (Courtesy of the Jefferson County Museum.)

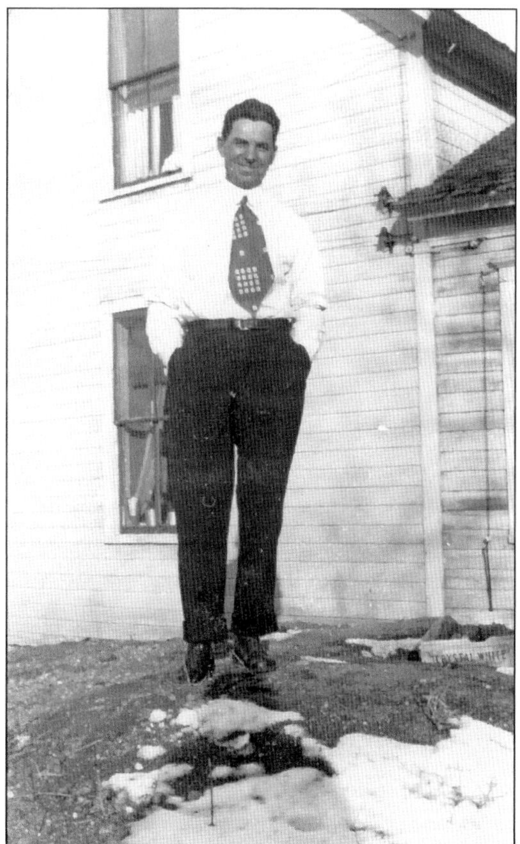

Jess Ripley, an employee at the Steele Mercantile Store in Boulder, Montana, smiles for the camera. (Courtesy of the Jefferson County Museum.)

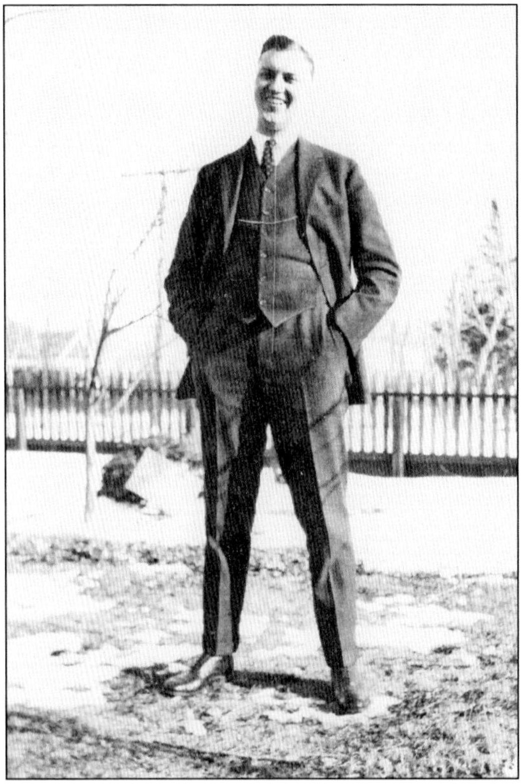

John Connely was a traveling salesman who stopped once a month at the Steele Mercantile Store to take orders for merchandise. (Courtesy of the Jefferson County Museum.)

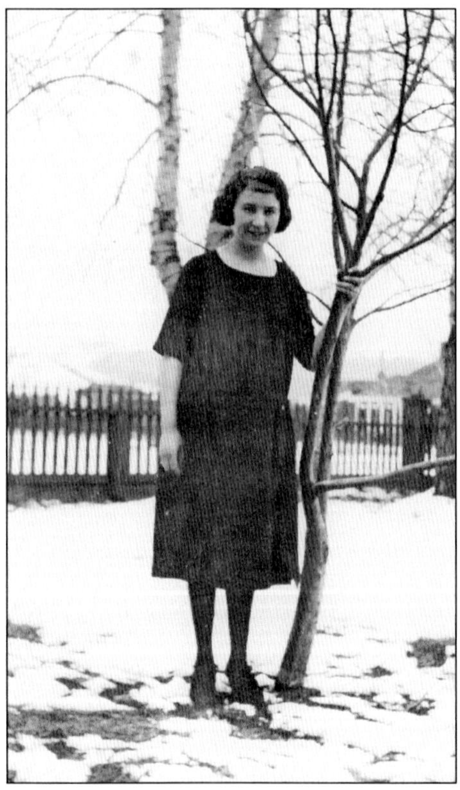

Boulder resident Ann McGonigle worked as a bookkeeper for the Steele Mercantile Store. (Courtesy of the Jefferson County Museum.)

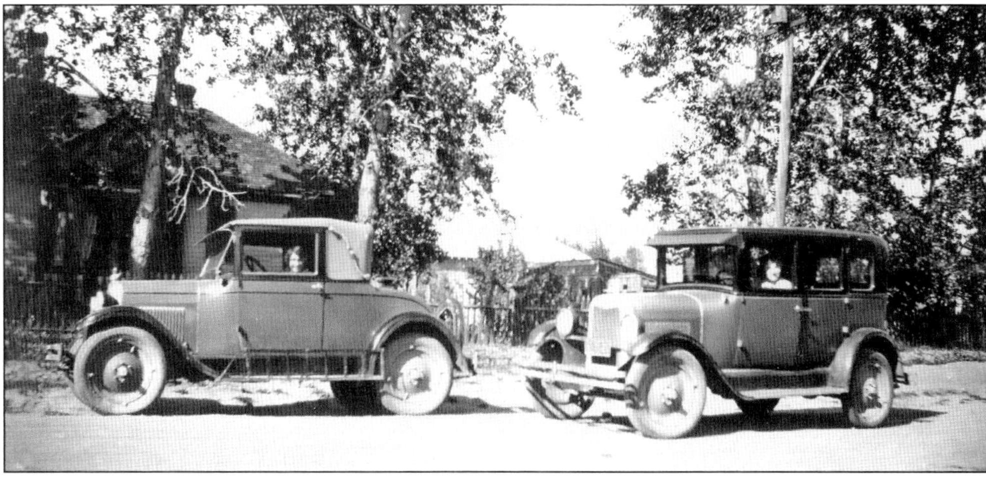

Cousins Lucille Steele and Jessie Steele, daughters of storeowners William and John Steele, show off their new cars for the camera. Lucille smiles from her sporty coupe, while Jesse drives a Chevy Coach. (Courtesy of the Jefferson County Museum.)

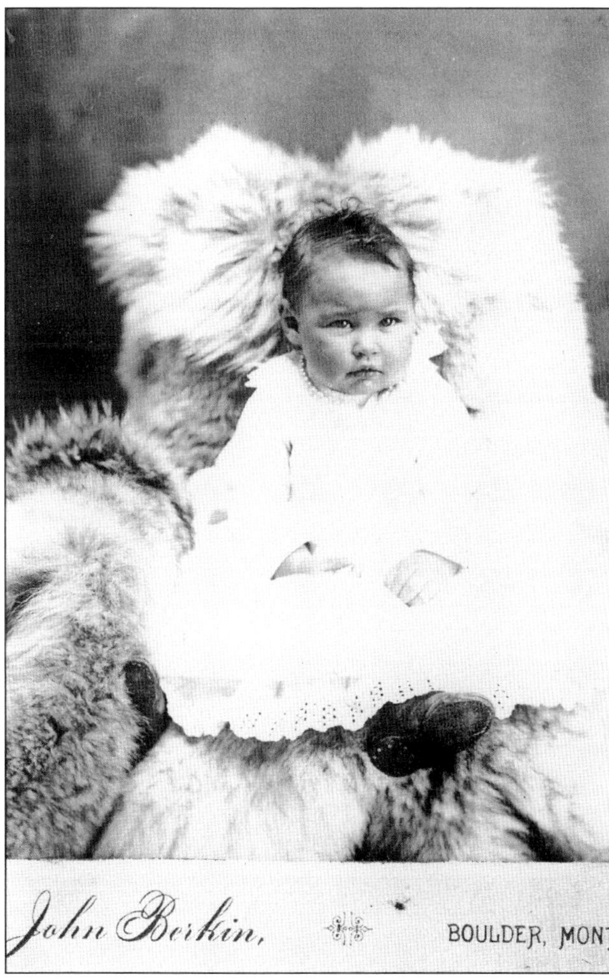

Photographer John Berkin grew up in Jefferson County after his family moved to Montana from England. His father, William Berkin, was an early freighter in Jefferson County. John grew up riding in the freight wagon with his father. He learned to hunt and became a skilled taxidermist. Later he settled in Boulder and opened a photography studio. His photographs of Jefferson County residents often featured one of his furs or game trophies as props to add interest. (Courtesy of the Jefferson County Museum.)

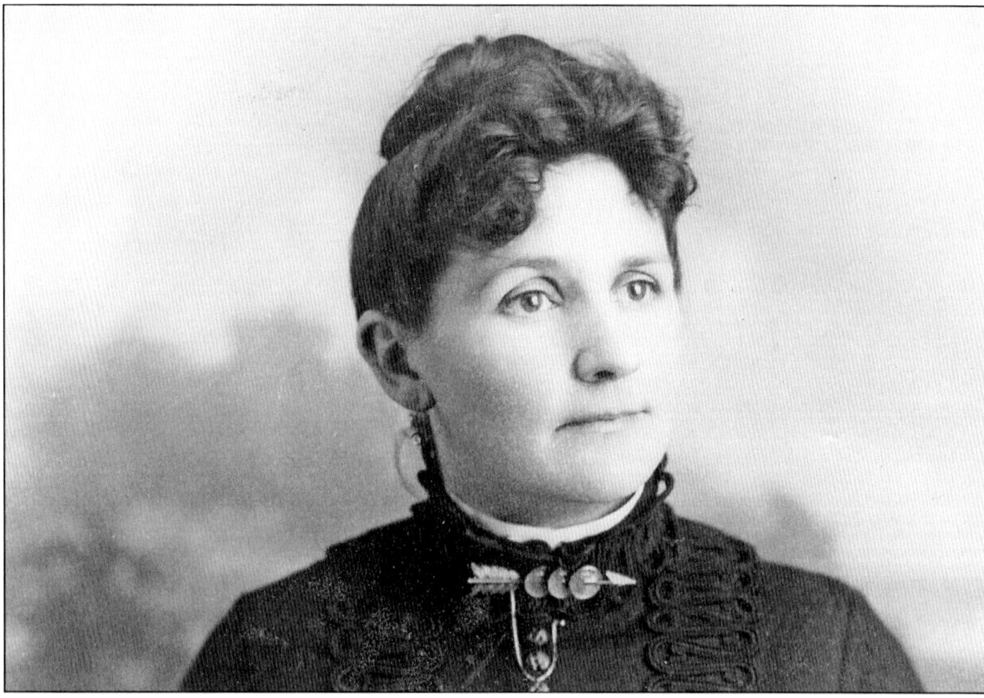

This photograph of a Boulder resident was taken by photographer John Berkin. In addition to portraits, Berkin took railroad photographs for the Oregon Short Line Railroad. He later closed his photography office and served as a member of the seventh session of the Montana State Legislature. (Courtesy of the Jefferson County Museum.)

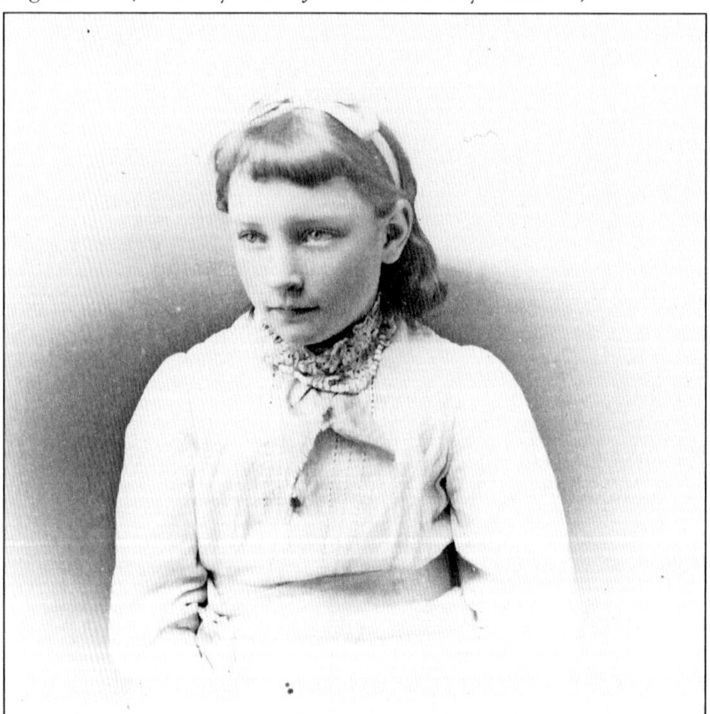

A child sits for her photograph, taken by Boulder photographer John Berkin. (Courtesy of the Jefferson County Museum.)

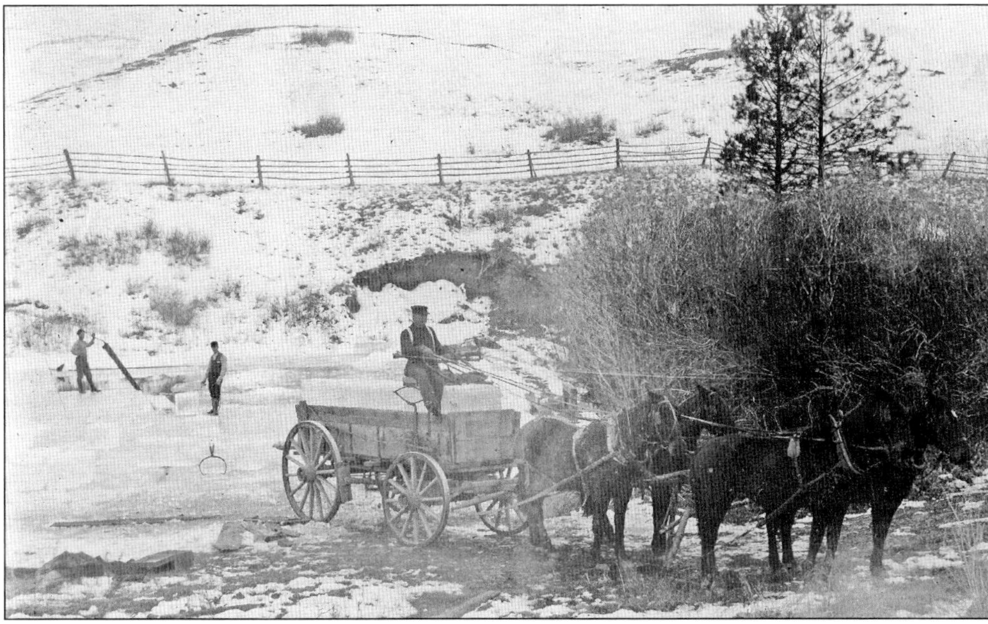

The Clancy photography company Ely and Haynes pictured these men cutting and loading ice for use in early refrigeration methods. While Clancy was not generally known for a thriving ice business, the town of Elk Park, at the southern end of Jefferson County, had its early beginnings in the ice business. Prior to dairy farmers moving into Elk Park, many of its residents earned a living transporting ice into nearby Butte. (Courtesy of the Jefferson County Museum.)

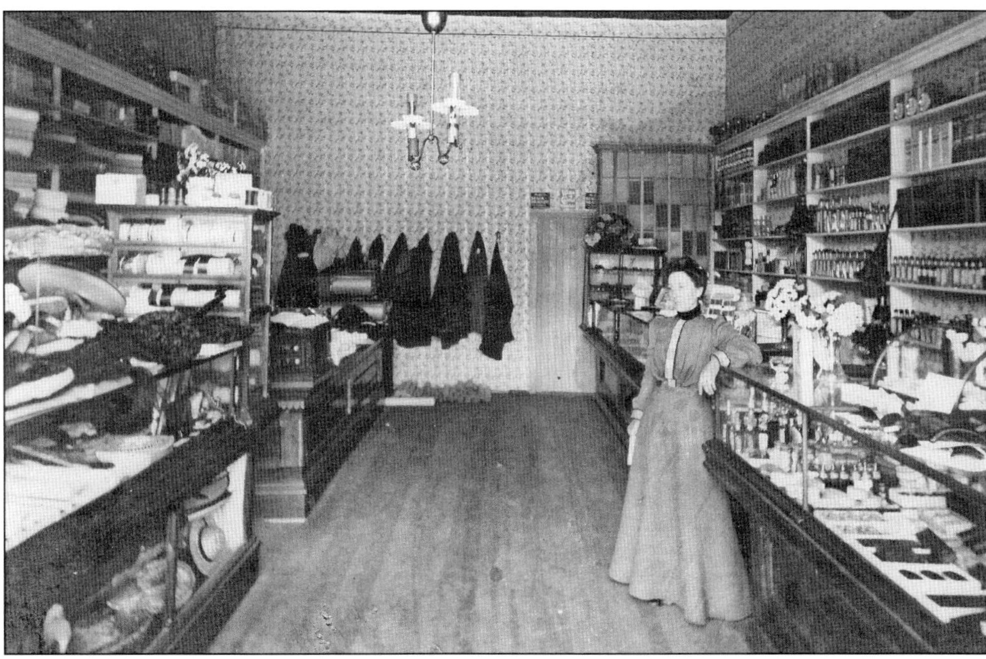

As businesses grew in Jefferson County, residents prospered, but sometimes storeowners met with tragedy. This well-stocked general mercantile store burned down shortly after this photograph was taken. (Courtesy of the Jefferson County Museum.)

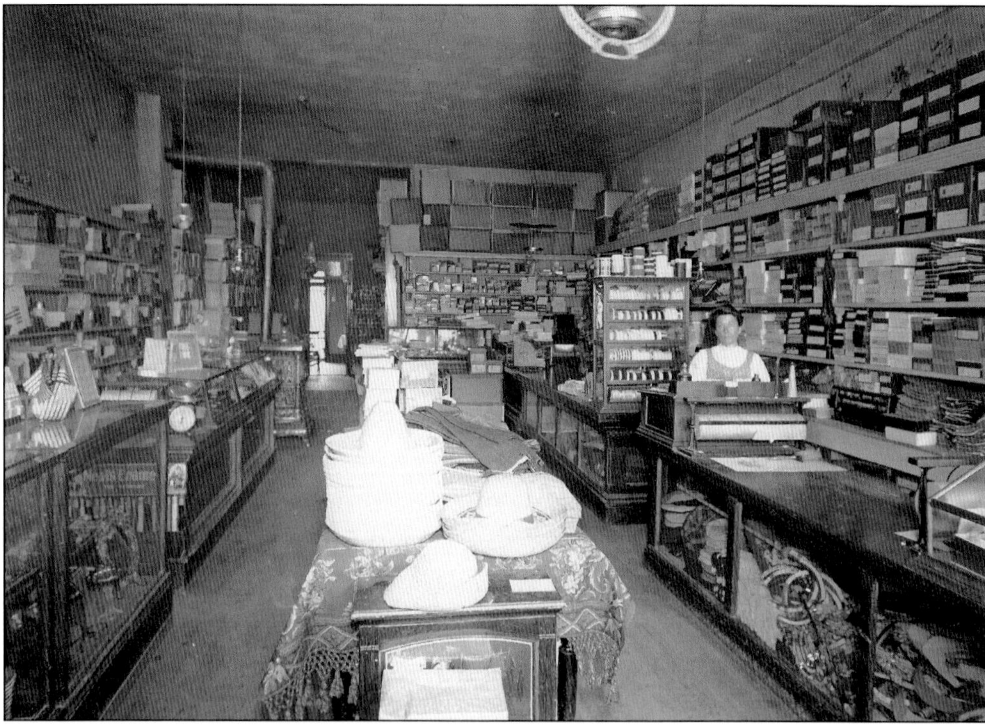

This young proprietress patiently stands behind her well-stocked counter, waiting for customers to purchase some of her wares. (Courtesy of the Jefferson County Museum.)

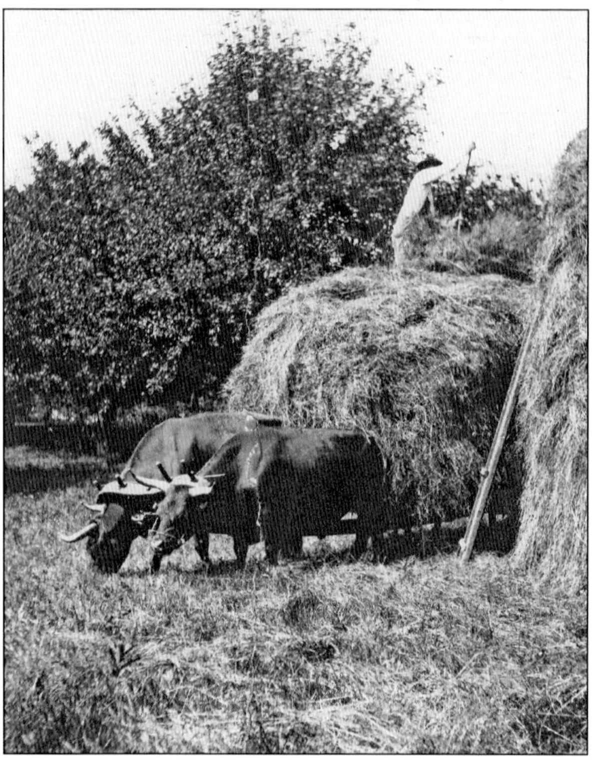

An unidentified man loads hay onto the back of an ox-drawn wagon. Hay was an important commodity in Montana. After the severe winter of 1897, when thousands of cattle froze to death, farmers and ranchers realized that herds needed a supplemental food source during the winter months and could not be expected to rely on the grass beneath the snow for sustenance. (Courtesy of the Jefferson County Museum.)

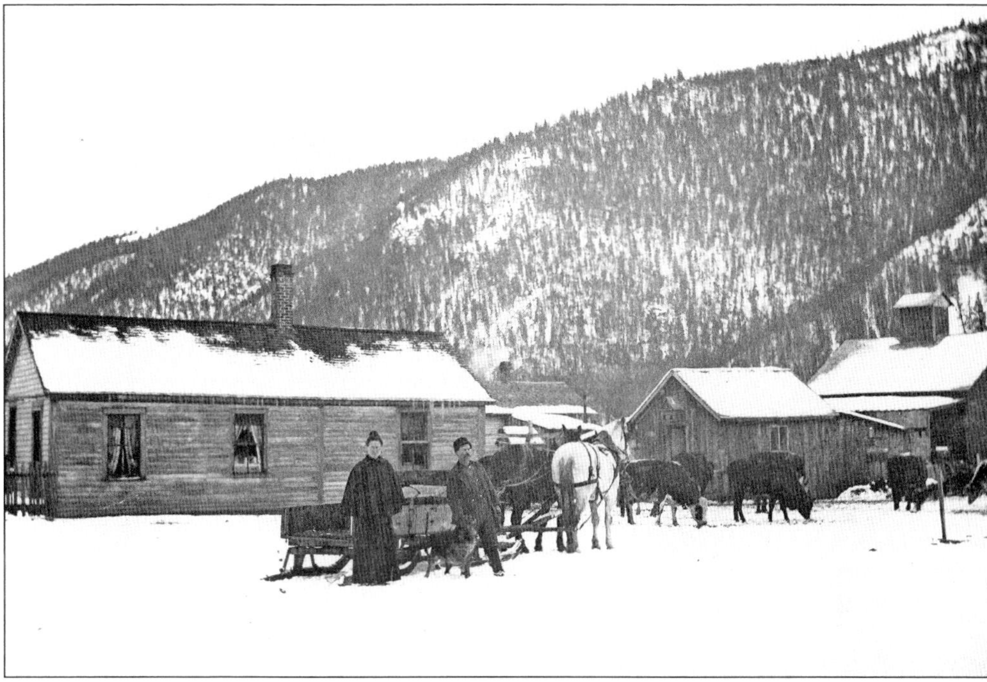

Alfred and Emma Sockerson of Basin use their sled to feed their cattle. Alfred came to Montana from Sweden. He married Emma York in 1900, and together they had four children. Sadly, in 1912, Alfred committed suicide. (Courtesy of the Jefferson County Museum.)

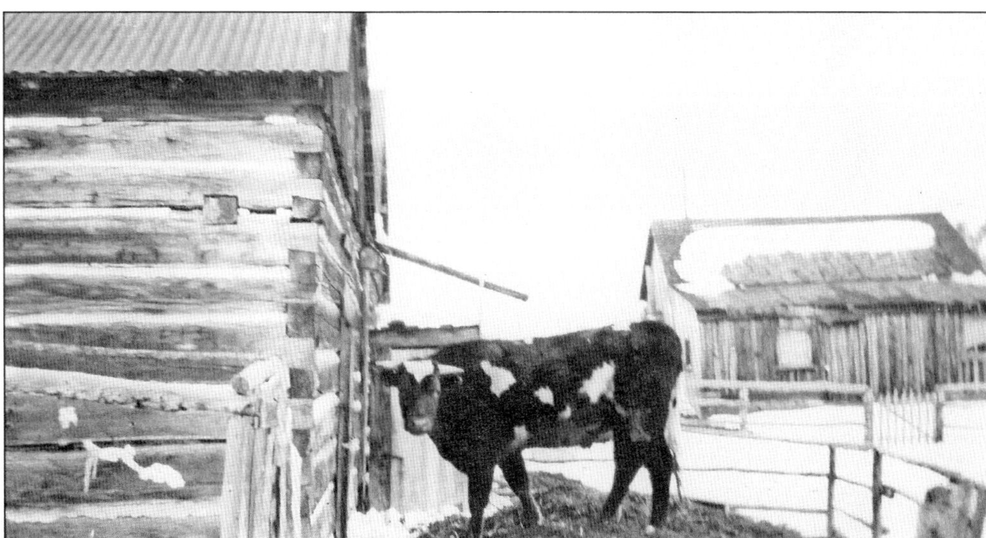

While working the mines in Comet, the Mattson family raised cattle to provide extra income and food for themselves. Sometimes that meant that their cattle lived close to the family home. (Courtesy of the Jefferson County Museum.)

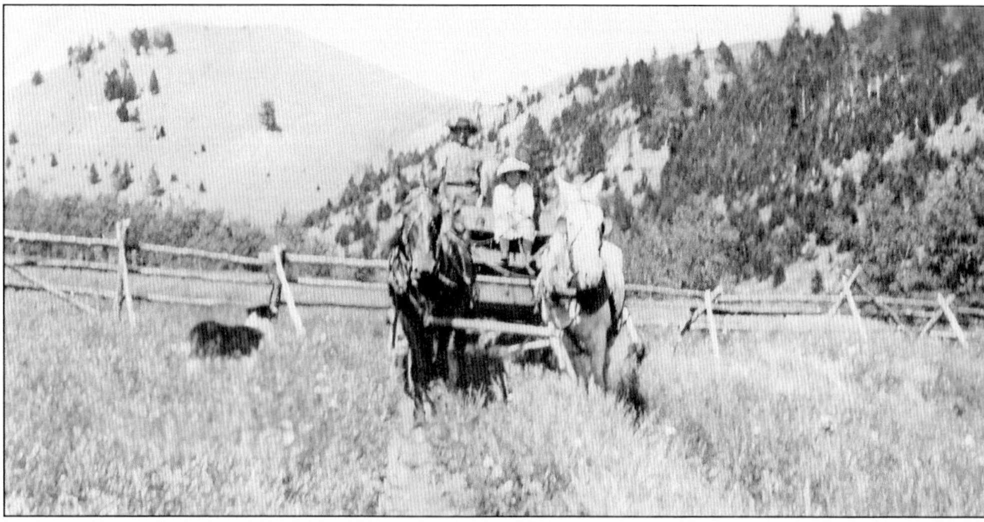

A large horse-drawn wagon, like the one pictured here, was an important piece of ranching equipment. (Courtesy of the Jefferson County Museum.)

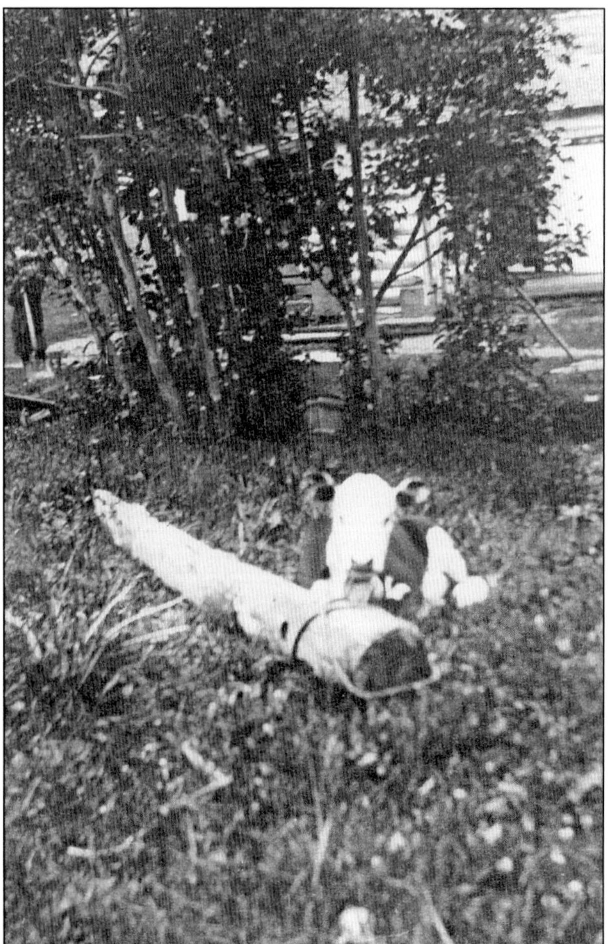

This cow rests after pulling logs to the location of a new log structure for the Mattson family in Comet. (Courtesy of the Jefferson County Museum.)

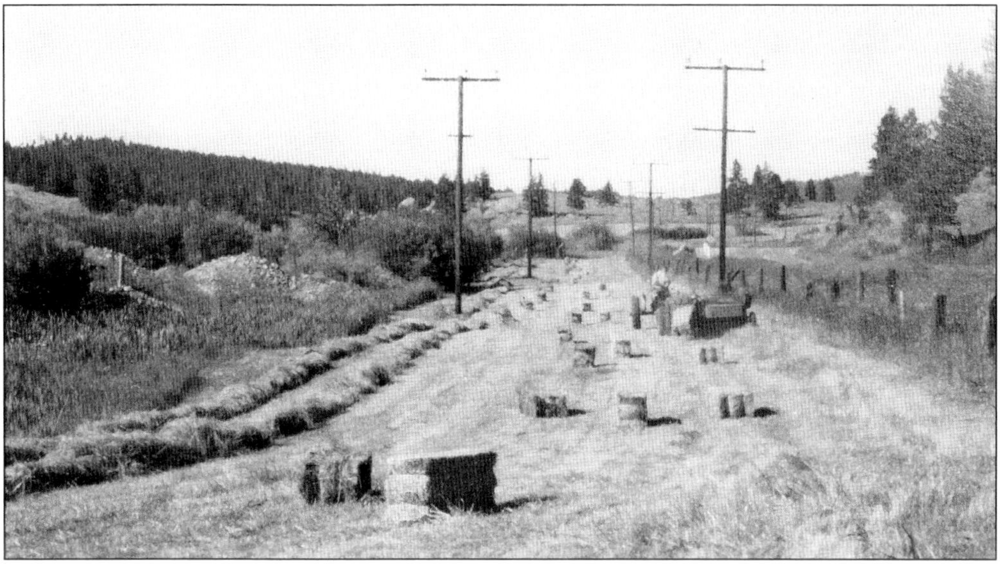

John Haab of Clancy is photographed harvesting his crop of hay. The Haab family owned farmland that was later replaced by Interstate 15 and the housing developments of Blue Sky Heights and Forest Park Estates in Clancy. (Courtesy of the Haab family, Clancy, Montana.)

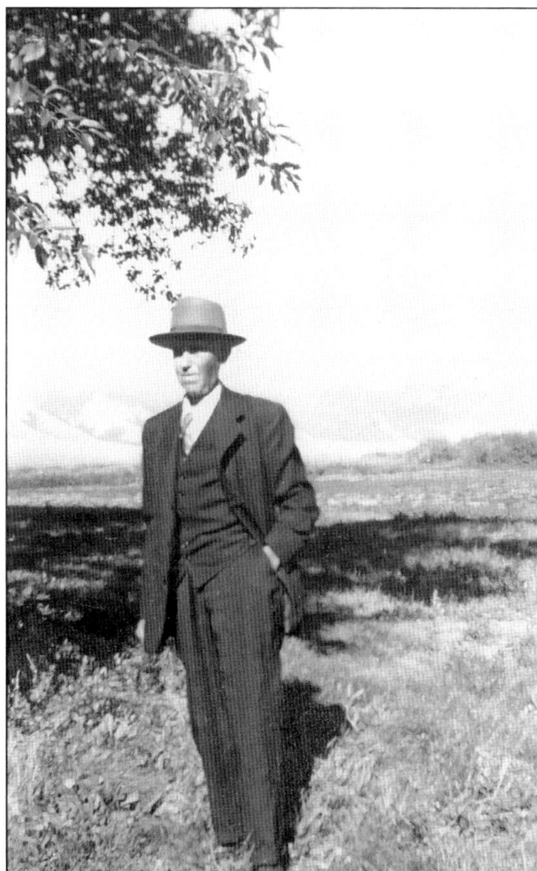

Jefferson County resident Henry Schmidt of the Boulder Valley worked for area ranches and made his home with his brother near the Flood ranch. (Courtesy of the Jefferson County Museum.)

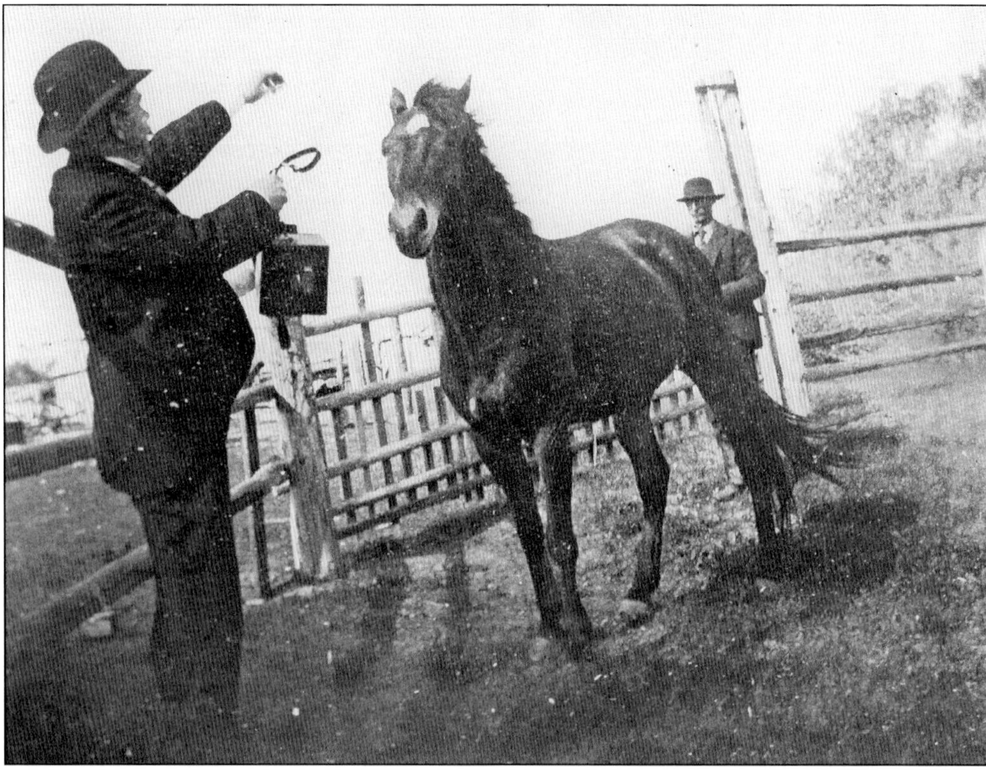

Horses were an important commodity in the early days of Jefferson County. This horse clearly was not ready to have his photograph taken. (Courtesy of the Jefferson County Museum.)

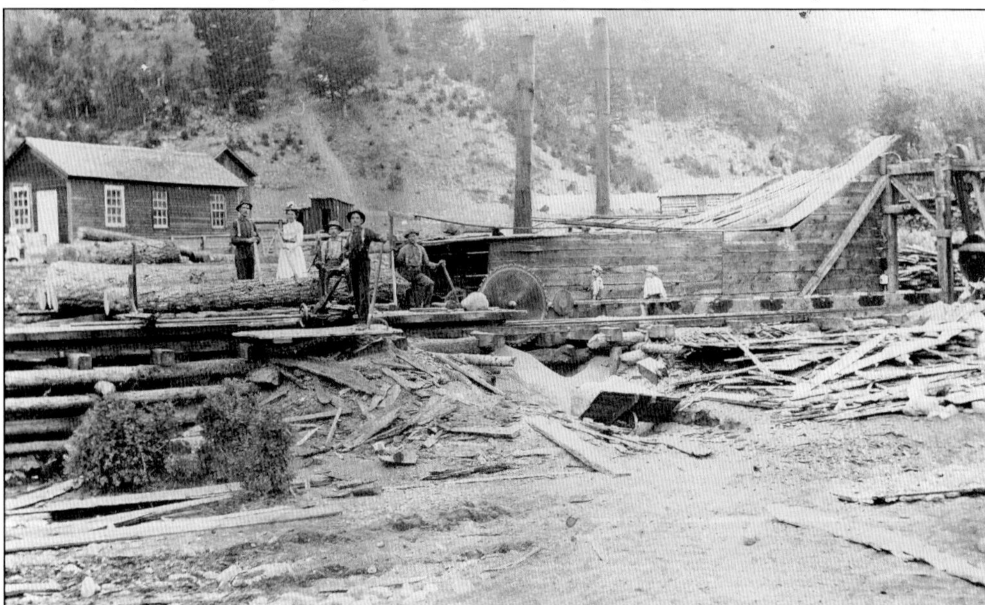

The Fuller Sawmill, owned by Wilbur F. Jackson of Basin, was located between Boulder and Basin. The Montana Central Railway had a scheduled stop at Fuller, making it easy for Jackson to load his products for shipment. (Courtesy of the Jefferson County Museum.)

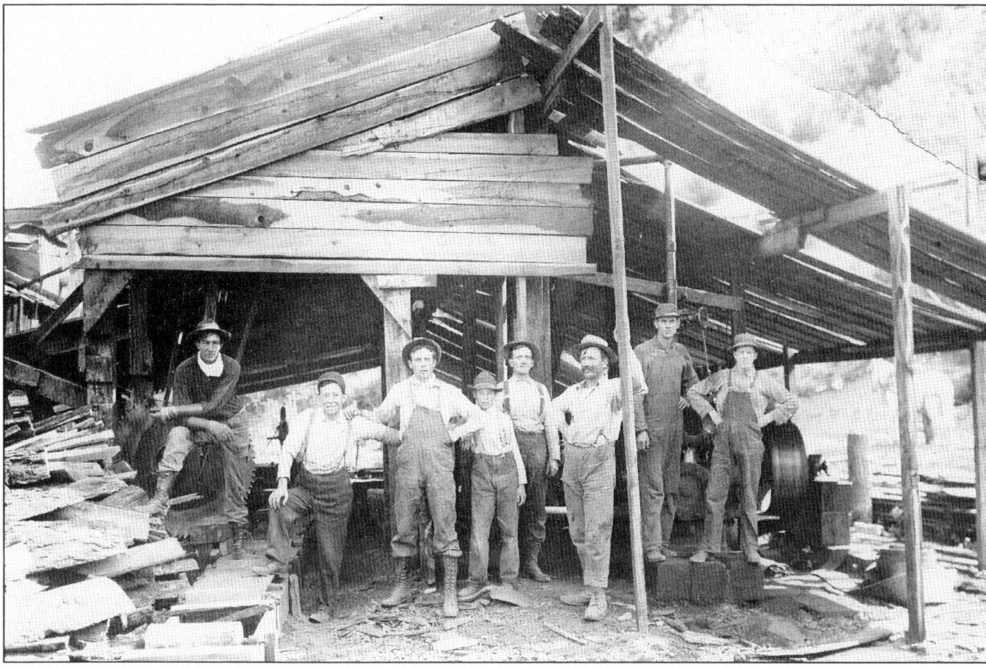

The men working at the Fuller Sawmill take a break from their work to have their picture taken. From left to right are Clarence Waldie, John Hoot, Wilbur Jackson, four unidentified, and Truman Hopkins at the extreme right. (Courtesy of the Jefferson County Museum.)

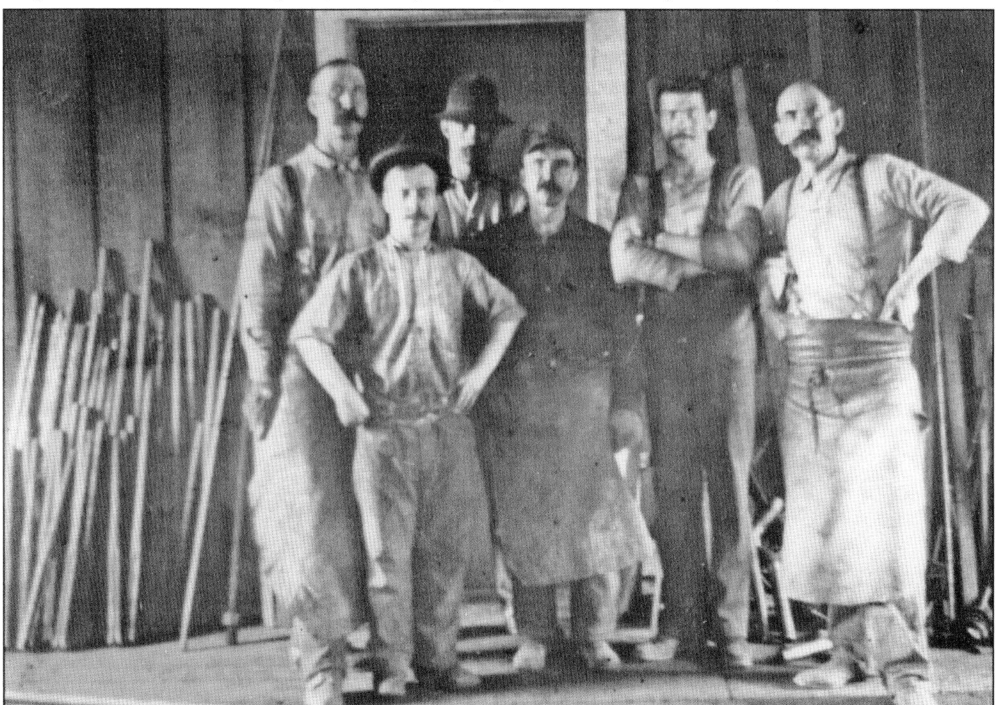

Blacksmith John Gow (far right) and friends gather outside the blacksmith shop in Wickes. (Courtesy of the Jefferson County Museum.)

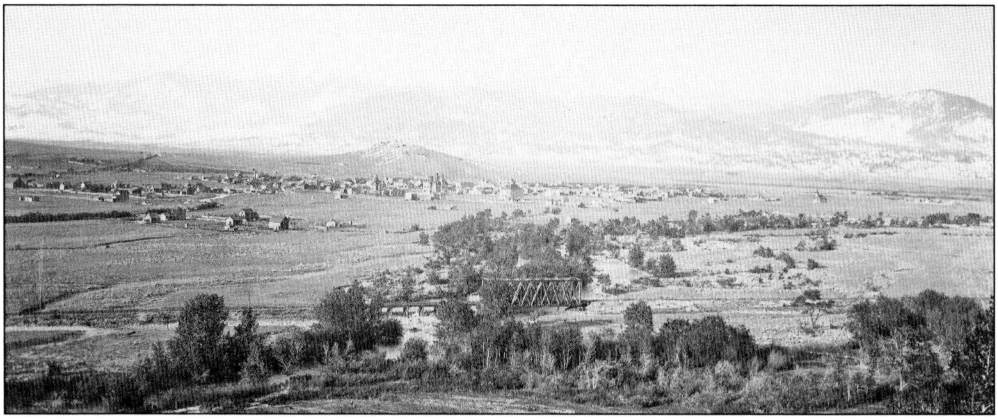

This photograph of Boulder was taken on June 9, 1895. (Courtesy of the Jefferson County Museum.)

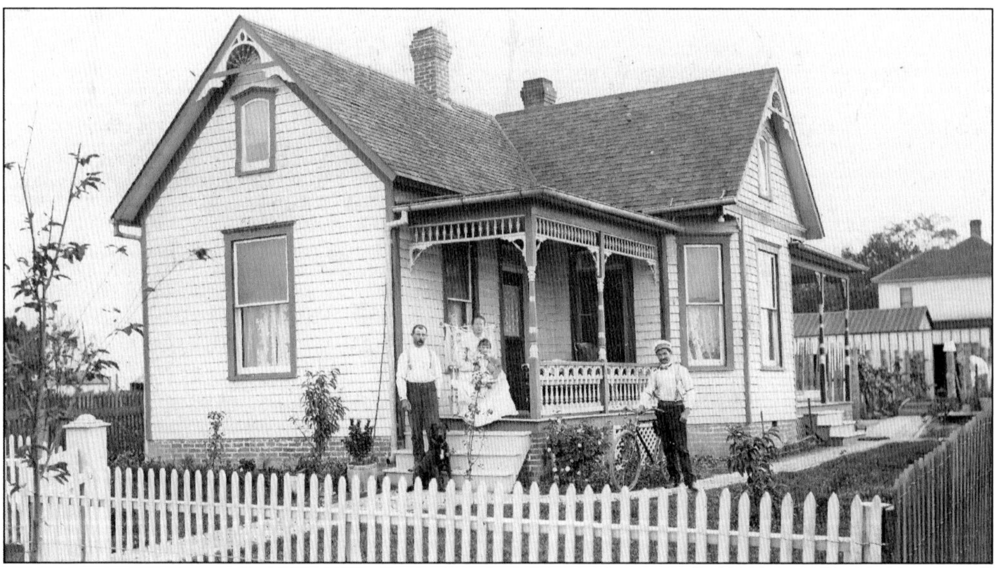

Once the home of William Wolters, owner of the first bus line and taxi service in Boulder, this building was located on South Elder Street in Boulder. William married Margaret King in 1882, and together they had eight children. Their daughter Freda Margaret married Jess Ripley in 1905. William Wolters sold his bus to Jess and Freda in 1925. (Courtesy of the Jefferson County Museum.)

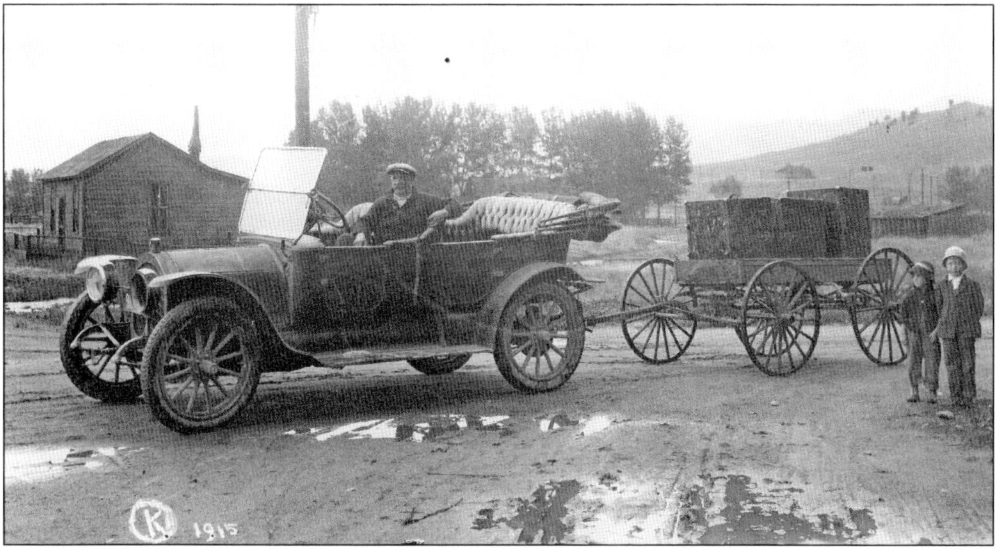

In 1915, William Wolters grins from his "Lightning Express," used for his taxi business in Boulder. Wolters operated the first taxi service in Boulder and often transported people from the Boulder train depot to the Boulder Hot Springs. (Courtesy of the Jefferson County Museum.)

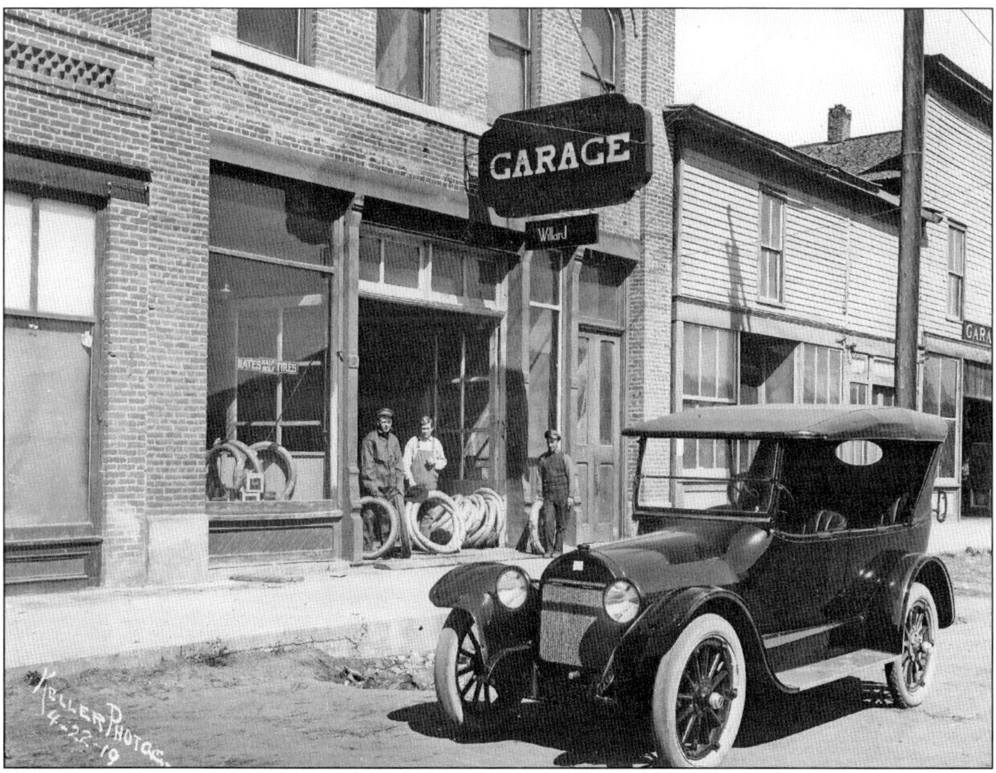

On April 22, 1919, a beautiful polished Buick parked outside Willard's Corner Garage in Boulder waits for the return of its owner. In 1915, Buick introduced the first ventilating windshield. Buicks were mid-priced automobiles starting around $1,200. (Courtesy of the Jefferson County Museum.)

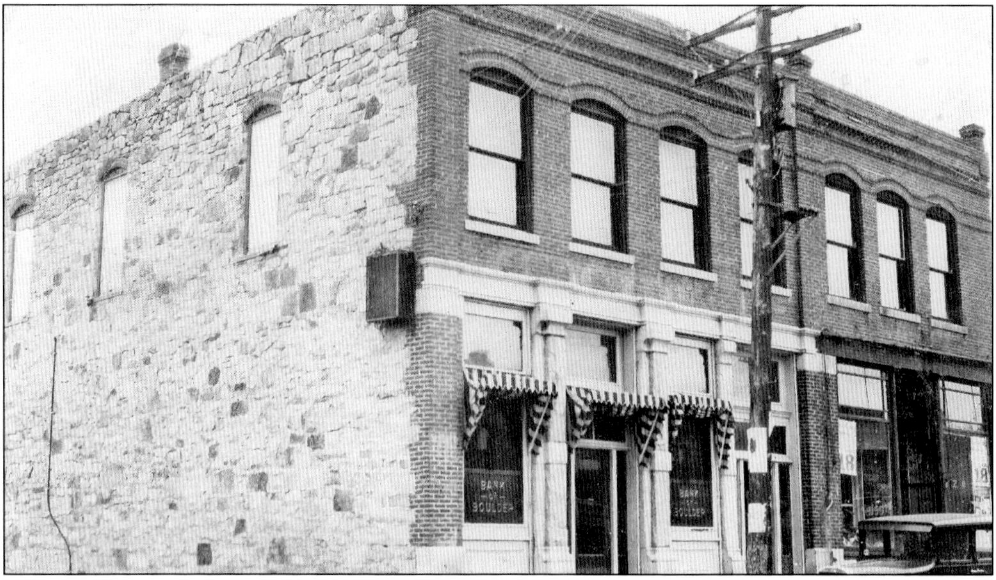

The Bank of Boulder was built in 1888 on Boulder's Main Street. This photograph of the Bank of Boulder and Gaffney's Mercantile was taken about 1926. (Courtesy of the Jefferson County Genealogy and Heritage Center, Boulder, Montana.)

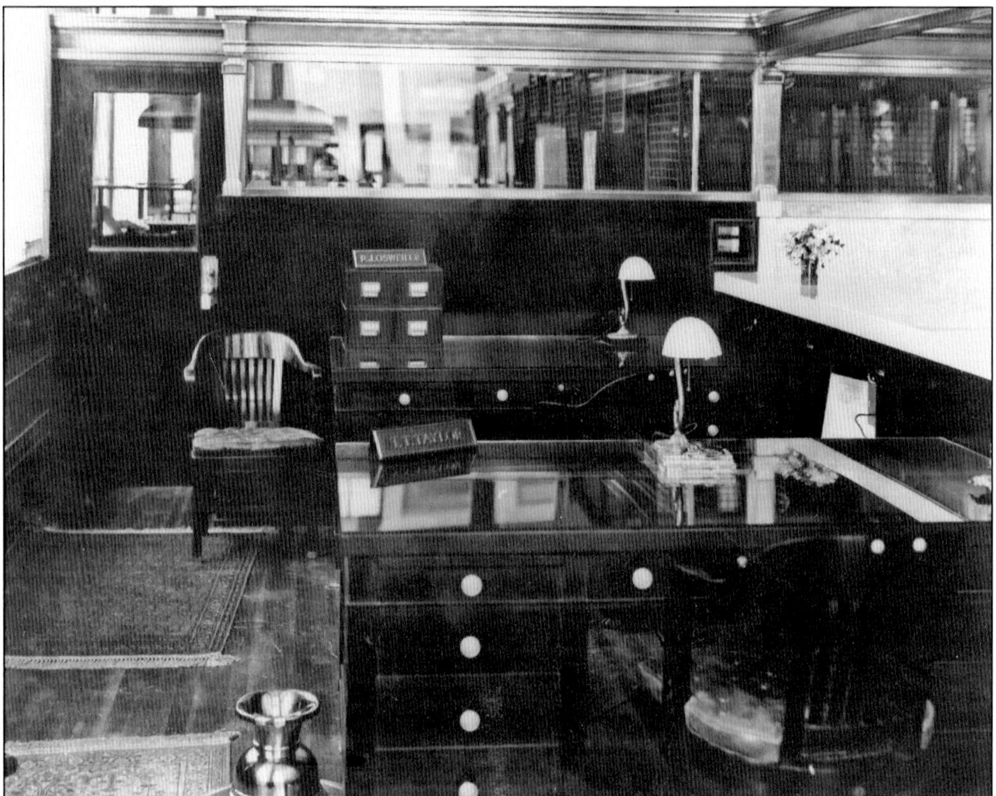

This picture shows Bank of Boulder officer Thomas T. Taylor's desk; he worked at the bank from 1928 to 1929. (Courtesy of the Jefferson County Genealogy and Heritage Center, Boulder, Montana.)

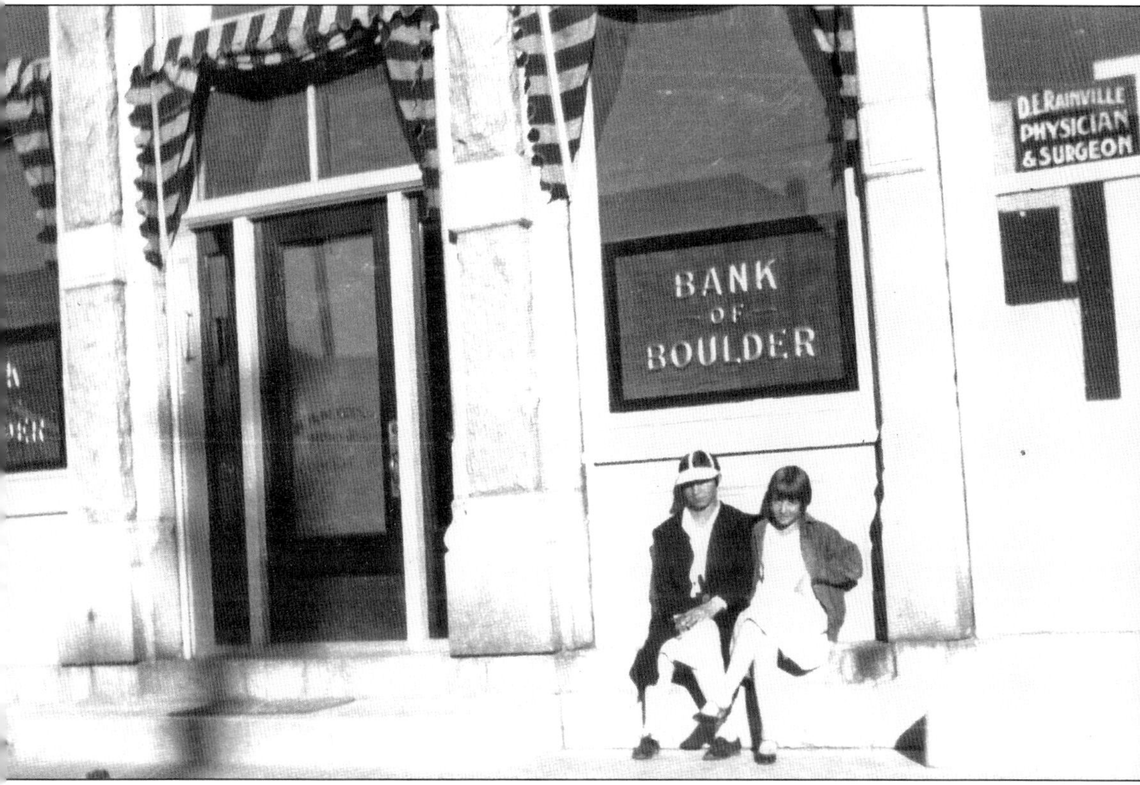

Two girls take a break outside the Bank of Boulder. Dr. D. E. Rainville's office was located next door to the bank when this photograph was taken. Dr. Rainville moved to Boulder in 1914 after he accepted a medical position with the State School for the Deaf and Blind, which he held until 1919. In 1922, he actively promoted the use of vaccinations against the increase in smallpox in Jefferson County. In February 1933, more than 100 travelers were stranded in Boulder as a result of heavy snow. Many left their cars on the road and walked into Boulder. The exposure to the elements caused some to suffer from frostbite. Dr. Rainville worked long into the night to help them. In private practice from 1919 until his death in 1937, he was a member of numerous organizations in Jefferson County, like the Fraternal Order of the Eagles in Basin and the Knights of Maccabeus. (Courtesy of the Jefferson County Genealogy and Heritage Center, Boulder, Montana.)

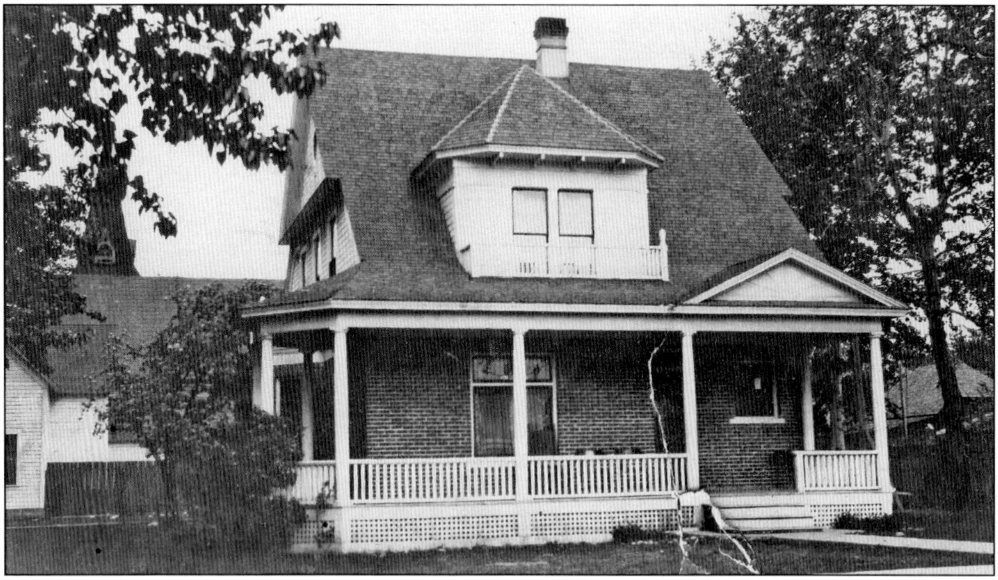

The home of Dr. Ira Leighton was built in 1902 in Boulder. As a physician, Dr. Leighton cared for the Boulder community for many years. He also served as mayor for the town. At one time, his office was located in the upstairs portion of the Bank of Boulder on Main Street in Boulder. Dr. Leighton went on to be elected to the Montana State Senate in 1911 and 1922. He died in 1926 from cancer. (Courtesy of the Jefferson County Genealogy and Heritage Center, Boulder, Montana.)

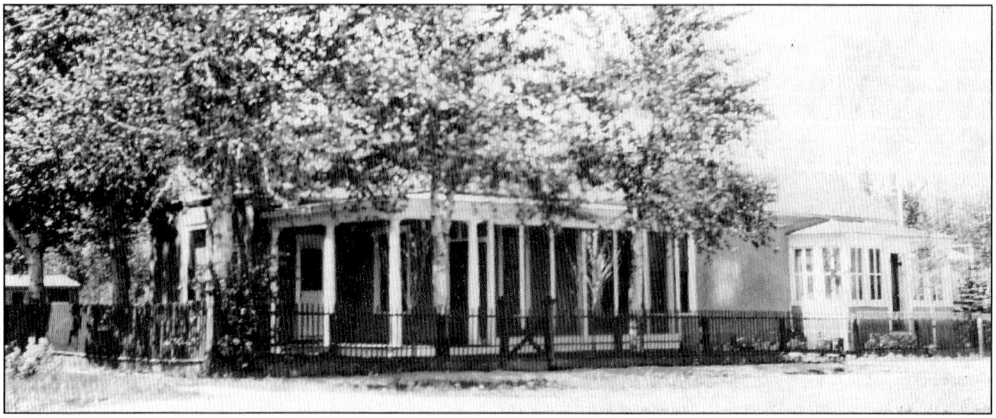

Pharmacist J. A. Riedel lived in this home while he operated his drugstore in Boulder. He purchased the store in 1900 and operated it until 1928, when he sold it to his assistant Art Aspengren. (Courtesy of the Jefferson County Genealogy and Heritage Center, Boulder, Montana.)

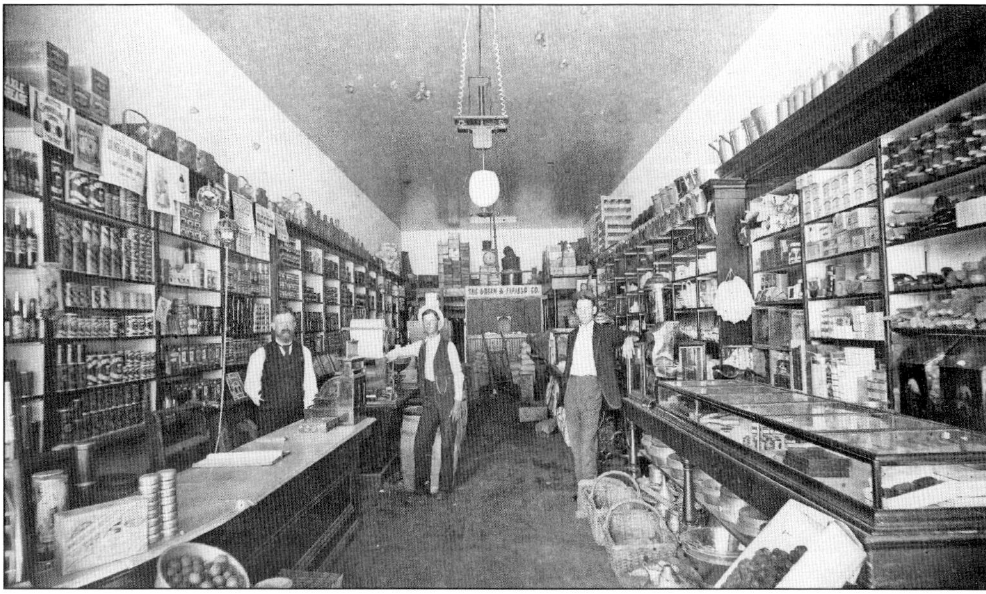

The interior of the Enos Thomas Store in Boulder shows a large inventory of canned goods. Enos Thomas moved to Montana from Iowa. His daughter Mary married John Steele in 1897. (Courtesy of the Margaret Quinn Estate.)

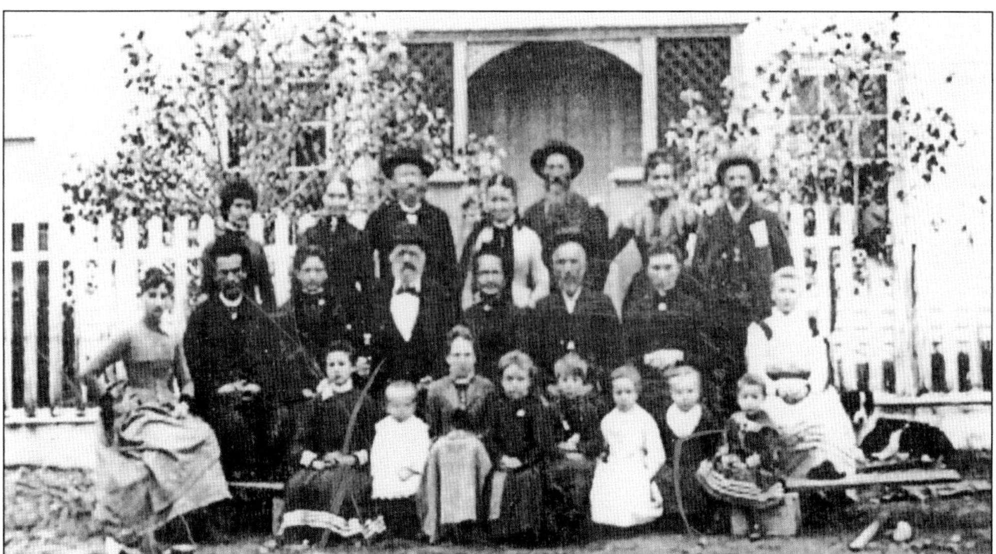

Jefferson County pioneers Hiram and Mary Cook sit for this photograph surrounded by family and friends in 1888. Hiram Cook moved to Montana in 1868 and later owned the first hotel in Boulder. (Courtesy of the Jefferson County Genealogy and Heritage Center, Boulder, Montana.)

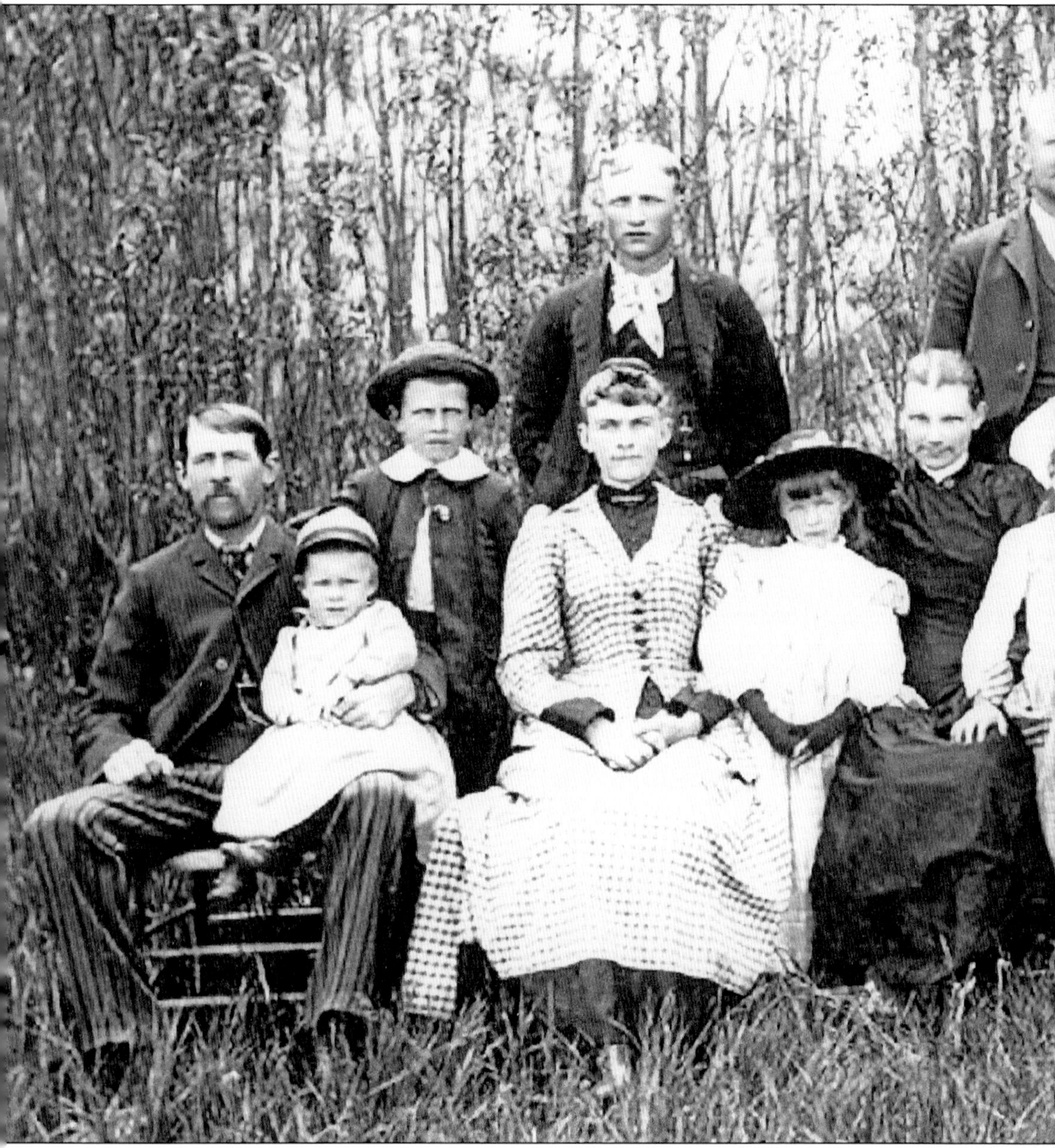

George and Calista Douglas (both center, seated) gather with members of their family to have their picture taken in 1891. George was employed by the Milwaukee and Mississippi Railroad for a short time before he became a farmer in Nebraska. He married Calista Allen on Christmas Day, 1861, and together they raised a large family. In 1864, they traveled by covered wagon from

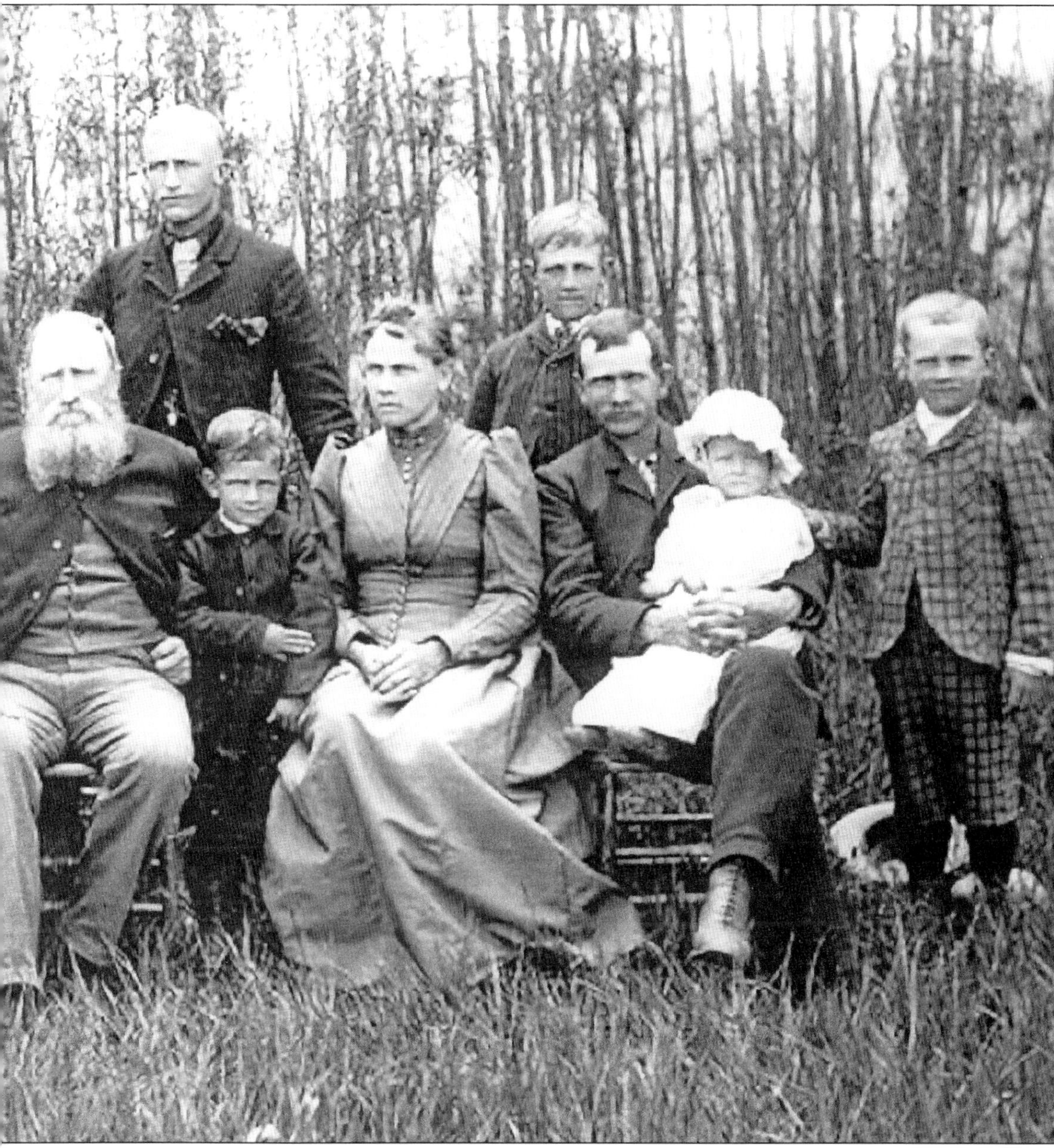

Nebraska to Montana. Although they originally planned to live in Virginia City, by 1865, George and Calista had moved to Jefferson County. They homesteaded land at the intersection of the current Whitetail Road and the original Boulder Hot Springs Road. (Courtesy of the Jefferson County Genealogy and Heritage Center, Boulder, Montana.)

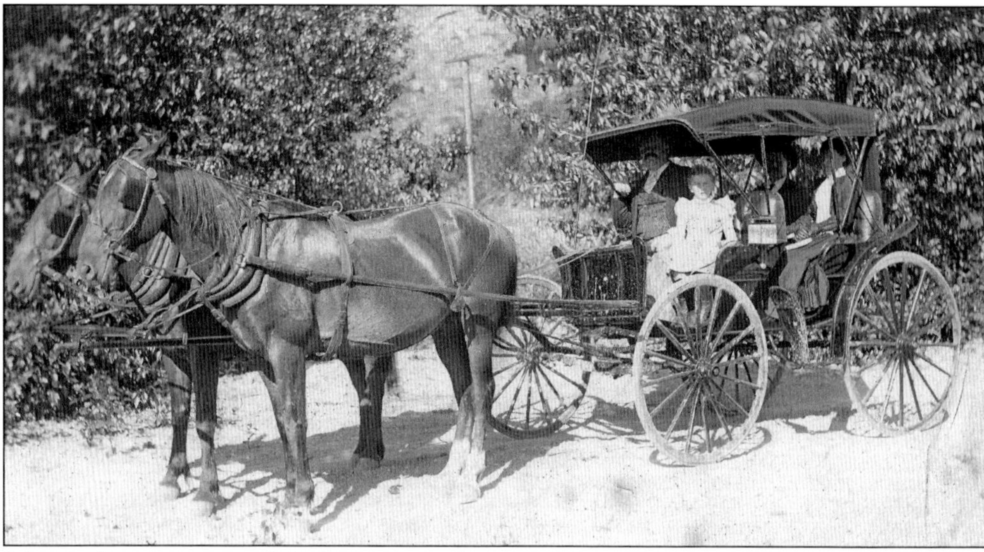

John Sockerson, owner of the Basin Bar, takes his brother's family out for a ride. John and his brothers, Alfred and Charles, immigrated to Montana from Sweden in 1882. (Courtesy of the Jefferson County Museum.)

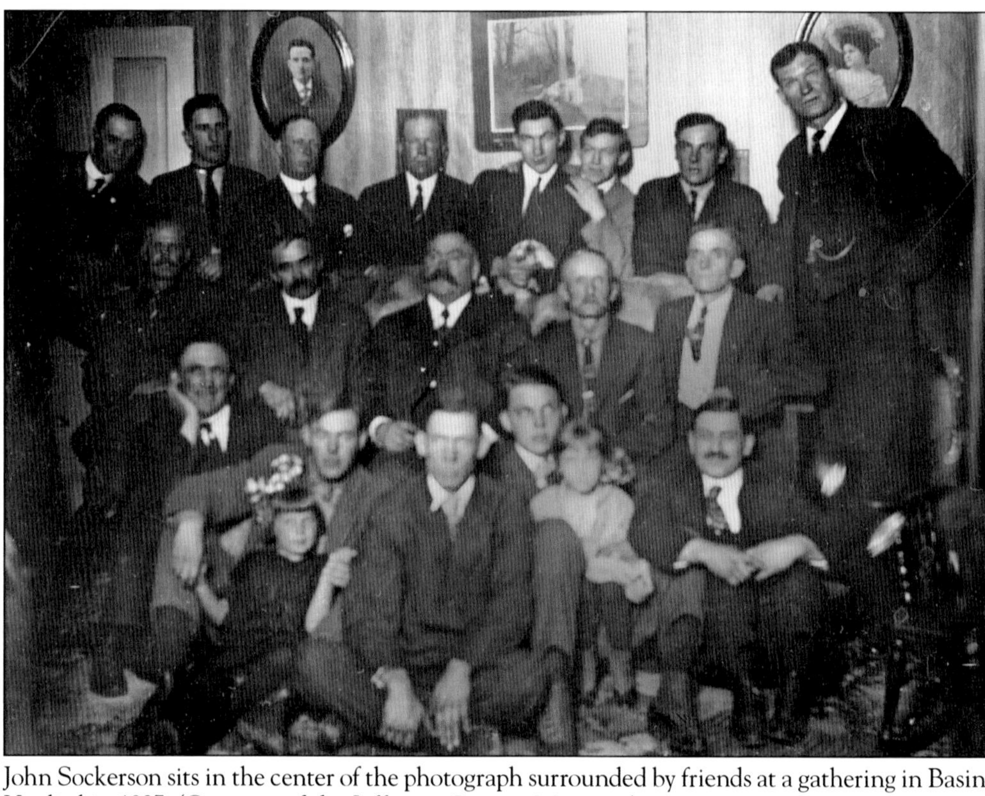

John Sockerson sits in the center of the photograph surrounded by friends at a gathering in Basin. He died in 1927. (Courtesy of the Jefferson County Museum.)

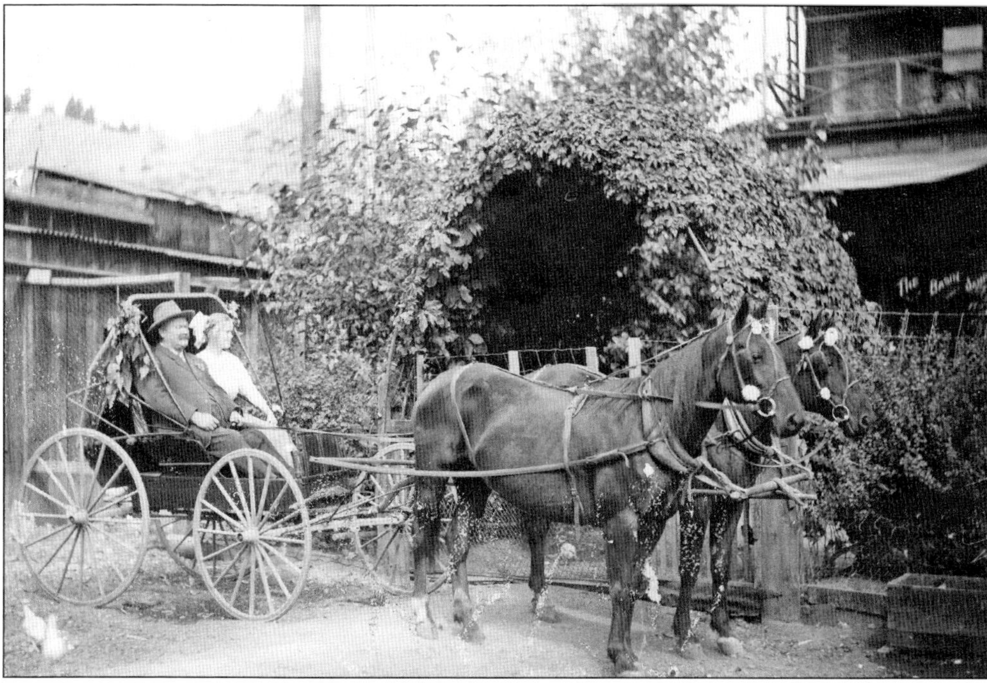

Florence Sockerson sits at the edge of her seat as her uncle, John Sockerson, drives his flower-bedecked horse and buggy. Florence graduated from Jefferson County High School in 1915, but after her marriage to David Hansen in 1919, she moved away from Basin. (Courtesy of the Jefferson County Museum.)

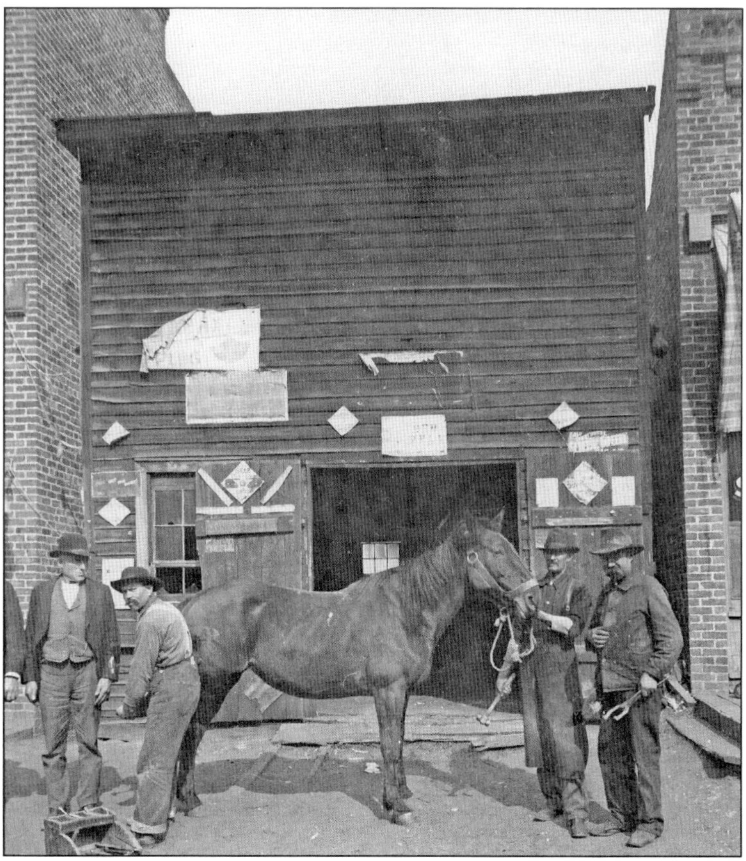

Alfred Sockerson was shoeing a horse when this picture was taken outside the Basin blacksmith building. (Courtesy of the Jefferson County Museum.)

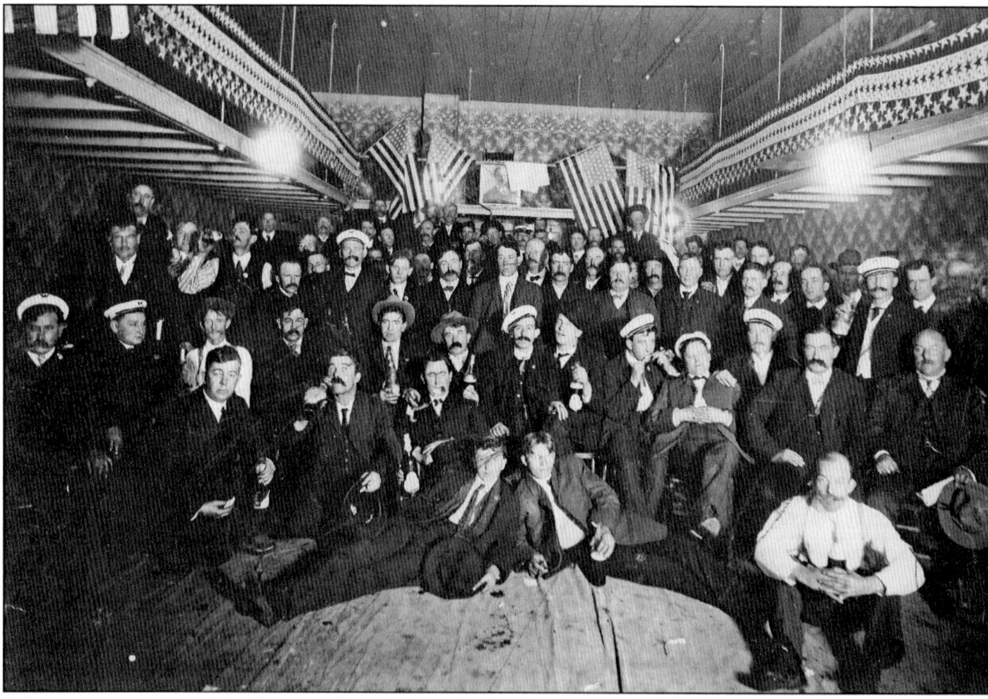

Charter members of the Fraternal Order of the Eagles in Basin pose for a photograph on October 23, 1904. Members of the lodge included Dr. D. E. Rainville and John Sockerson, both prominent men in Basin and Boulder. (Courtesy of the Jefferson County Museum.)

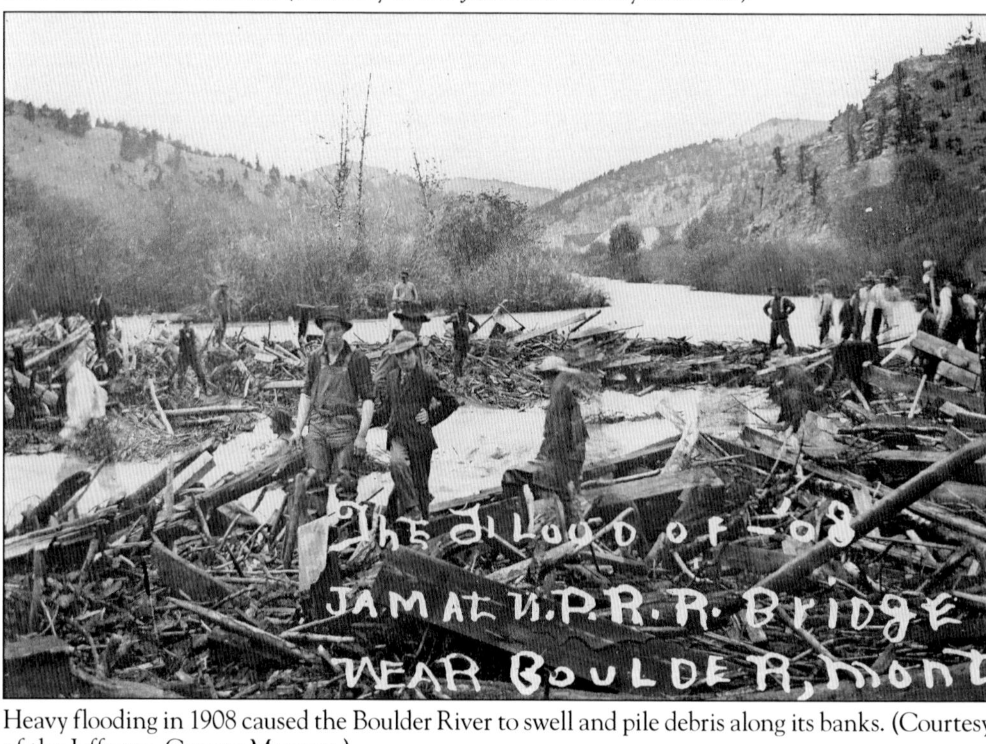

Heavy flooding in 1908 caused the Boulder River to swell and pile debris along its banks. (Courtesy of the Jefferson County Museum.)

Six

STATELY ARCHITECTURE

In 1883, Boulder was selected as the permanent location for the seat of local government for Jefferson County. On April 25, 1888, Jefferson County voters approved a bond issue of $40,000 to construct a new courthouse in Boulder. The two-and-a-half-story building was designed by architect John C. Paulsen. The courthouse was built in the Greek style of architecture. The sandstone foundation extending approximately 4 feet above the ground created a lofty structure for government offices. To match the grand exterior, the interior contained hardwood floors, wainscoting, and ornate door jams, and a carved newel post with turned balustrade formed the staircase to the second floor. In addition to the Jefferson County Courthouse, Paulsen designed the original Montana Deaf and Dumb Asylum, a school for deaf and blind children a short distance from the courthouse. He planned an impressive building made of locally manufactured brick and trimmed with copper. It combined Italianate and Renaissance Revival styles, uncommon in Montana. A pitched gable and hipped roof with two stories of large, semicircular arched windows dominated its front facade. Sadly, Paulsen did not live to see the finished building. He died in 1897. His partner, C. S. Haire, oversaw the completion of the building. After finishing the Montana Deaf and Dumb Asylum, C. S. Haire designed a new school in Clancy. The original structure contained an entry, bell tower, and two schoolrooms. It was constructed of cut local granite and brick. The interior consisted of decorative hardwood trim, ornate ceiling tiles, and maple hardwood floors. In order to pay for the new school, Clancy taxpayers approved a $5,000 bond issue in 1898. The bond provided for the cost to build and furnish the new school building. The Jefferson County Courthouse, the Montana Deaf and Dumb Asylum, and the Clancy School were just a few examples of the stately buildings constructed in Jefferson County. Other buildings, like the original Whitehall and Boulder Schools, were destroyed and rebuilt, but a few architecturally significant buildings remain as a testament of the hard work and determination of early Jefferson County residents.

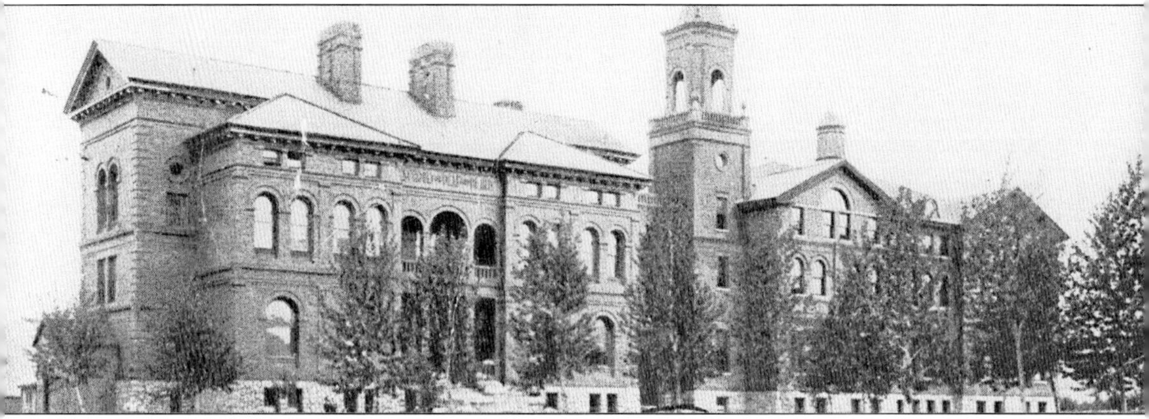

On September 1, 1893, the Montana Legislature agreed to open a state school to teach the deaf, blind, and mentally handicapped in Boulder. Originally called the Montana Deaf and Dumb Asylum, the school accepted deaf and blind children between the ages of 6 and 21 and mentally challenged children and adults. Eventually, separate facilities for the mentally impaired were built. In January 1934, the Montana Legislature voted to build new facilities for the deaf and blind students in Great Falls, and the Boulder location became a training school for the mentally disabled. The design of the building was undertaken by the architectural firm of Paulsen and Haire. John C. Paulsen was the Montana state architect. As state architect, he was possibly involved in a corrupt building scheme with the Montana Capitol Commission. Before a grand jury investigation could hear Paulsen's testimony, he died under mysterious circumstances. When Paulsen died in April 1897, the completion of the Deaf and Dumb Asylum was left to his partner, C. S. Haire. (Courtesy of the Jefferson County Museum.)

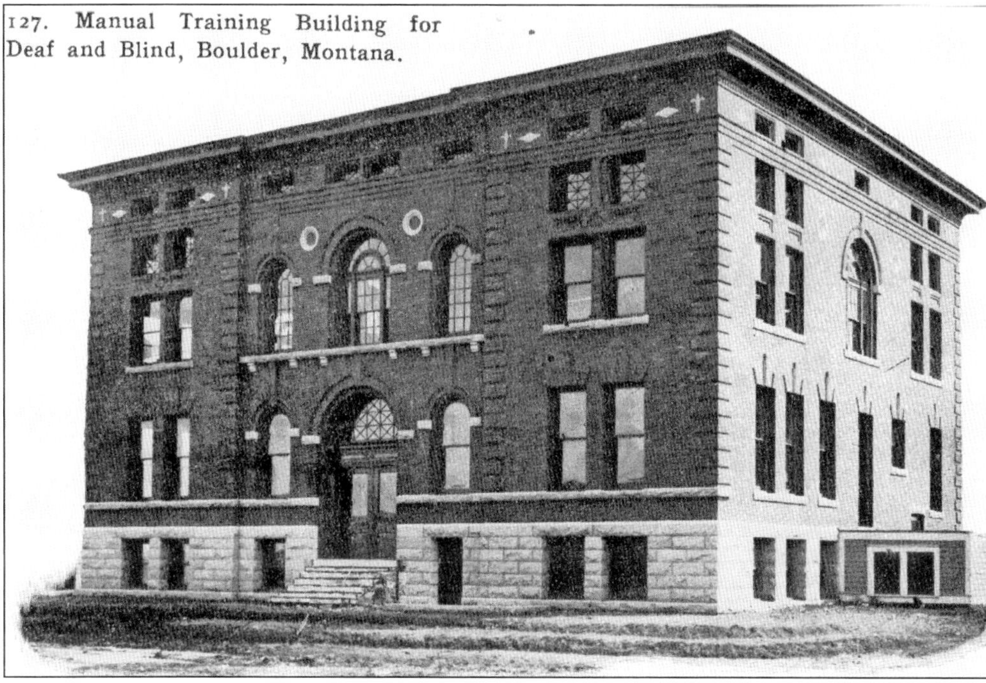

Pictured is one of the buildings used for training at the school for the deaf and blind children in Boulder. (Courtesy of the Jefferson County Museum.)

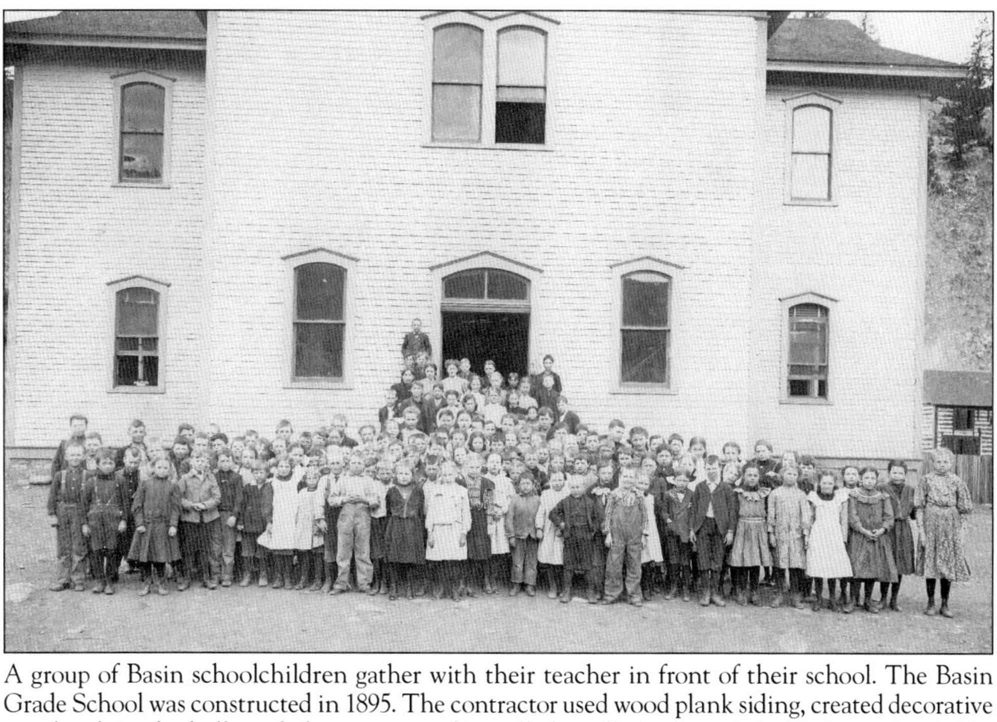

A group of Basin schoolchildren gather with their teacher in front of their school. The Basin Grade School was constructed in 1895. The contractor used wood plank siding, created decorative woodwork in the halls and classrooms, and installed small circular windows. A wooden belfry was built for the school bell. (Courtesy of the Jefferson County Museum.)

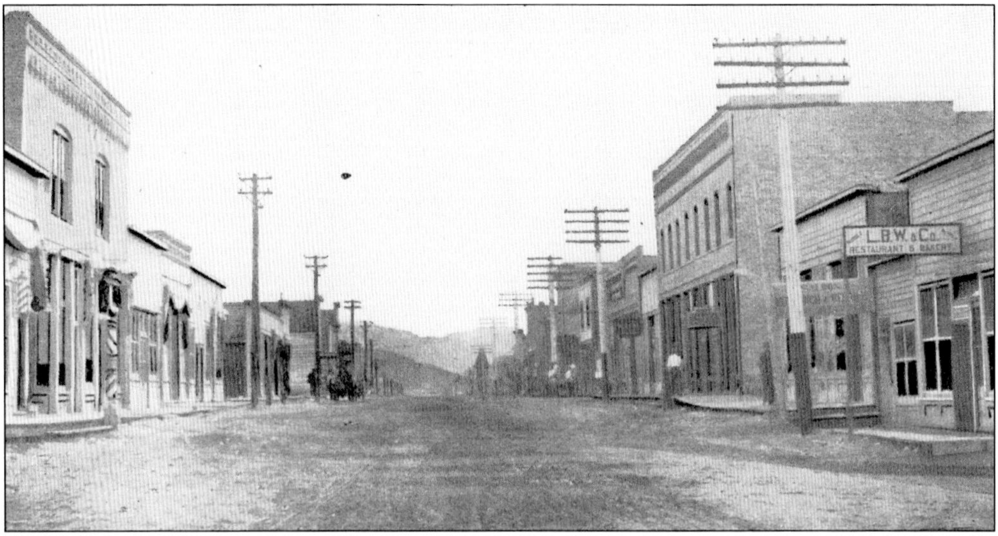

Along Basin Street in Basin in 1908 was a collection of wooden, false-front structures and sturdy brick buildings. (Courtesy of the Jefferson County Museum.)

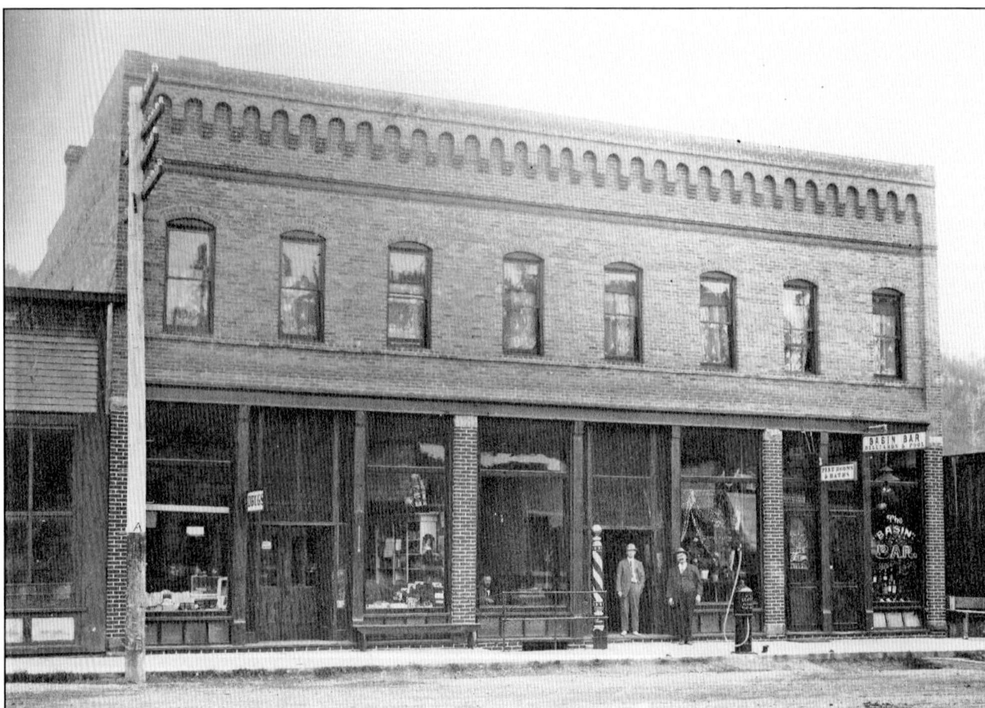

Building and bar owner John Sockerson (right) and barber Red Kohler stand outside the Basin Bar and Hotel and the Basin Barber Shop. The sturdy brick building is still on Basin's Main Street and while fine rooms are no longer available to rent, the building still contains a bar and restaurant. (Courtesy of the Jefferson County Museum.)

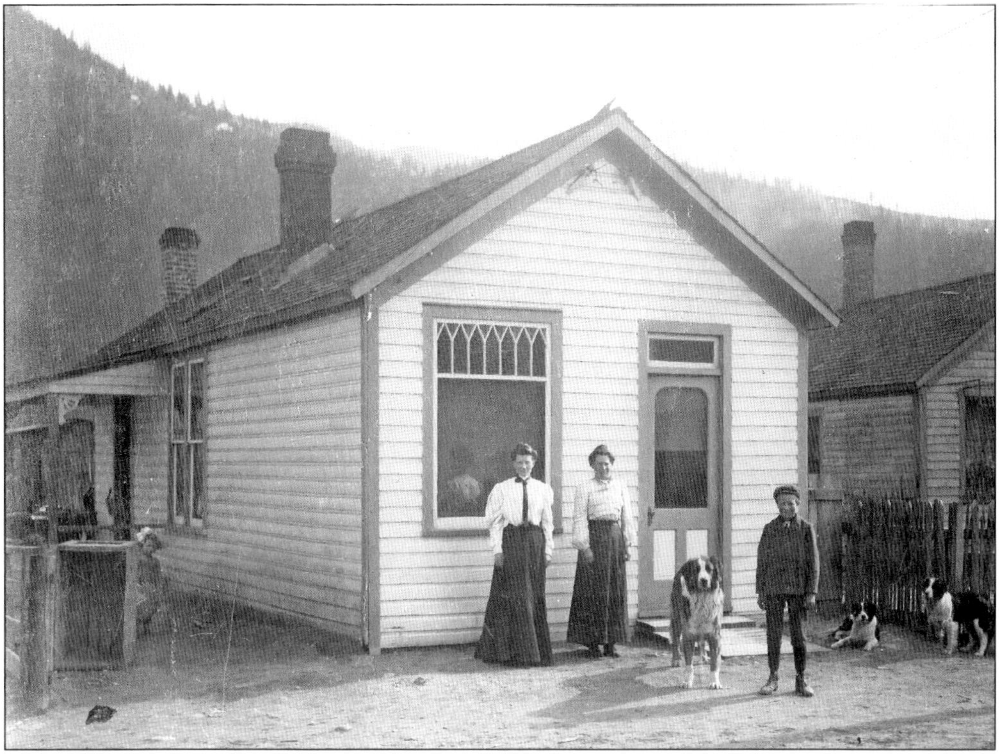

A family stands in front of their neat and tidy home in Basin. (Courtesy of the Jefferson County Museum.)

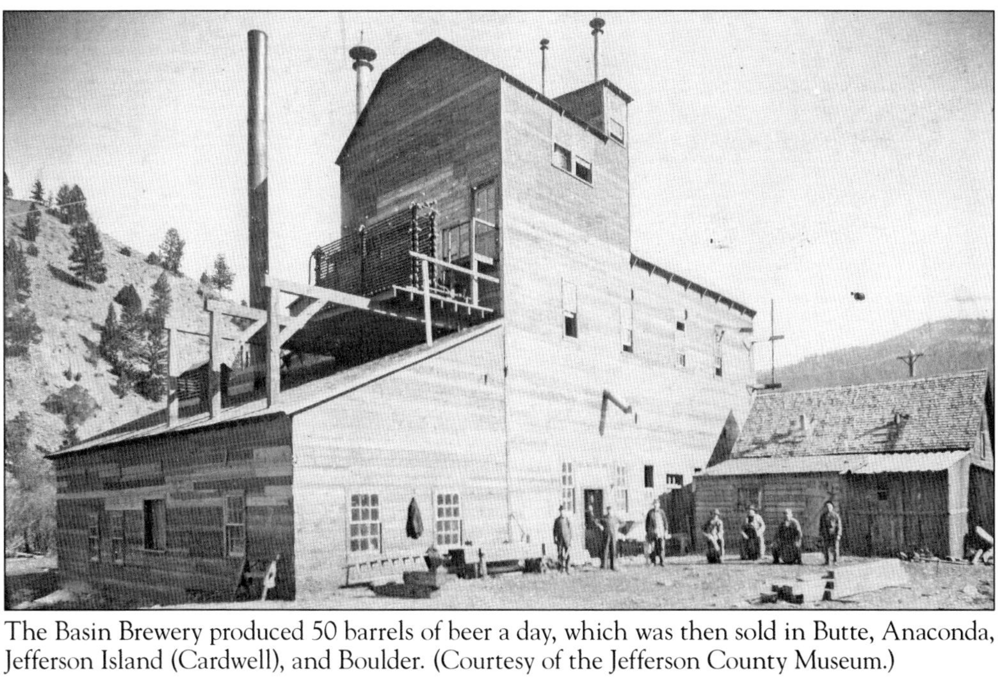

The Basin Brewery produced 50 barrels of beer a day, which was then sold in Butte, Anaconda, Jefferson Island (Cardwell), and Boulder. (Courtesy of the Jefferson County Museum.)

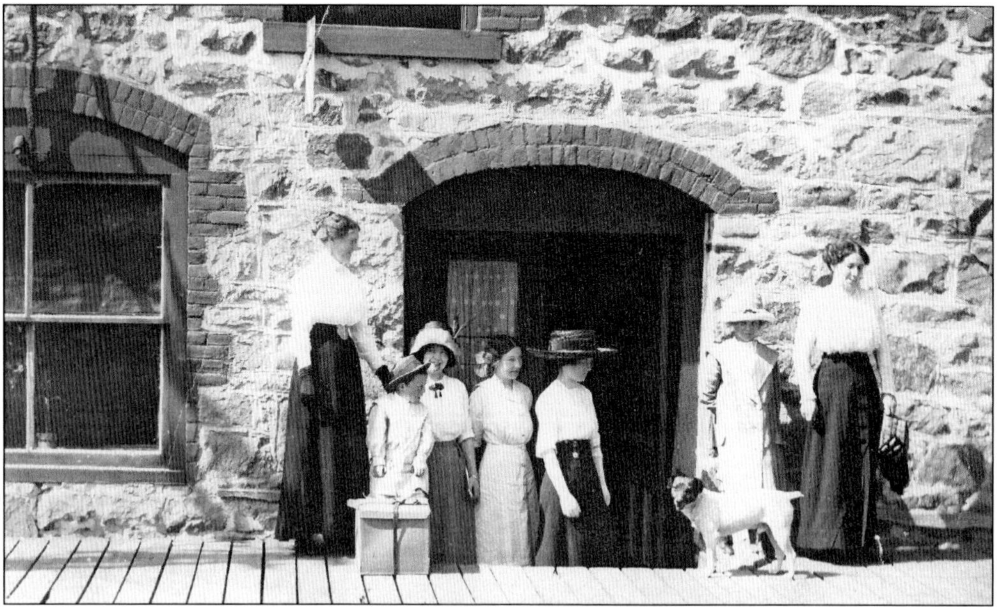

The Stone Annex, located in Basin, was completed in 1892 of stone and wood construction and joined the wood plank–constructed Hout Hotel next to it. The Stone Annex gave the Hout Hotel additional space for guests. (Courtesy of the Jefferson County Museum.)

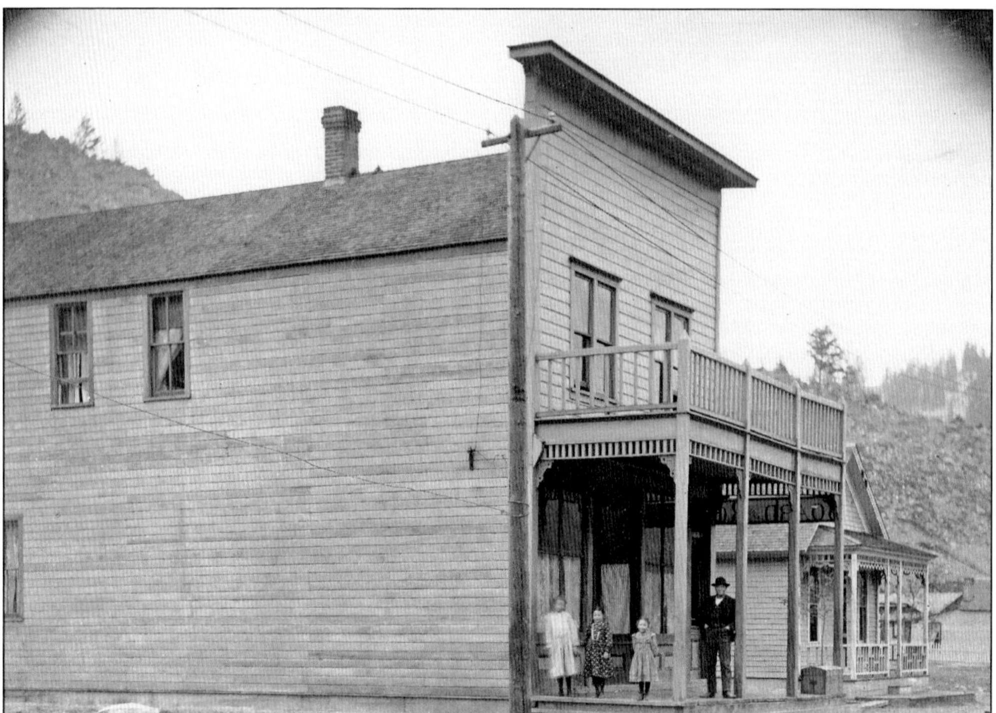

The Carlson Boarding House in Basin was owned by Oscar and Matilda Carlson. Their son, Charles, tore down the building and reused the lumber to build an addition onto his home in Bernice. (Courtesy of the Jefferson County Museum.)

Although Basin had numerous saloons, the town never had an abundance of churches. This little church served its Catholic members until it was torn down in 1951. (Courtesy of the Jefferson County Museum.)

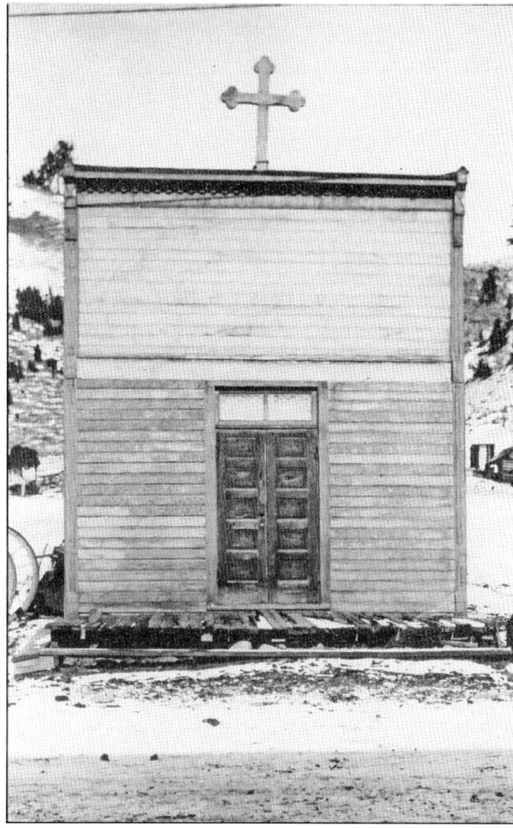

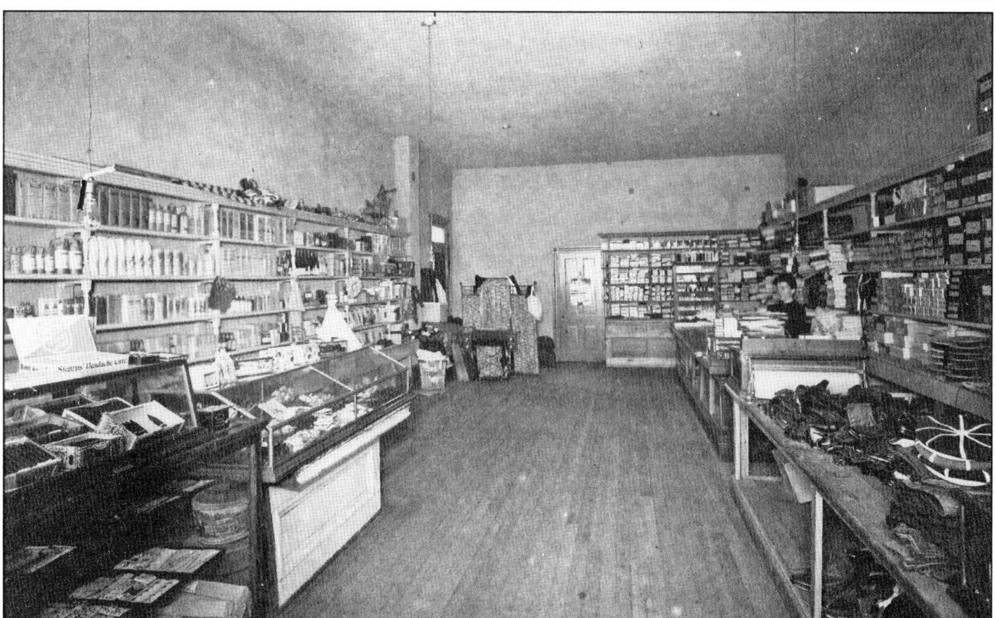

This photograph shows the inside of the Basin Store, which was owned by Kate Weber Berry. (Courtesy of the Jefferson County Museum.)

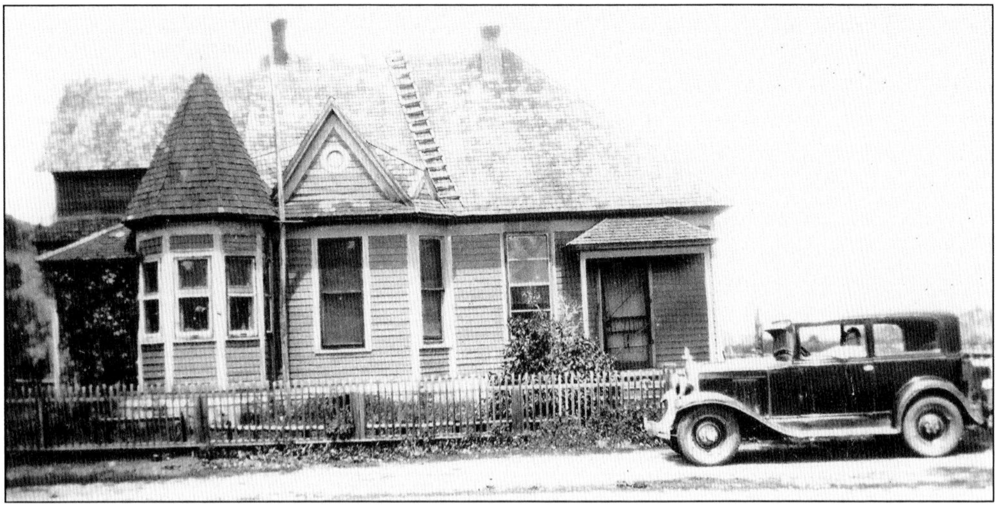

Walter Westover sits in his car outside his one-time residence in Clancy. The home was originally built by Clancy general store owner T. J. Chestnut. (Courtesy of the Jefferson County Museum.)

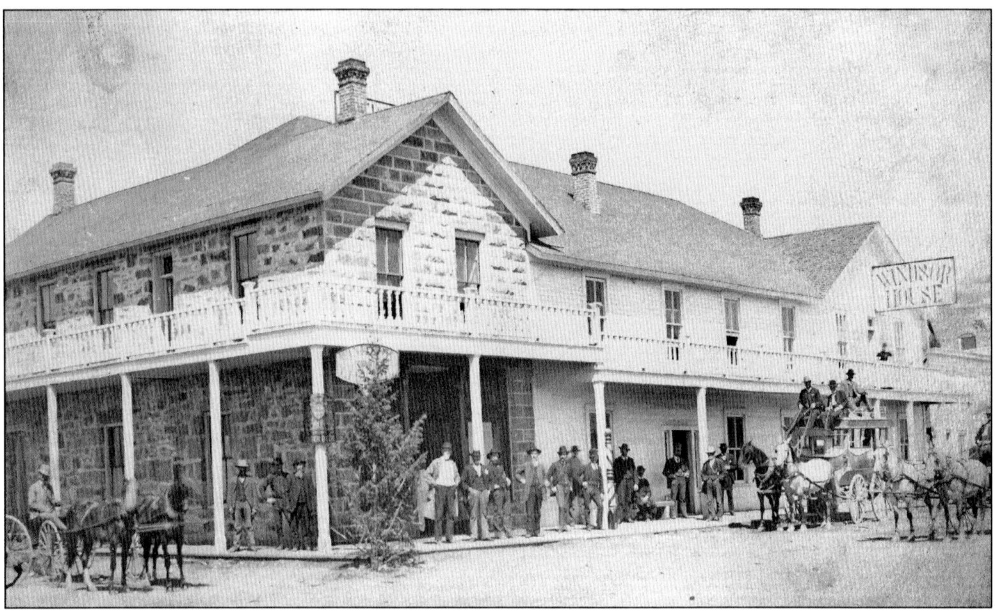

This photograph of the Windsor House (Bar) in Boulder, Montana, was taken in 1886. The bar offered rooms for rent and a place to eat and drink. In 1904, the building caught fire and burned down. Later that same year, it was rebuilt out of brick on the same location. (Courtesy of the Jefferson County Museum.)

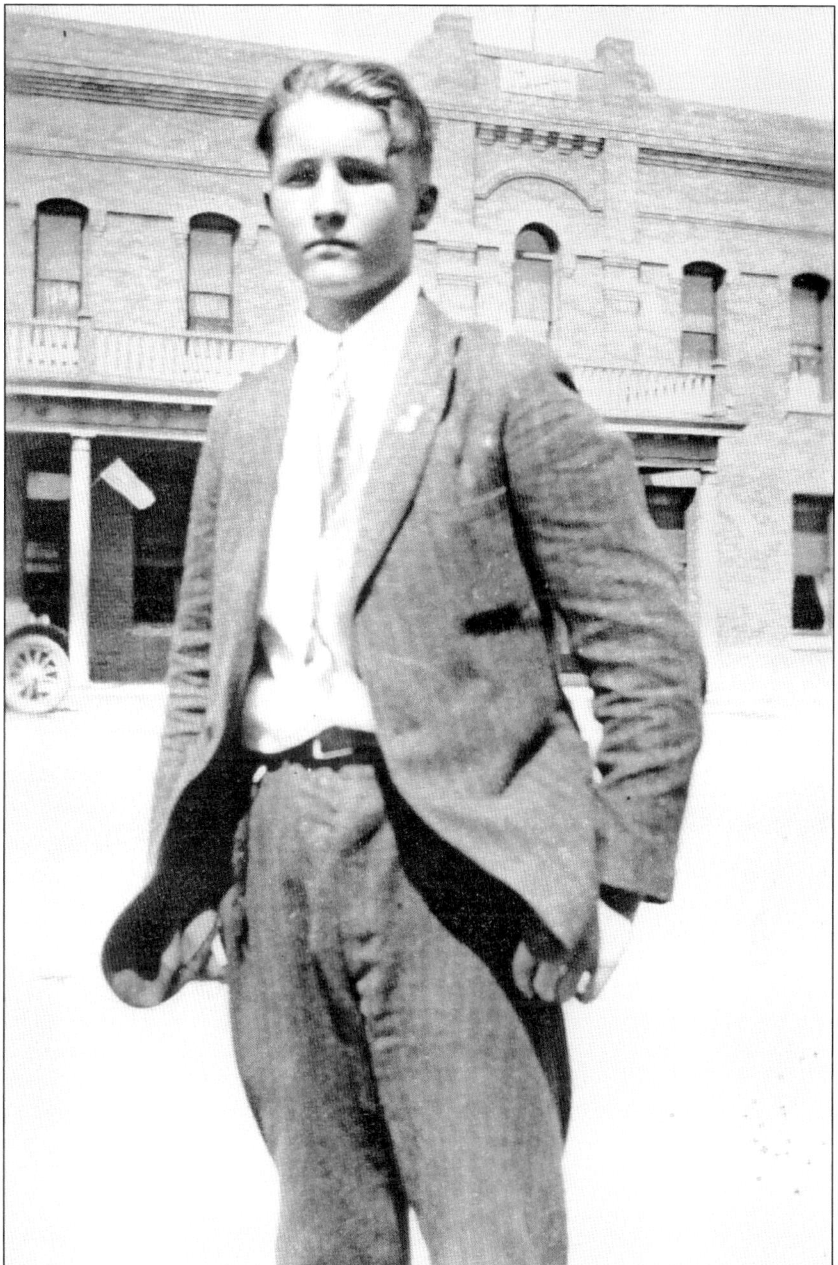

A young Sylavan Donagan stands outside of the newly rebuilt Windsor Hotel and Bar in Boulder. The original wooden Windsor House (Bar) was built in 1876 by Hiram Cook. On January 2, 1904, a fire started in the oil room below the stairway between the parlor and the office. Although the town fire bell was rung quickly to alert the sleeping hotel guests and Boulder residents, efforts to save the building were to no avail. In addition to the hotel, the adjoining stone bar and another building to the north were destroyed. Water thrown on the buildings across the street prevented further destruction of the town of Boulder. The following month, construction began on the new Windsor. The new building was made of brick and stone and contained 38 rooms. (Courtesy of the Jefferson County Museum.)

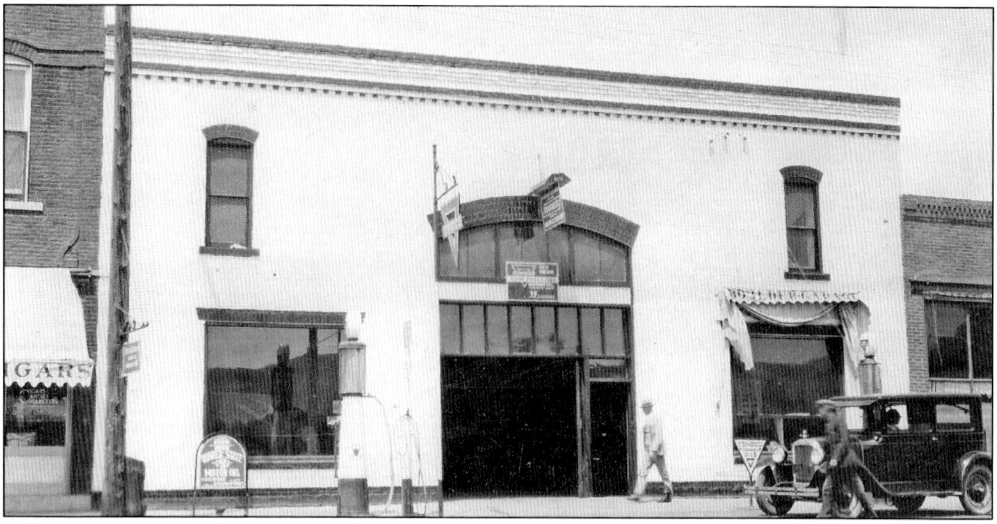

The Boulder Service Station and Garage was located on Main Street in Boulder. (Courtesy of the Jefferson County Genealogy and Heritage Center, Boulder, Montana.)

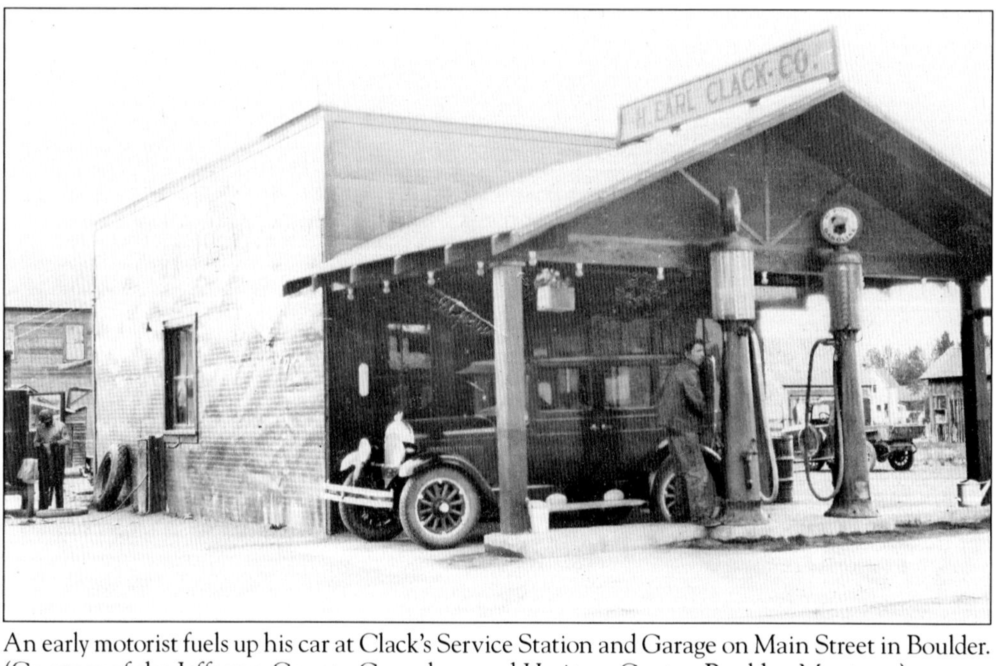

An early motorist fuels up his car at Clack's Service Station and Garage on Main Street in Boulder. (Courtesy of the Jefferson County Genealogy and Heritage Center, Boulder, Montana.)

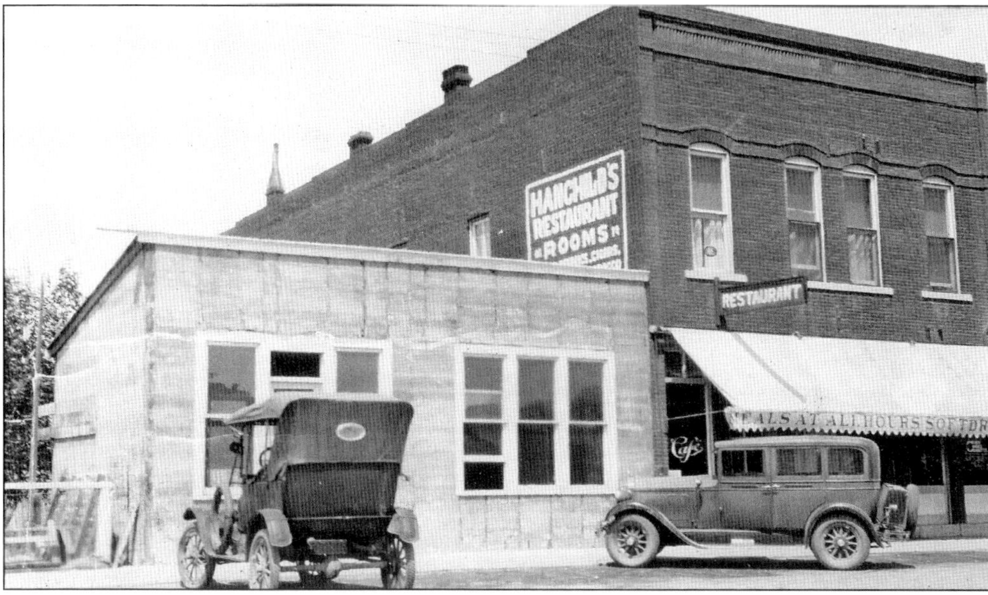

Guests at Hanchild's Restaurant in Boulder enjoyed food served at all hours and a cigar if they chose. (Courtesy of the Jefferson County Genealogy and Heritage Center, Boulder, Montana.)

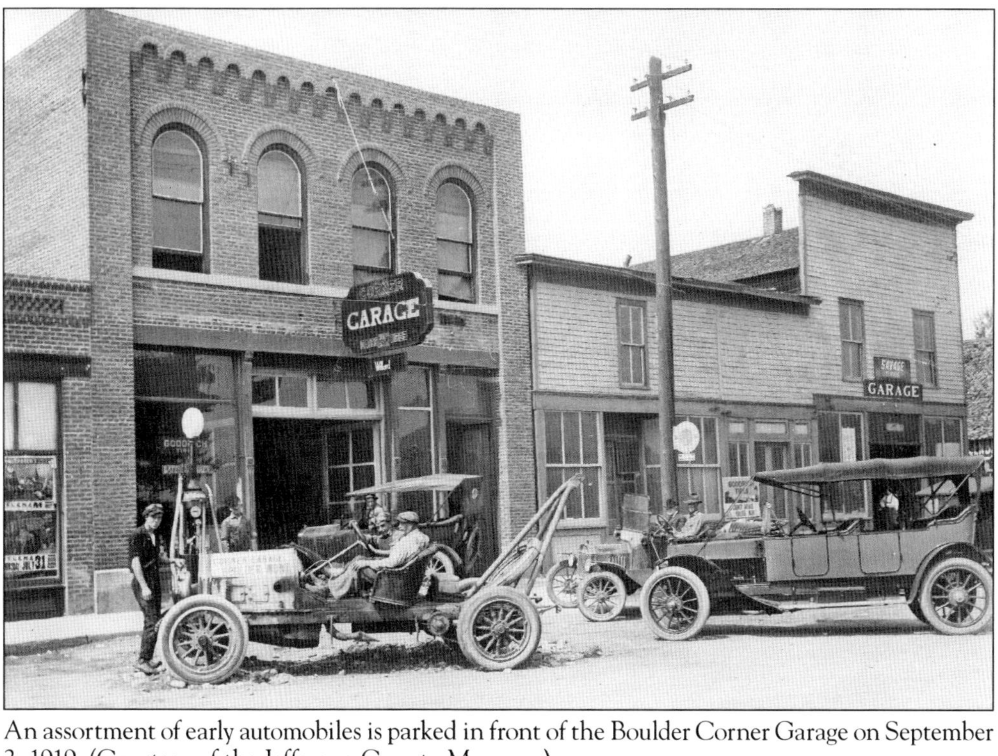

An assortment of early automobiles is parked in front of the Boulder Corner Garage on September 2, 1919. (Courtesy of the Jefferson County Museum.)

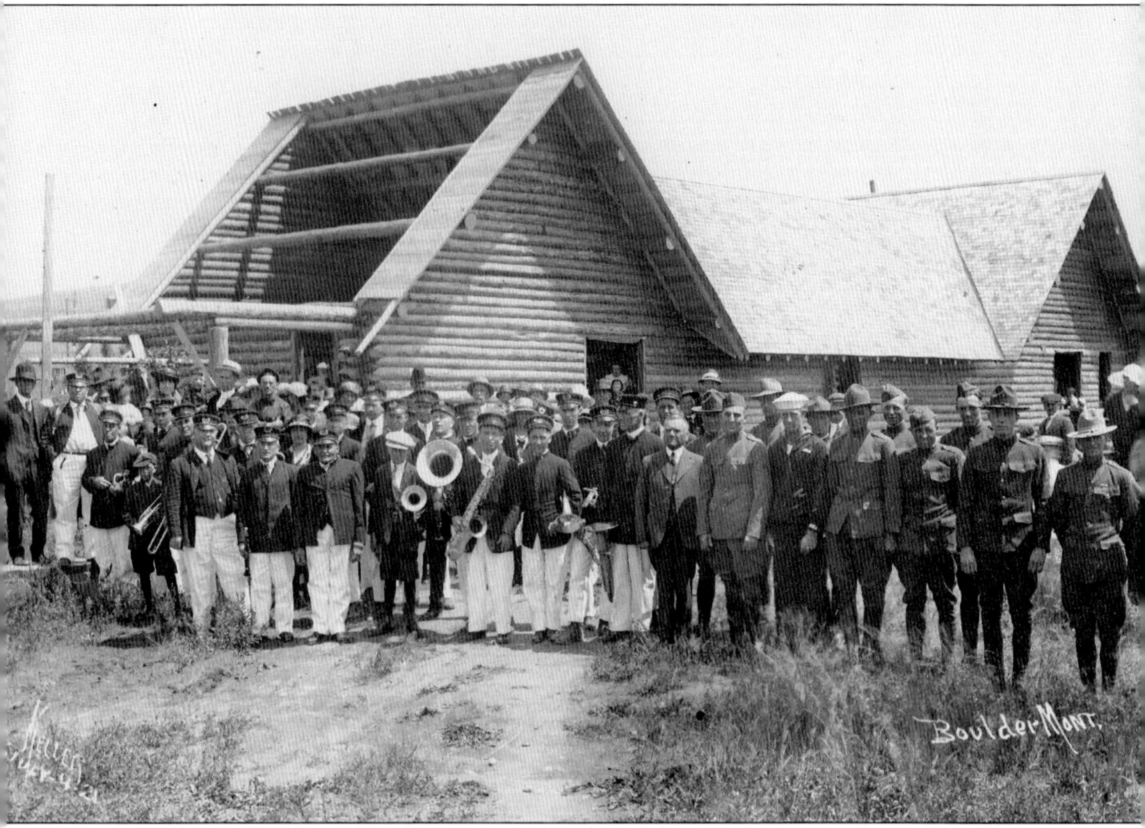

The American Legion Club House, which now contains the offices for the government of the City of Boulder, was constructed in 1921 as a place for Legionnaires to hold meetings and social gatherings. At a dedication ceremony on July 4, 1921, those in attendance were Boulder mayor Ira Leighton; Hon. Edward Phelan; the Women's Auxiliary; Whitehall band members; and veterans of the Civil War, Spanish-American War, and World War I. Local residents that served in the Civil War were Capt. George Ten Eyck, A. S. Kellogg, William Kennedy, Frank Hoopes, Tom Basye, William Hoopes, Horace Taylor, S. S. Street, Joel Bresee, Vining Cook, Charles Sargent, J. H. Nelson, and M. W. Weber. By 1921, only one local veteran of the Civil War was able to attend the ceremony for the new American Legion Club House. After the dedication ceremony, guests attended a midnight supper at the Windsor Hotel. (Courtesy of the Jefferson County Museum.)

Seven

Picnics and Parties

When the 1921 graduating class of Jefferson County High School met for their end-of-school picnic down along the banks of the Boulder River, they enjoyed a day of festivities. During the course of the day, classmates swam in the river, ate good food, and staged a mock execution of one of their own. Later, with paint bucket in hand, they lowered themselves over the dam and painted a large "21" for all to see. High school graduation was not the only time Jefferson County residents enjoyed a fun picnic or party. Each time someone in the community got married or reached their first communion, friends and families had a party. National holidays were another excuse for a fun celebration. On July 4, 1917, brothers William and John Steele took their families on a picnic. The girls dressed in red, white, and blue dresses, and the car was decorated with holiday bunting. The Mattson family of Comet also enjoyed the day in their early-model Dodge covered with U.S. flags and red, white, and blue banners. During the fall harvest season, Jefferson County residents met for food fairs. This allowed neighbors to bring their produce together for display. Families enjoyed visiting and eating the fruits of their labors. Dances and balls frequently held at the Boulder Hot Springs added to the entertainment choices for the pioneering families in Jefferson County. While time was often spent with family in wholesome activities, when hardworking men desired a night out, they would visit the local drinking establishment or join a popular club. At one time, Basin offered 12 bars to distract the hardworking miners. While miners in Comet had 22 saloons to choose from, sometimes they just sat on the porch of someone's house and drank to their satisfaction. Picnics and parties were a sure way to remember loved ones, celebrate milestones, and just plain have fun. After long, backbreaking days of work, men and women of Jefferson County welcomed any chance to relax.

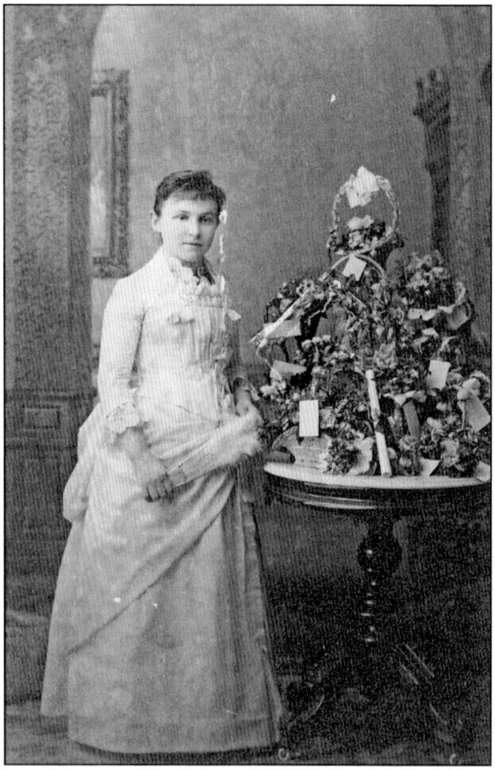

Jefferson County residents enjoyed celebrating milestones in each other's lives like first communions, graduations, and weddings. This photograph, saved from destruction when the former George Paradis home in Boulder was torn down, depicts an unknown young woman standing next to a table loaded with gifts. (Courtesy of the Jefferson County Museum.)

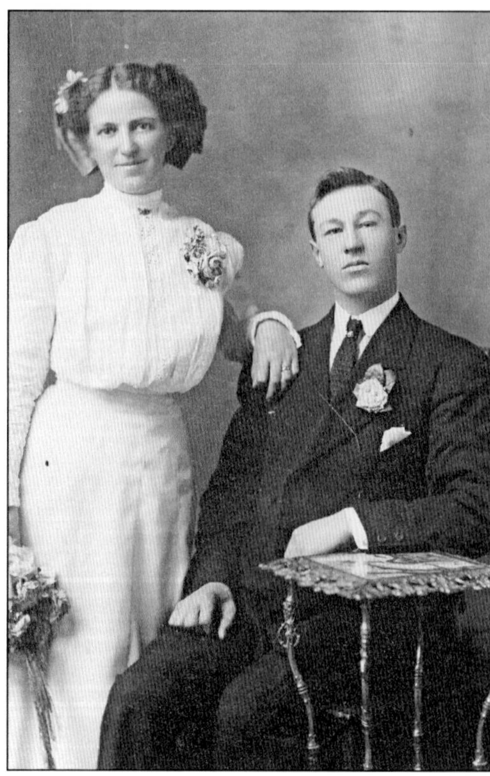

After their wedding, this unidentified happy couple poses for the camera. The bride made certain her new wedding ring was in the photograph. (Courtesy of the Jefferson County Museum.)

This young unidentified bride is dressed in her finery, including a corsage and pearls. (Courtesy of the Jefferson County Museum.)

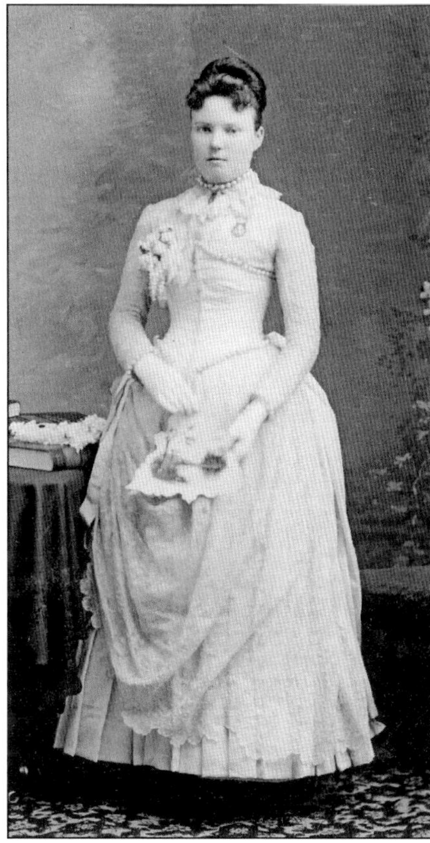

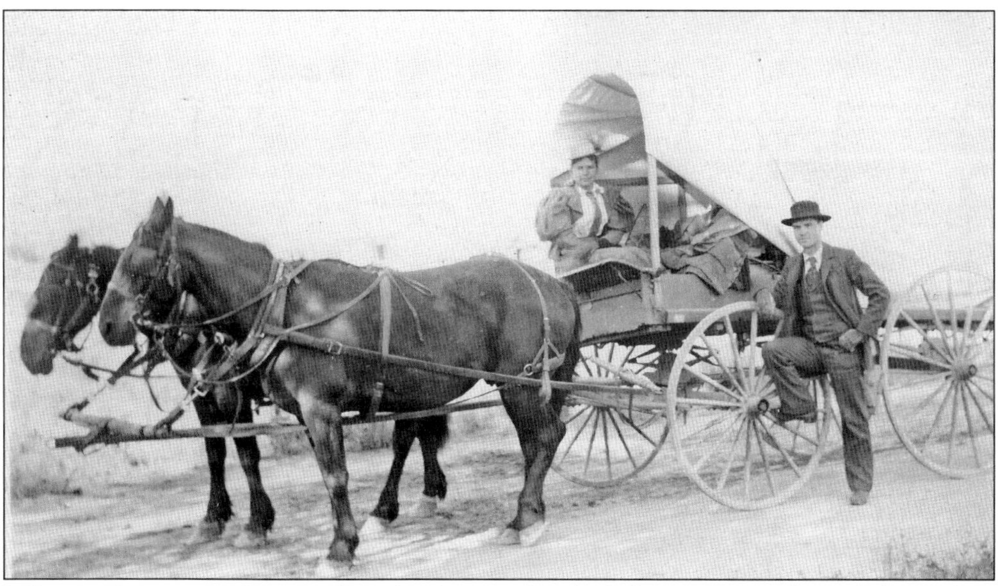

Jefferson County residents Will and Helen Wickes had their picture taken while on their honeymoon to Yellowstone National Park in 1896. William Woodbridge Wickes married Helen Stinson in July 1896. He worked for Wickes Dry Goods in Boulder. (Courtesy of the Jefferson County Museum.)

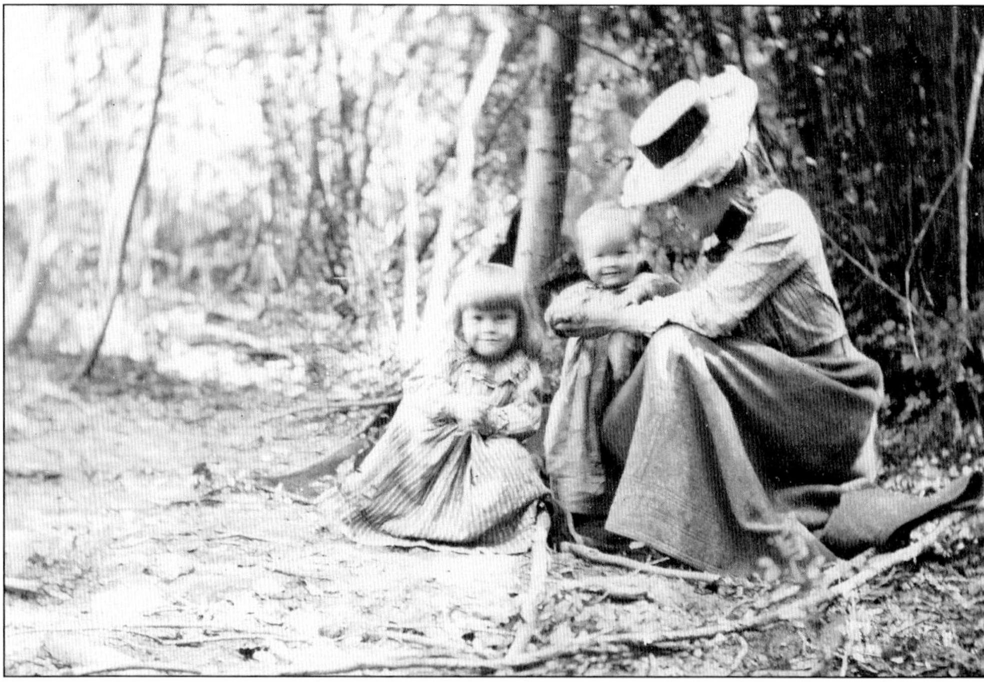

Jefferson County resident Helen Wickes holds her daughter Elizabeth while her daughter Margaret smiles for the camera in Yellowstone National Park in 1901. (Courtesy of the Jefferson County Museum.)

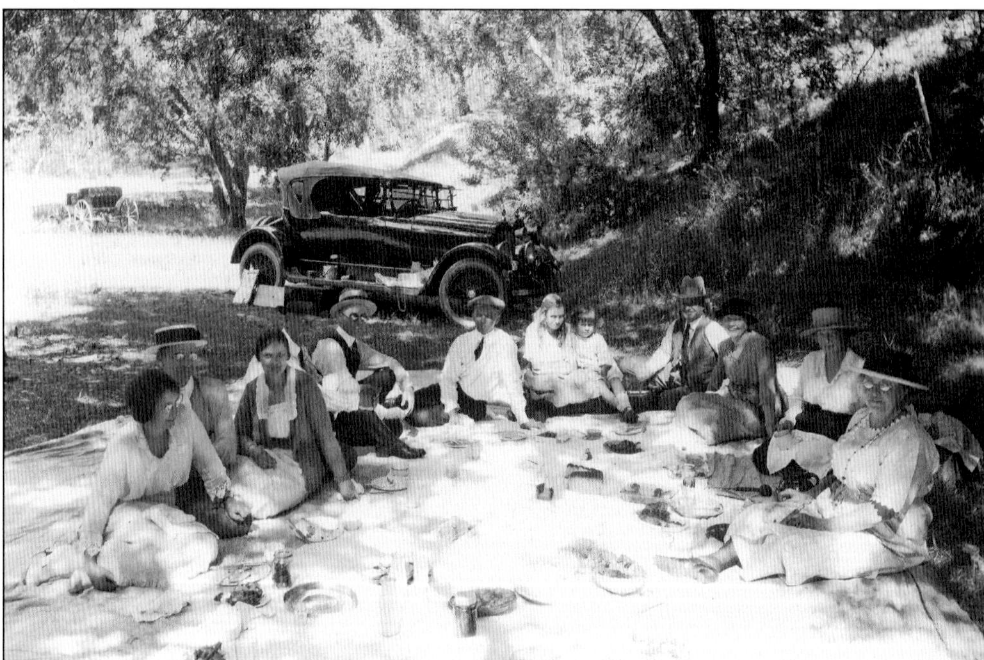

A family enjoys a picnic in 1922. Long before the use of disposable napkins, plates, or cups, this family used real dishes, silverware, and cups for their picnic. Even the pies were baked in sturdy pie plates. (Courtesy of the Jefferson County Museum.)

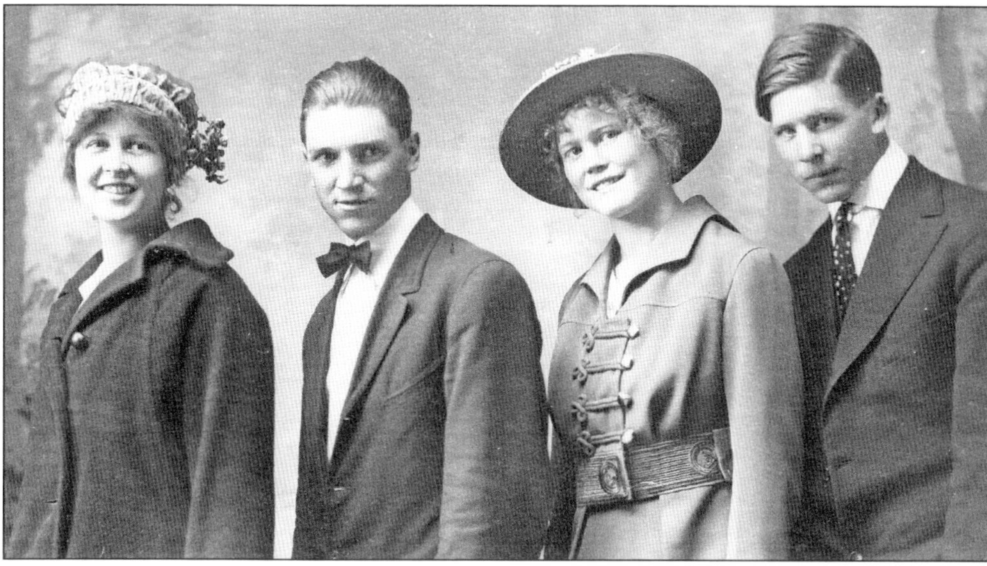

These young friends look forward to an evening out. Charles Carlson stands on the far right next to Florence Sockerson, and Ernest (Sam) Wilson stands next to Florence. The woman on the far left is unidentified. Sam and Florence graduated from Jefferson County High School in 1915. The Wilson family operated a ranch south of Boulder. In 1938, Sam found work as a foreman for the Civilian Conservation Corps camp in Winifred. Charles lived in Bernice, where he produced charcoal and ran his family's ranch. In 1919, he married Edna Williamson, daughter of the local forest ranger. Charles later served as Jefferson County commissioner and was elected to the Montana State House of Representatives. Florence Sockerson endured the loss of her father to suicide at a young age. Florence moved from Jefferson County after her marriage to David Hansen in 1919. (Courtesy of the Jefferson County Museum.)

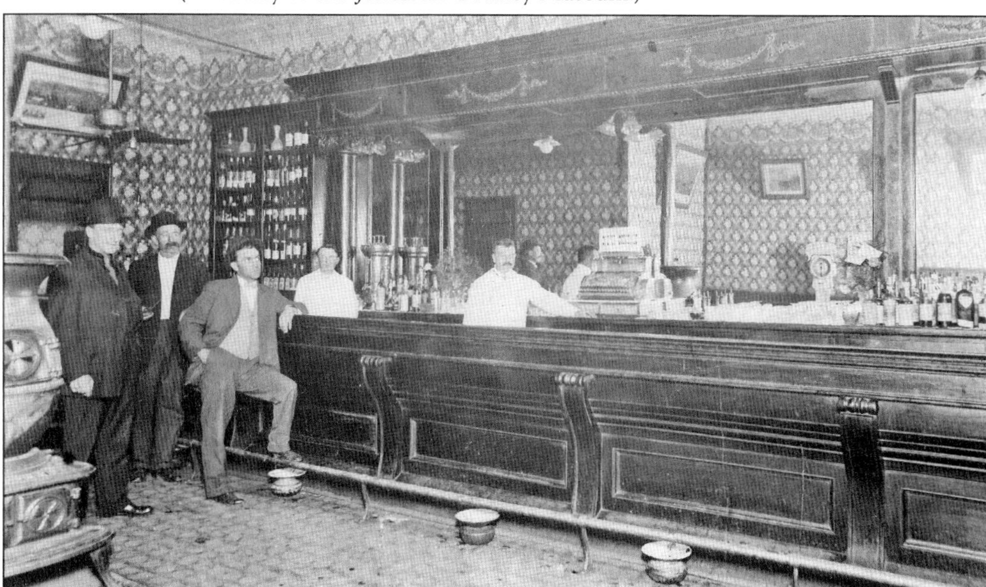

One form of entertainment in the mining community of Basin was to enjoy a drink at one of the bars. The ornate bar and fancy wallpaper of this watering hole is offset by the less-than-clean floor and well-used spittoons. (Courtesy of the Jefferson County Museum.)

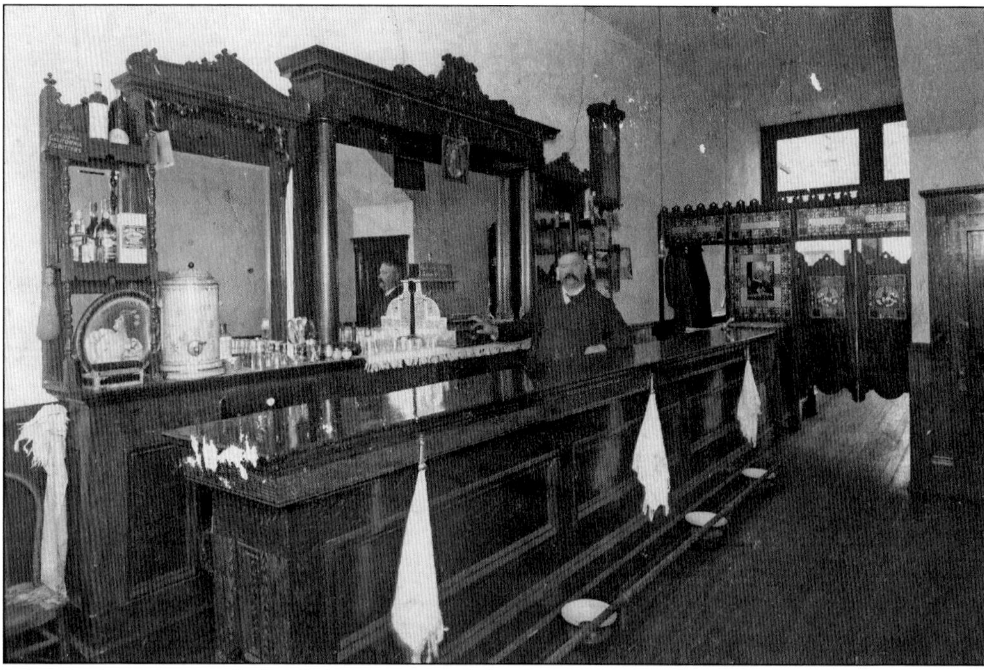

John Sockerson waits behind the counter of the Basin Bar for thirsty customers. (Courtesy of the Jefferson County Museum.)

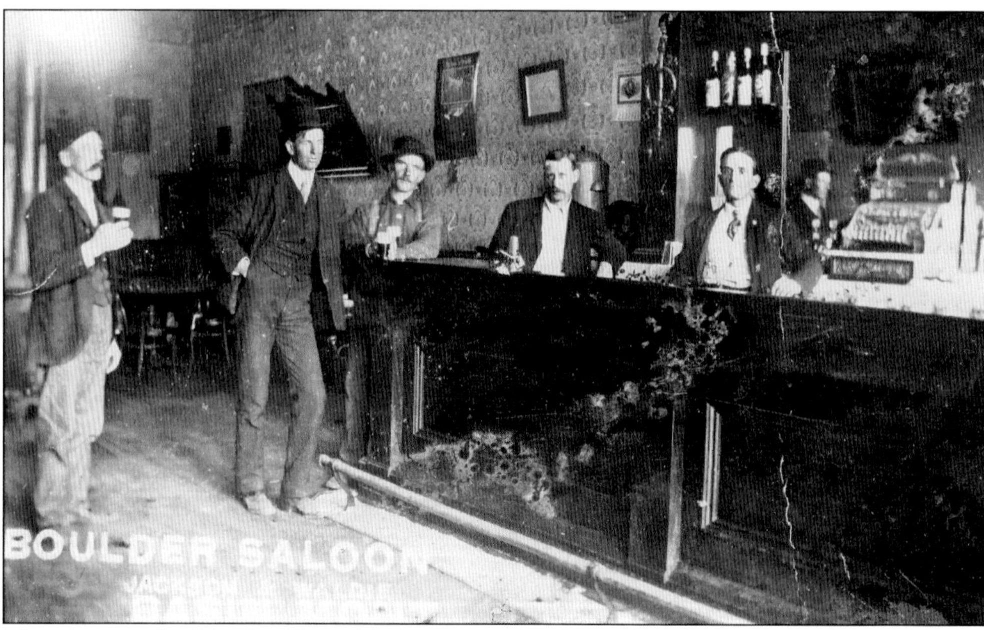

This photograph of the Boulder Saloon in Basin was taken in 1909. Wilber Jackson and Clarence Waldie co-owned the Boulder Saloon. (Courtesy of the Jefferson County Museum.)

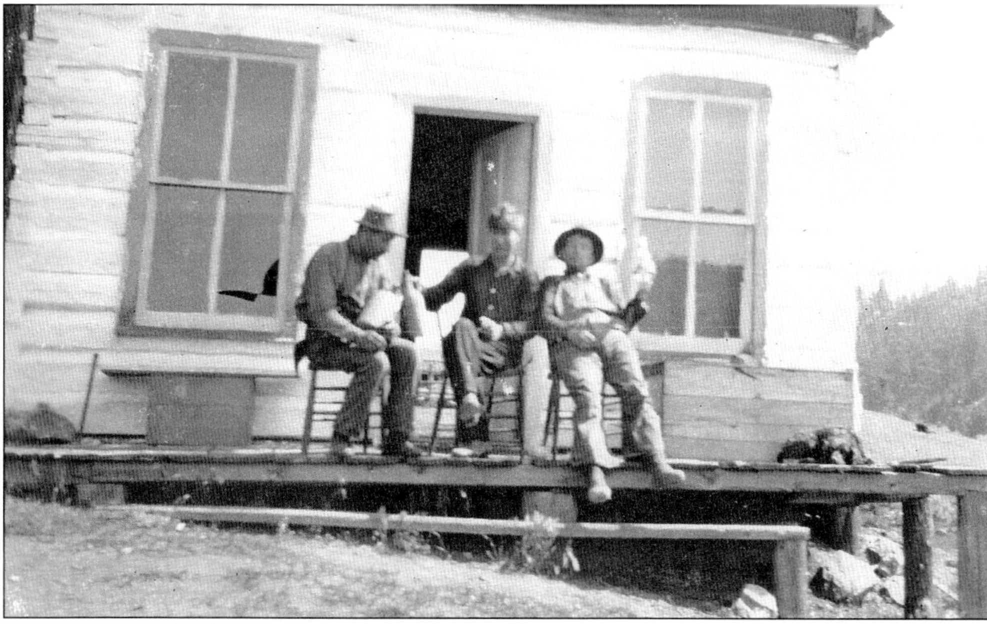

Miners enjoy a drink or two on the porch of a humble home in Comet, Montana. (Courtesy of the Jefferson County Genealogy and Heritage Center, Boulder, Montana.)

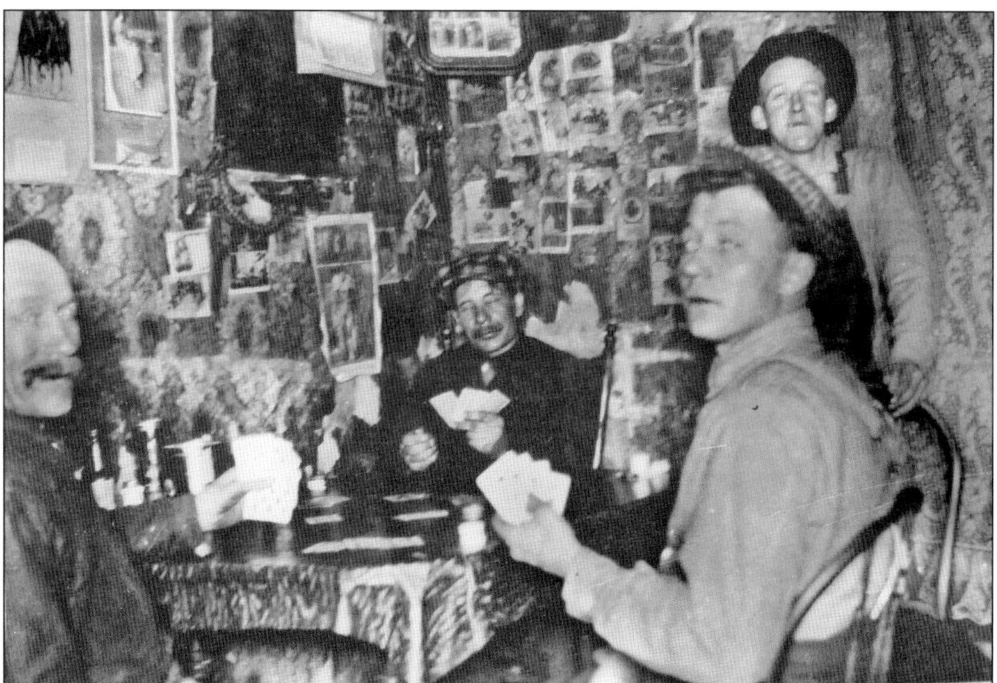

Playing card games was one form of entertainment enjoyed by these miners in Comet, Montana. (Courtesy of the Jefferson County Genealogy and Heritage Center, Boulder, Montana.)

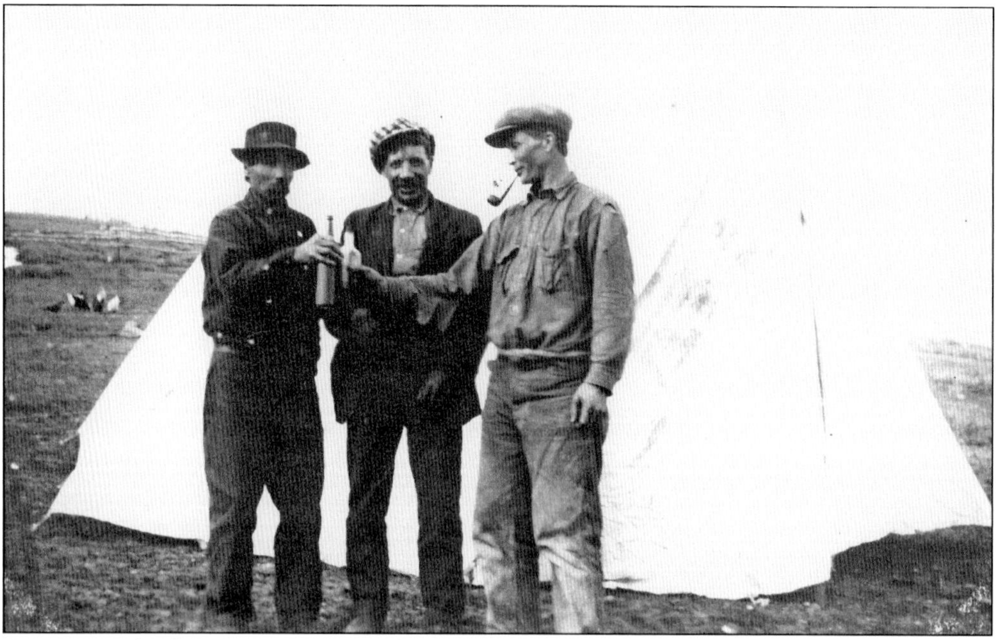

Camping with a large canvas tent was fun as long as these miners had something strong to drink. (Courtesy of the Jefferson County Genealogy and Heritage Center, Boulder, Montana.)

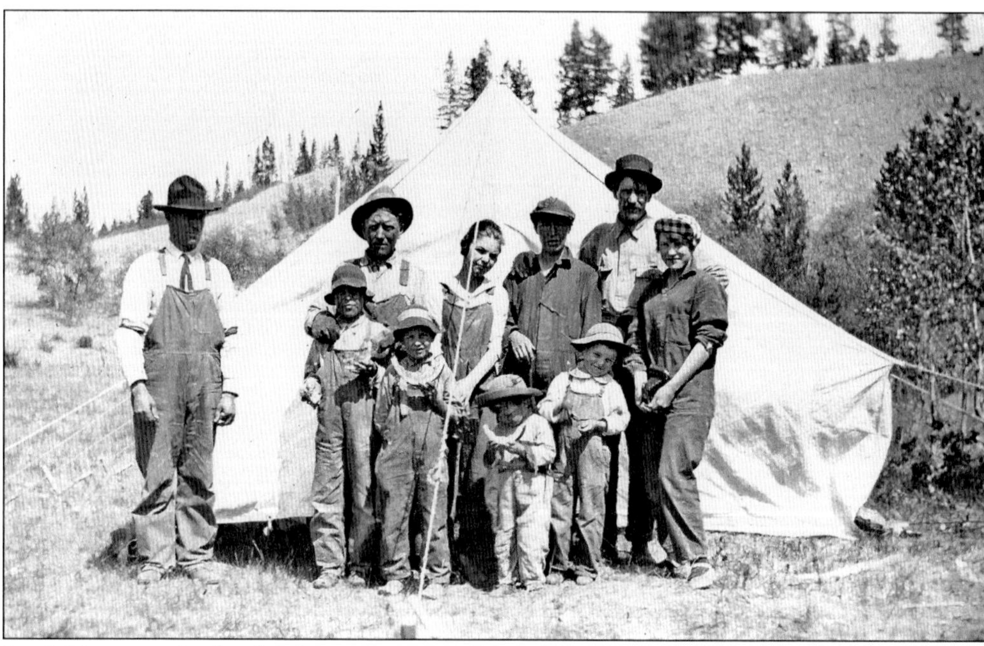

Jacob Mattson takes his family camping in Jefferson County. (Courtesy of the Jefferson County Genealogy and Heritage Center, Boulder, Montana.)

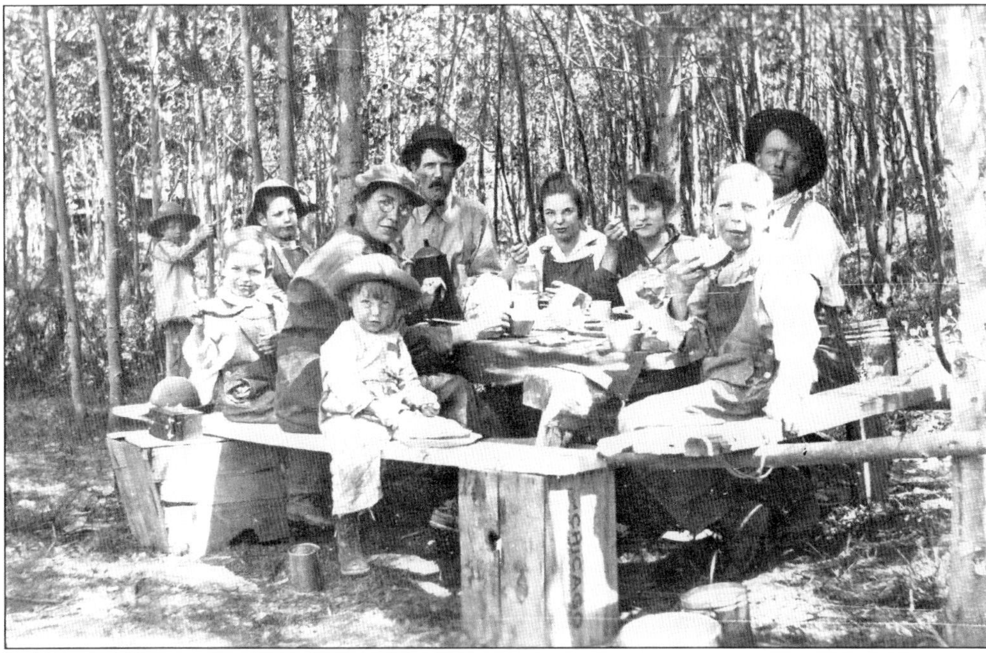

Comet residents Jacob Mattson (center, with mustache) and his family eat a picnic lunch at a rustic table. (Courtesy of the Jefferson County Genealogy and Heritage Center, Boulder, Montana.)

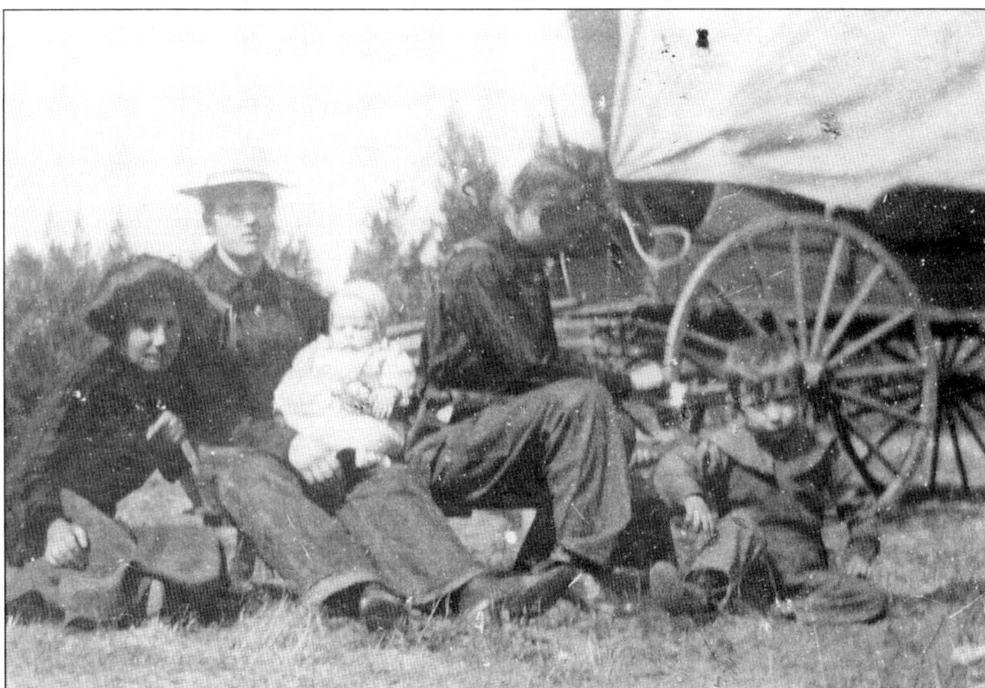

From left to right, Jefferson County residents Nina Allen, Nevada Hastie Glass, son Jim Glass, and Ada Glass Folkins with her stepson Joe Folkins take their covered wagon camping in 1904. (Courtesy of the Lindsay family, Clancy, Montana.)

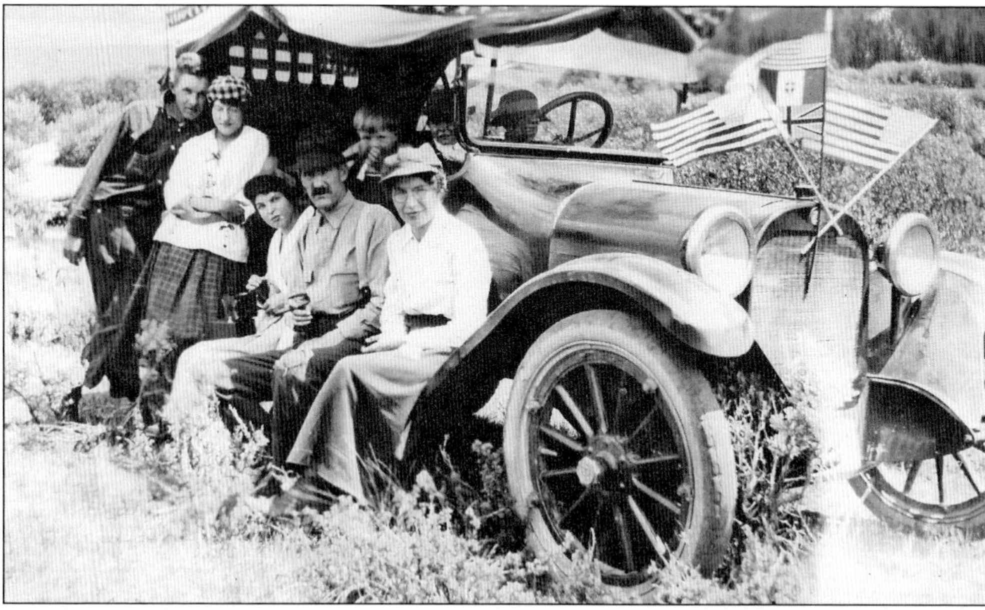

On July 4, 1917, the Mattson family decorated their car with flags and bunting to celebrate the holiday. (Courtesy of the Jefferson County Genealogy and Heritage Center, Boulder, Montana.)

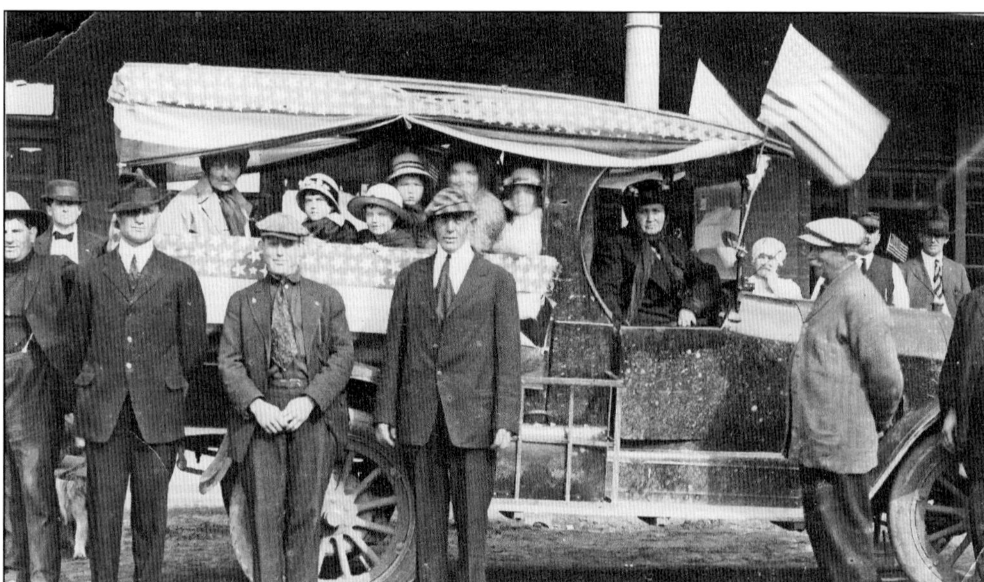

Boulder and Basin residents sit in an early bus decorated for the Fourth of July. William Wolter, who operated the first bus in Boulder, turns away from the camera to laugh at his busload of people. (Courtesy of the Jefferson County Museum.)

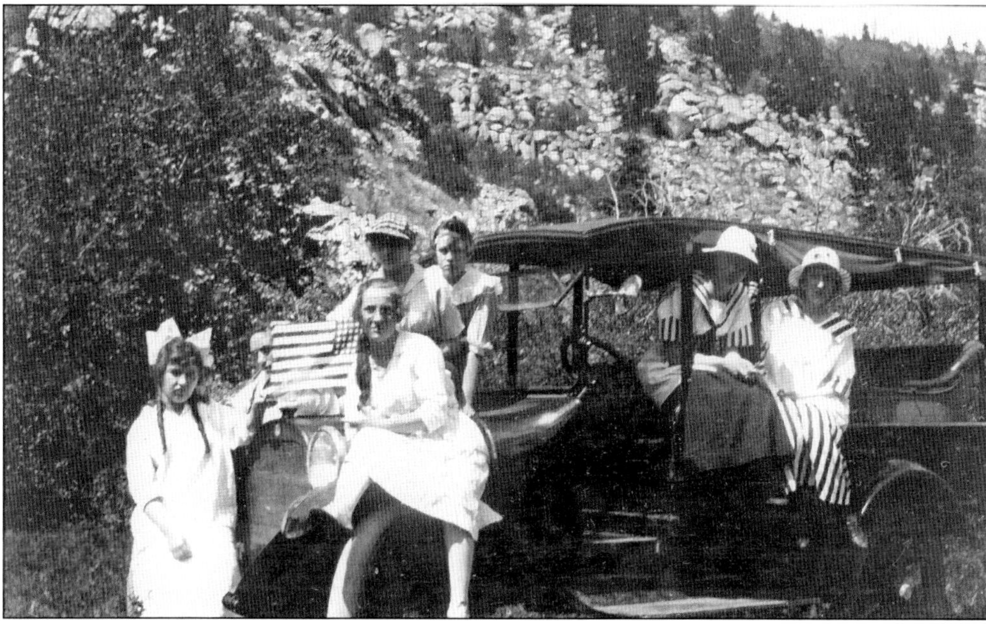

Jessie Steele of Boulder sits on the bumper of the car while helping to hold up a U.S. flag on July 4, 1917. (Courtesy of the Jefferson County Museum.)

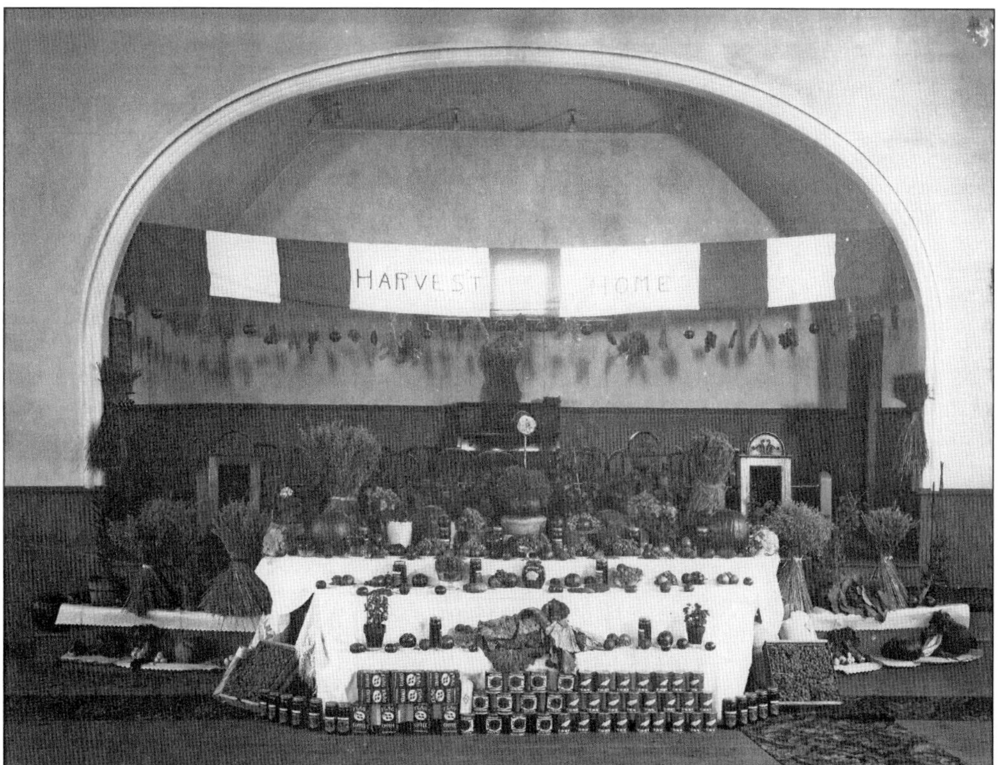

Jefferson County residents held fairs like the Harvest Home Fair to show off their prized vegetables and to socialize with neighbors. (Courtesy of the Jefferson County Museum.)

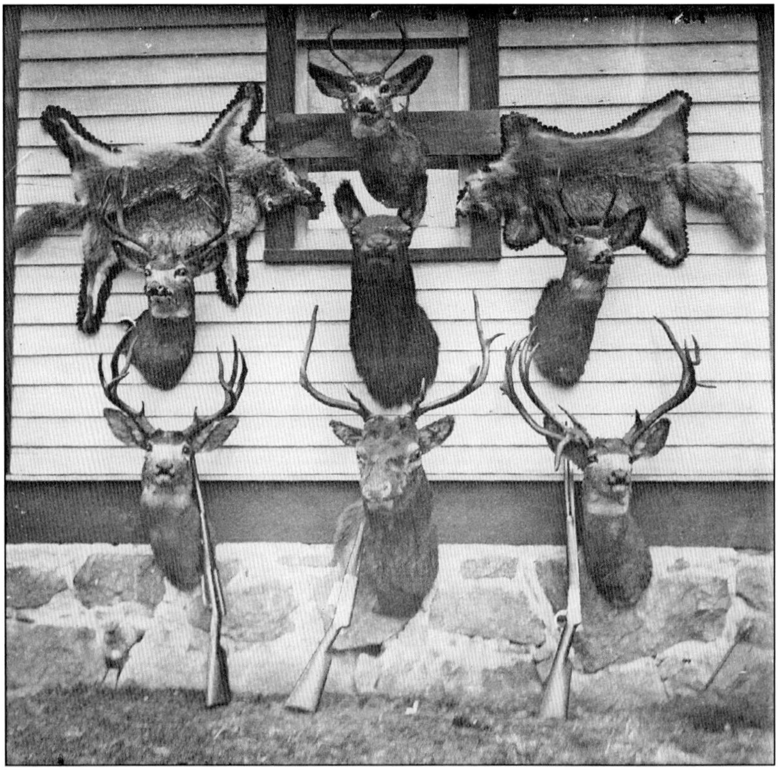

A favorite pastime for Wilber F. and Drew Jackson was hunting. They hung up their trophies on a building in Basin for this photograph, taken in 1919. (Courtesy of the Jefferson County Museum.)

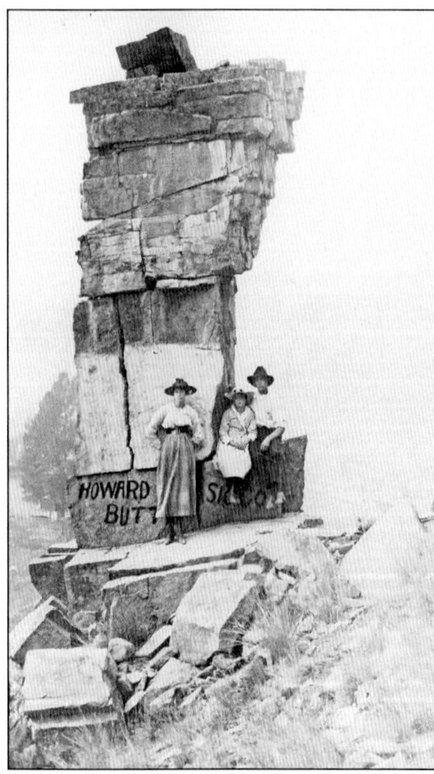

Sometimes Jefferson County residents enjoyed hiking for entertainment. This group hikes up to an interesting rock formation named "Pulpit Rock" by locals. (Courtesy of the Jefferson County Genealogy and Heritage Center, Boulder, Montana.)

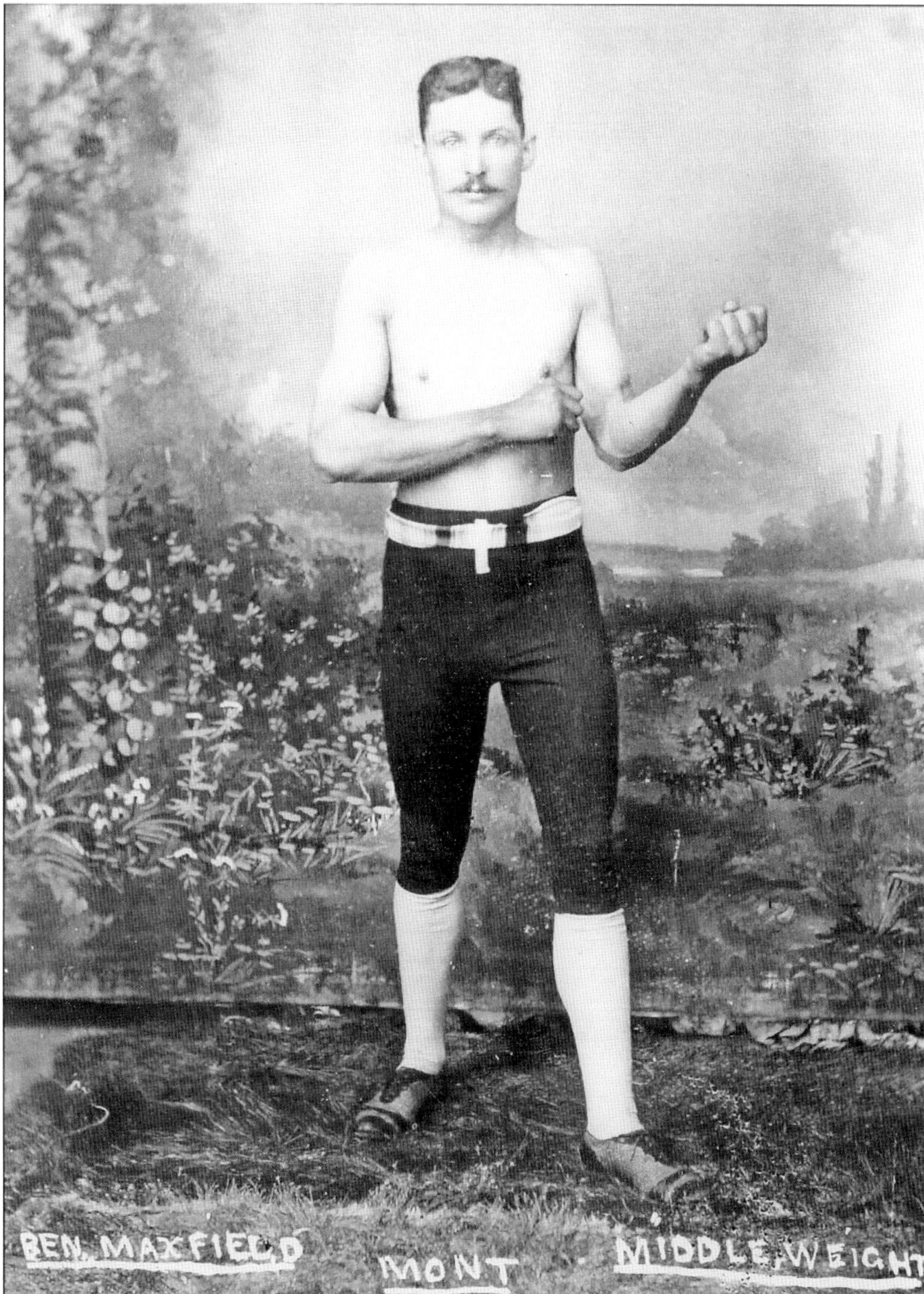

Middleweight boxer Ben Maxfield assumes a boxer's stance for photographer John Berkin to take his picture. Maxfield lived for a time in Boulder and owned property on Main Street. He originally came from Utah to train at the Boulder Hot Springs around 1888. (Courtesy of the Jefferson County Genealogy and Heritage Center, Boulder, Montana.)

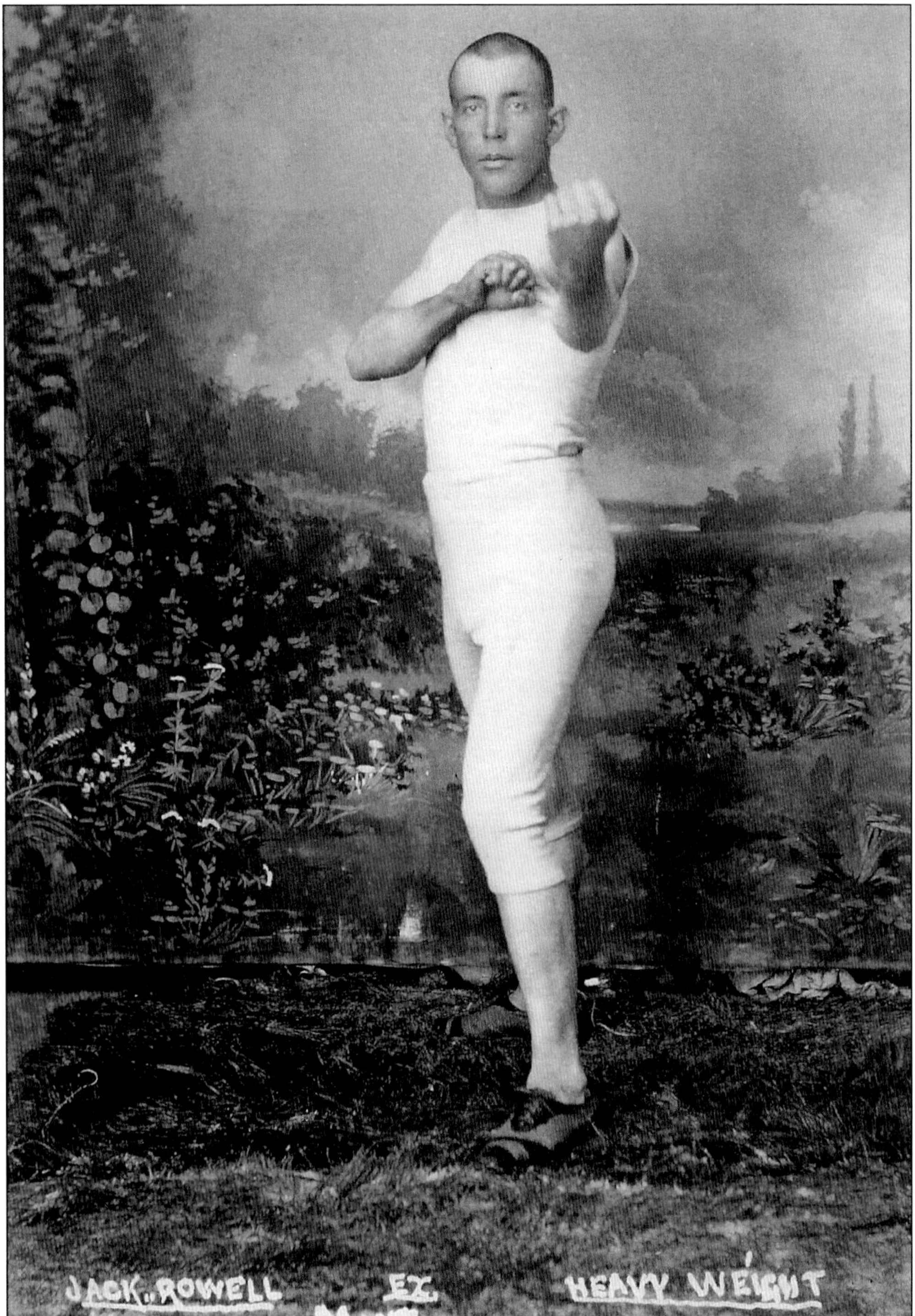

Ex-heavyweight boxer Jack Rowell also had his picture taken by John Berkin. (Courtesy of the Jefferson Genealogy and Heritage Center, Boulder, Montana.)

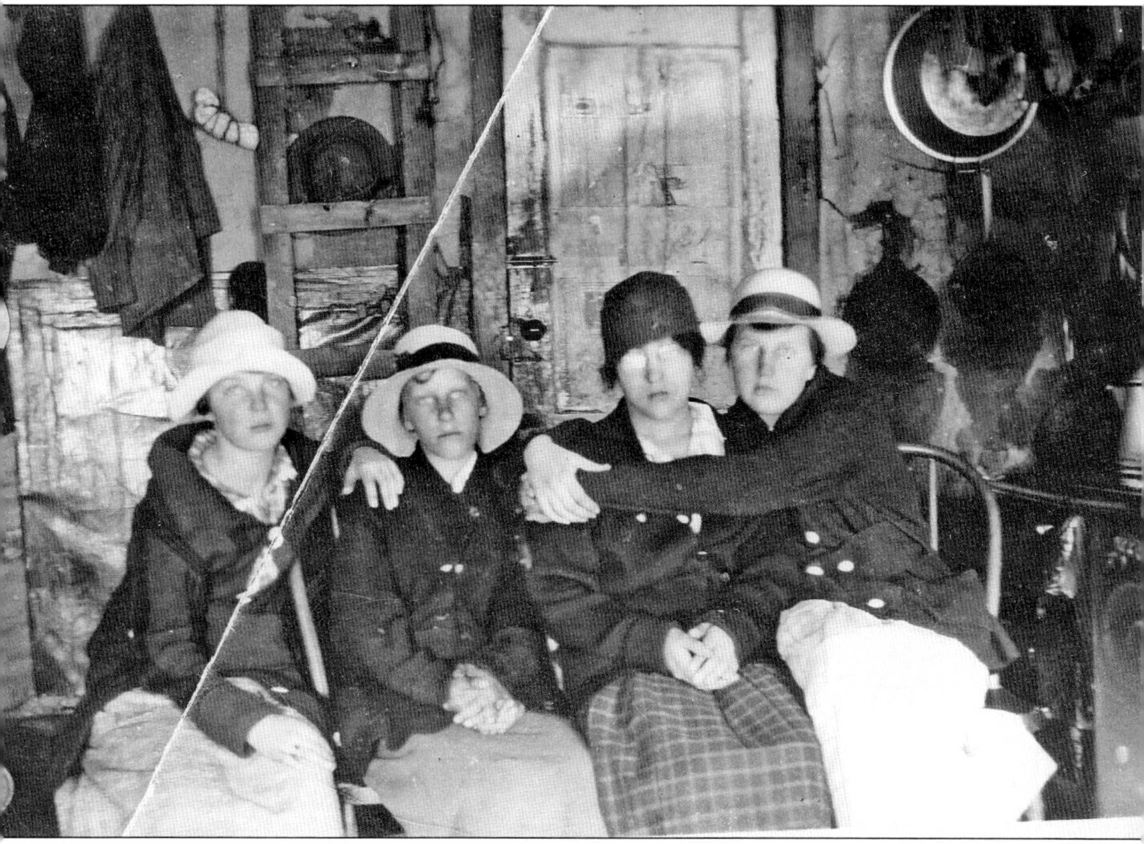

All dressed up for a party, these young ladies from Comet smile for the camera. (Courtesy of the Jefferson County Genealogy and Heritage Center, Boulder, Montana.)

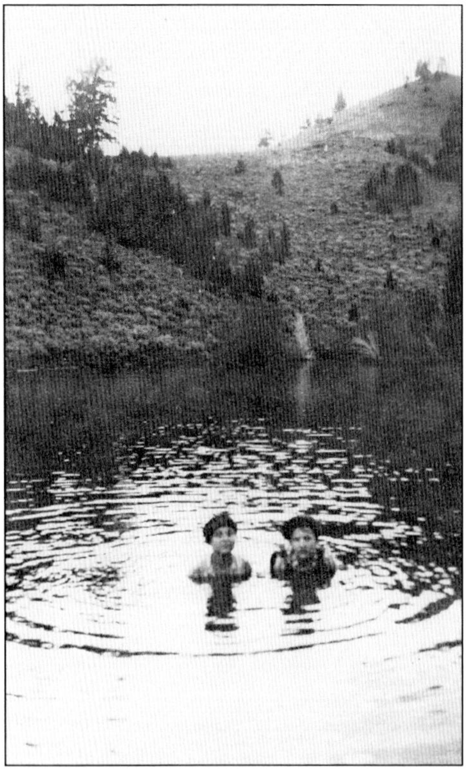

In 1917, these women decided not to wear any swimwear while they swam. They simply left their dresses and hats on while they cooled off. (Courtesy of the Jefferson County Genealogy and Heritage Center, Boulder, Montana.)

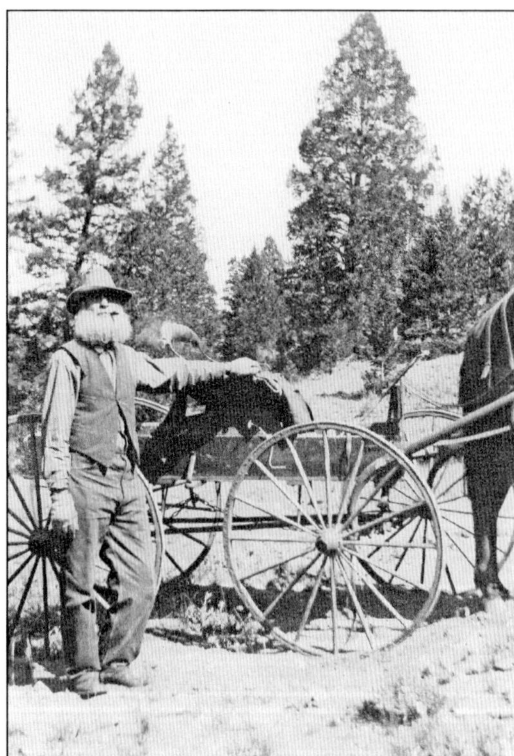

This Comet miner, thought to be Sam Peron, has his picture taken before he climbs into his buggy for an outing. (Courtesy of the Jefferson County Genealogy and Heritage Center, Boulder, Montana.)

Eight

Taking the Waters

Hot springs were discovered in the area now known as Jefferson County by First Peoples that traveled through the area on the way to traditional hunting grounds. Later European settlers in the towns of Pipestone, Boulder, and Alhambra built hotels and baths to capitalize on the warm waters. Prospector James E. Riley claimed the Boulder Hot Springs in 1863. Unfortunately, James Riley did not live long enough to complete his dream of building a hotel at the location. Later owners completed a hotel, but it was not until 1909, when Butte millionaire James A. Murray purchased the property, that an opulent renovation took place. Murray hired an interior decorator from New York City to redecorate the card room in a Chinese motif and do fancy fresco work in the huge lobby. Murray also hung 12-foot ceiling lights of amber glass in the lobby. He added stucco to the exterior arches and fountains to the hot springs building. The result was a large building resembling a Spanish mission. Meanwhile, in Pipestone, early proprietress J. N. Kirk operated a complex of hotel buildings at Pipestone Creek. The main hotel had a long covered porch that connected two brick buildings. Visitors would be picked up at a nearby train depot and transported to the hot springs. If tourists traveling to Jefferson County wanted to sample all the thermal areas, they could also travel north to Alhambra Hot Springs. By the time Mike Sullivan owned the Alhambra Hot Springs Hotel near Warm Springs Creek, the establishment included a two-story hotel, small cottages for long-term guests, indoor plunges, a lake for fishing or canoeing, a large dining room for meals, and a train depot within easy walking distance. The hotel staff catered to the every whim of the visitors and offered rooms with electric lights and steam heat. A few days spent in the thermal hot springs of Jefferson County ensured that tourists would go home rested and warm, even if they might not be cured of all their ailments.

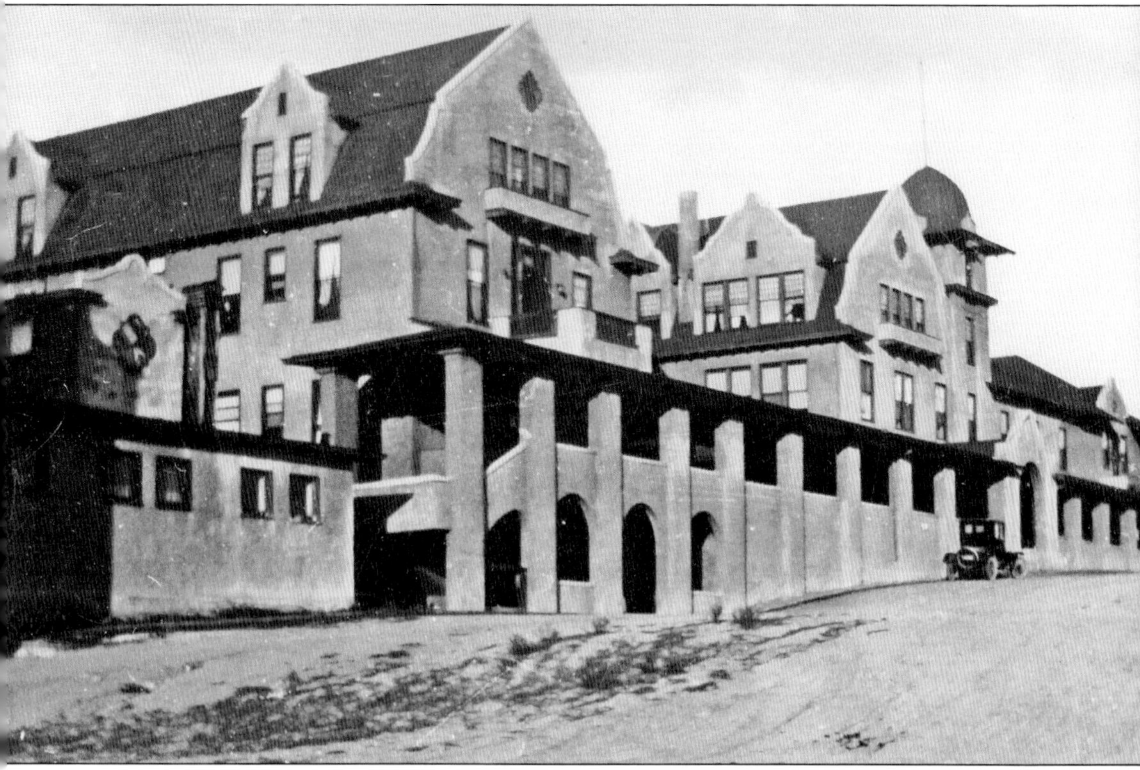

This photograph of the Boulder Hot Springs most likely was taken when Butte millionaire James Murray owned it. Murray purchased the property in 1909 and began restoration work in 1910. The Murray family owned it until 1940, when C. L. Smith purchased it. Smith changed the name to the Diamond S Ranchotel. It was called the Diamond S until Stewart Lewin purchased the building in 1978. He changed the name back to Boulder Hot Springs and had it placed on the National Historic Register. Lewin rebuilt the bathhouse and the walkway leading to the outdoor pool, opened one wing of rooms, put in a new kitchen and a small restaurant, and made other repairs. Lewin closed the property in 1989. By 1990, the Hot Springs was purchased by a limited partnership including Anne Wilson Schaef. After a great deal of time and money was spent on renovation and repairs, the Boulder Hot Springs again opened in the summer of 1991. The spa buildings, the small dining room, and the east wing of the hotel have been completely refurbished. (Courtesy of the Jefferson County Museum.)

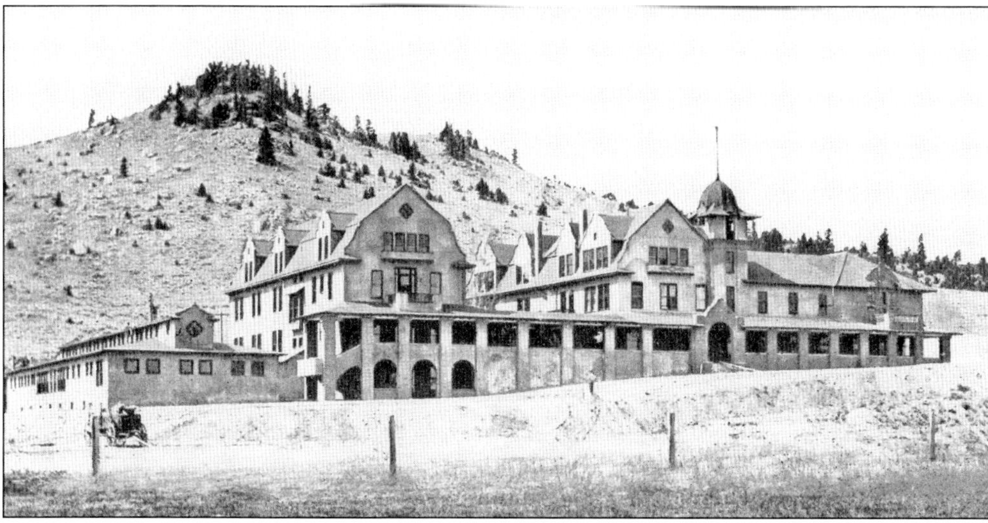

Sarah Hutchins wrote in 1911 from the Boulder Hot Springs that she was enjoying a week of much-needed rest. She and her husband had ridden the train out from Vermont for a vacation. (Courtesy of the Jefferson County Museum.)

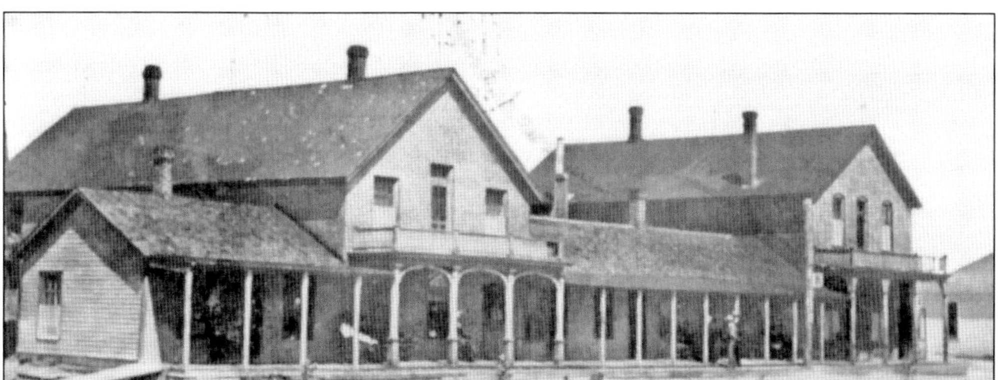

Visiting the numerous hot springs located in Jefferson County was often a treat for county residents. This photograph shows the Pipestone Hot Springs Hotel in 1909. Hazel Johnson, staying at the hotel with her family, wrote to her grandfather Bartlett Hepp explaining a more sobering reason for her visit: her father was very sick. (Courtesy of the Jefferson County Museum.)

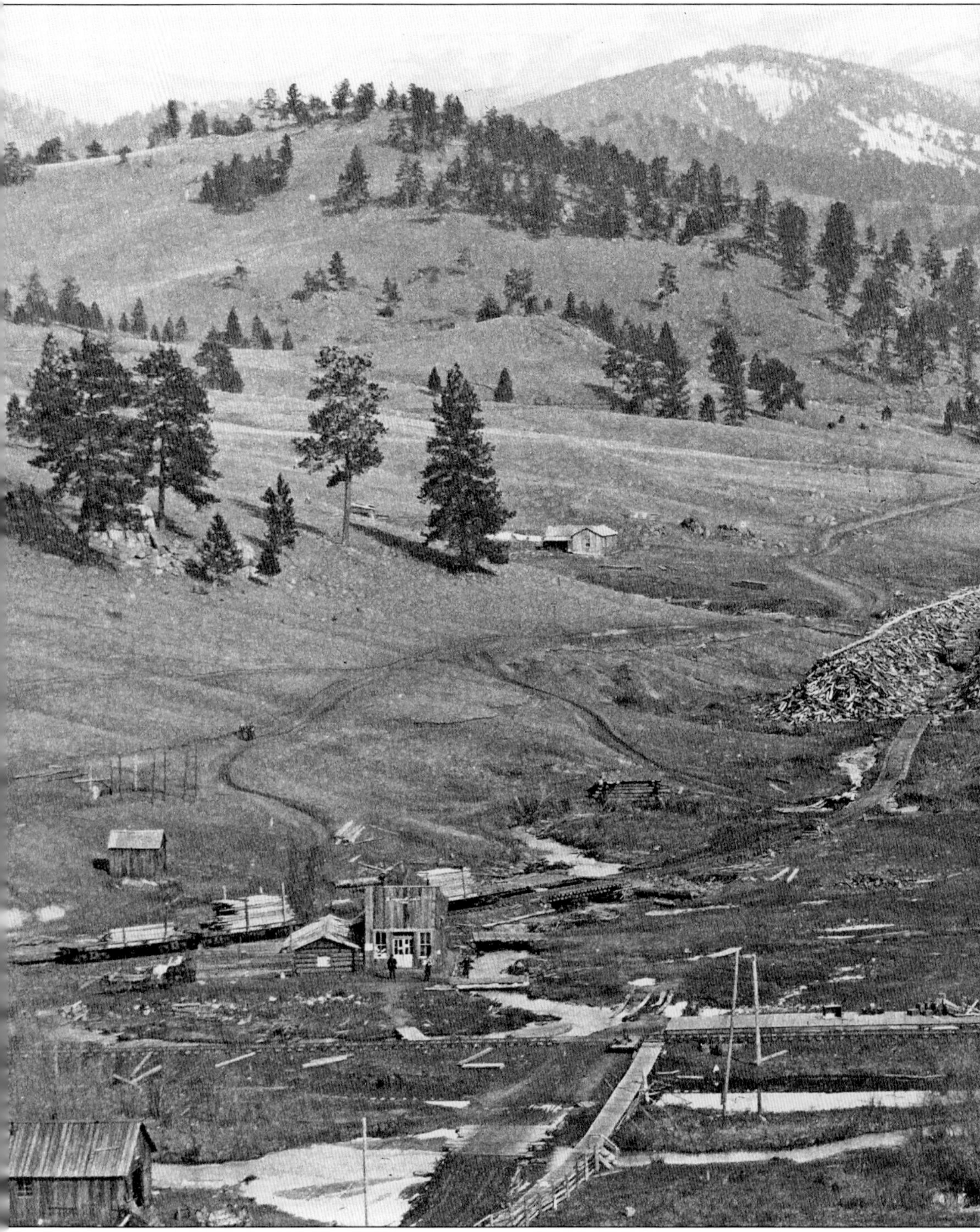

Alhambra Hot Springs, in the tiny community of Alhambra, was a luxury resort offering fine dining, lodging, and natural hot springs for soaking. When this picture was taken, the community of Alhambra still relied on the mining industry for a stable economy. However, the hot springs soon offered residents alternative employment. The Alhambra Hot Springs opened a hot springs

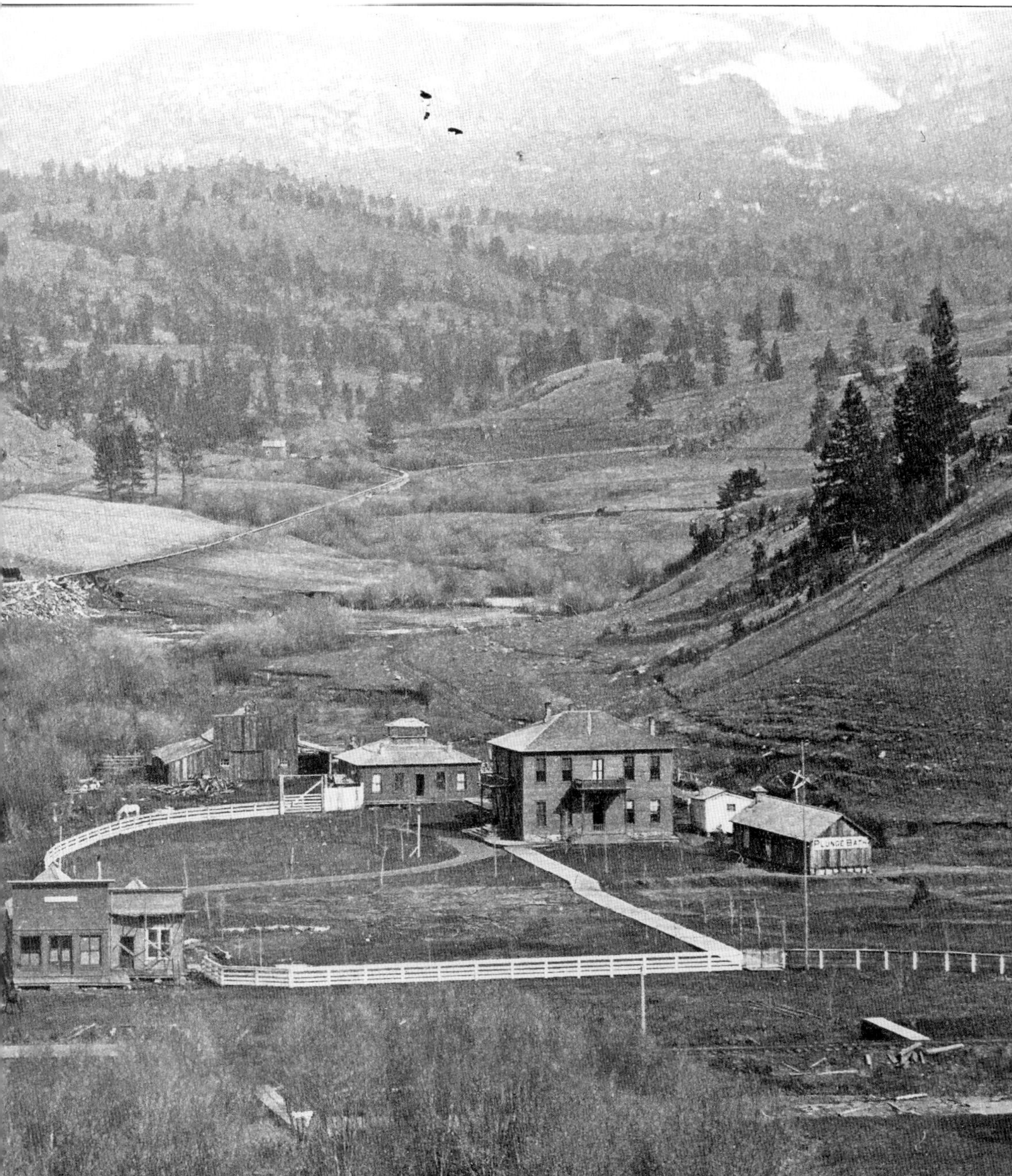

plunge bath in the smaller building to the right of the hotel. This photograph was taken prior to the addition of a grand porch on the main building and the railroad stop. The hotel later promoted the ease of rail travel by constructing a conveniently located railroad depot near the hotel. (Courtesy of the Jefferson County Museum.)

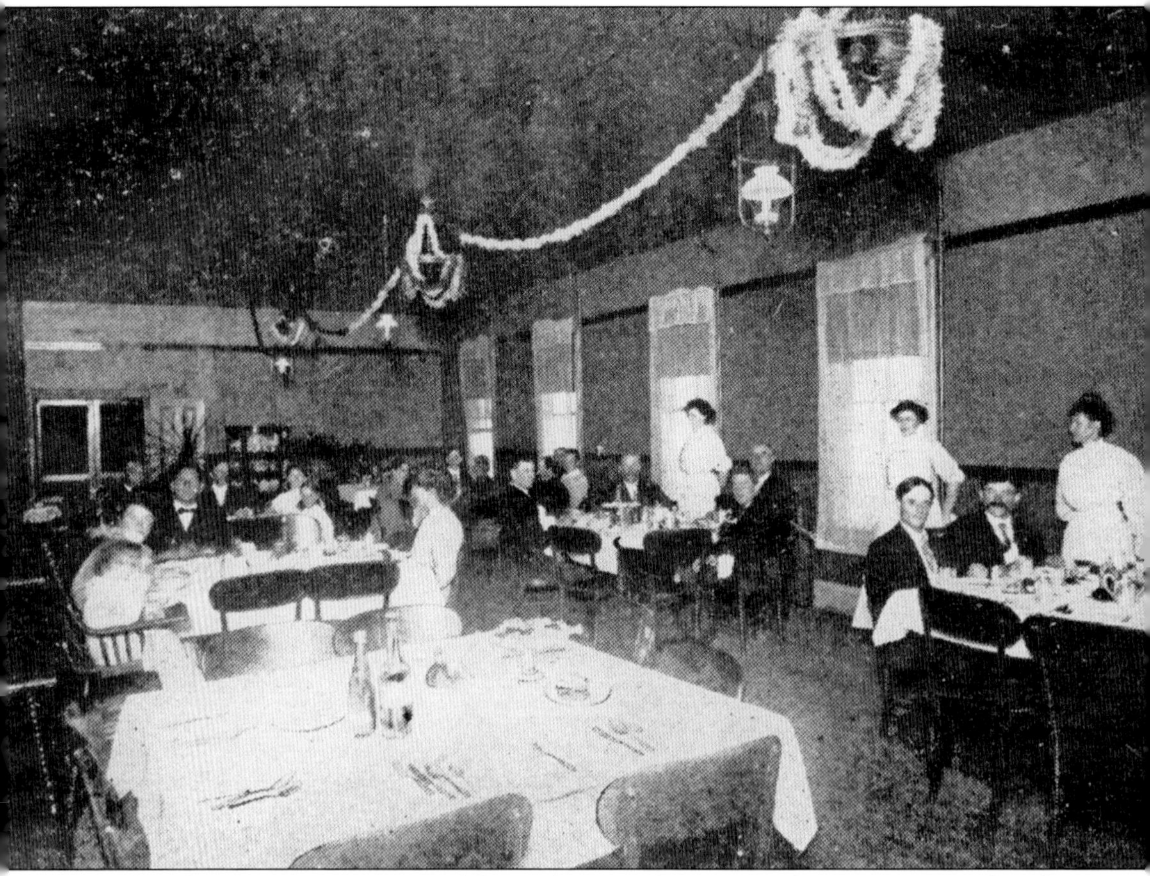

The Alhambra Hot Springs Hotel featured a main dining room for guests to enjoy fine dining and a glass of the mineral water. The on-staff doctors urged visitors to drink at least two quarts of the mineral water a day for medicinal purposes. While enjoying food from the hotel's kitchen, those staying at the hotel could read their mail or one of the daily newspapers. Guests were promised newspapers "almost as soon as if they were in the city." When visitors arrived who needed special attention, care was given to make them feel comfortable. If they were unable to eat in the dining room, the hotel would bring the meal to them in their rooms. (Courtesy of the Jefferson County Museum.)

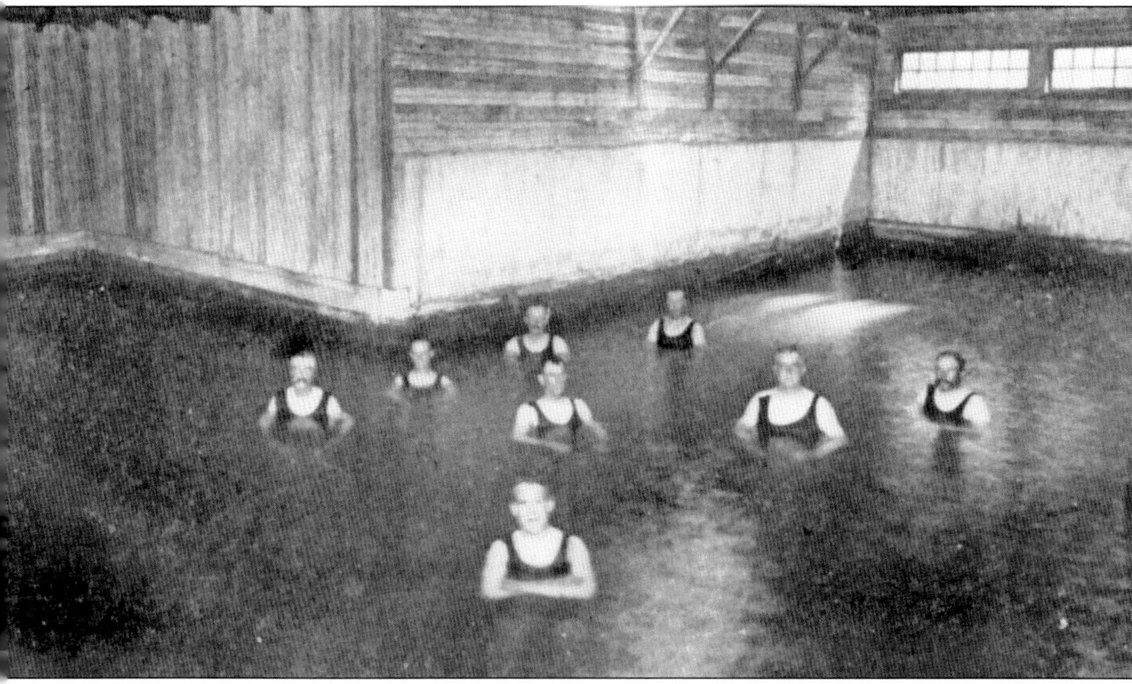

These men enjoy the indoor men's plunge bath at the Alhambra Hot Springs. The hotel contained a large public plunge in the main bathhouse for men and women to enjoy together. In addition, separate baths were available for men and women. While plunge baths were the most popular, the hotel offered segregated steam and mud baths as well. The Alhambra Hot Springs catered to individuals suffering from arthritis and advertised that attendants were on staff at all hours of the day or night to assist guests. (Courtesy of the Jefferson County Museum.)

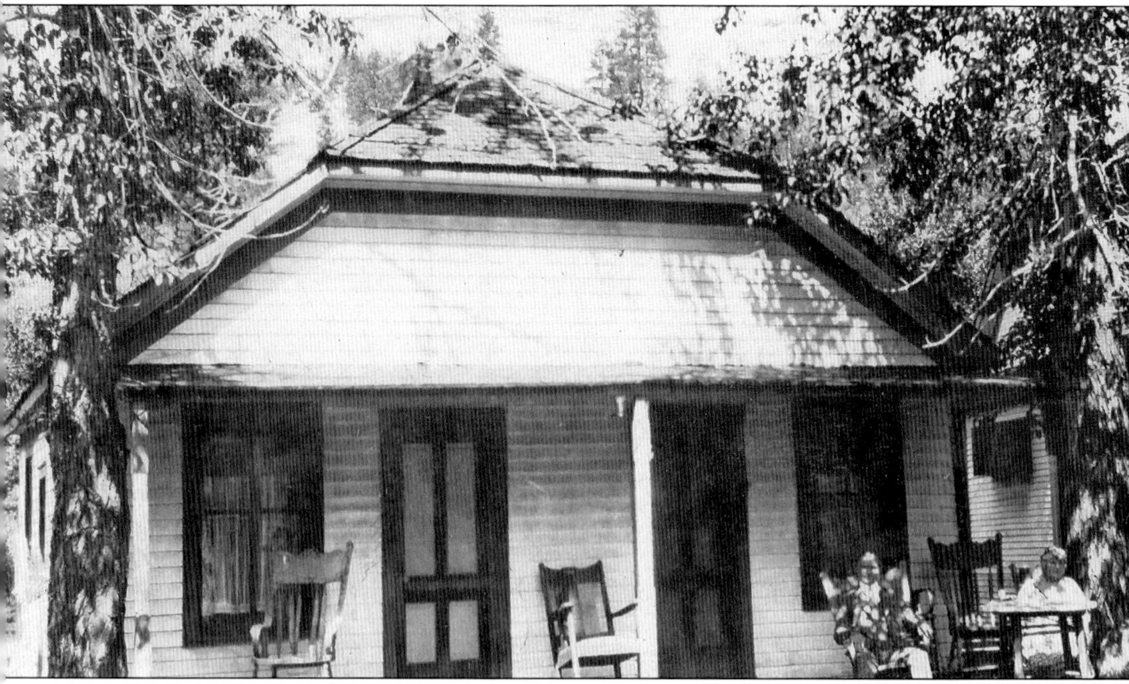

The Alhambra Hot Springs resort offered vacationers the chance to rent cottages at the rear of the main hotel building. (Courtesy of the Jefferson County Genealogy and Heritage Center, Boulder, Montana.)

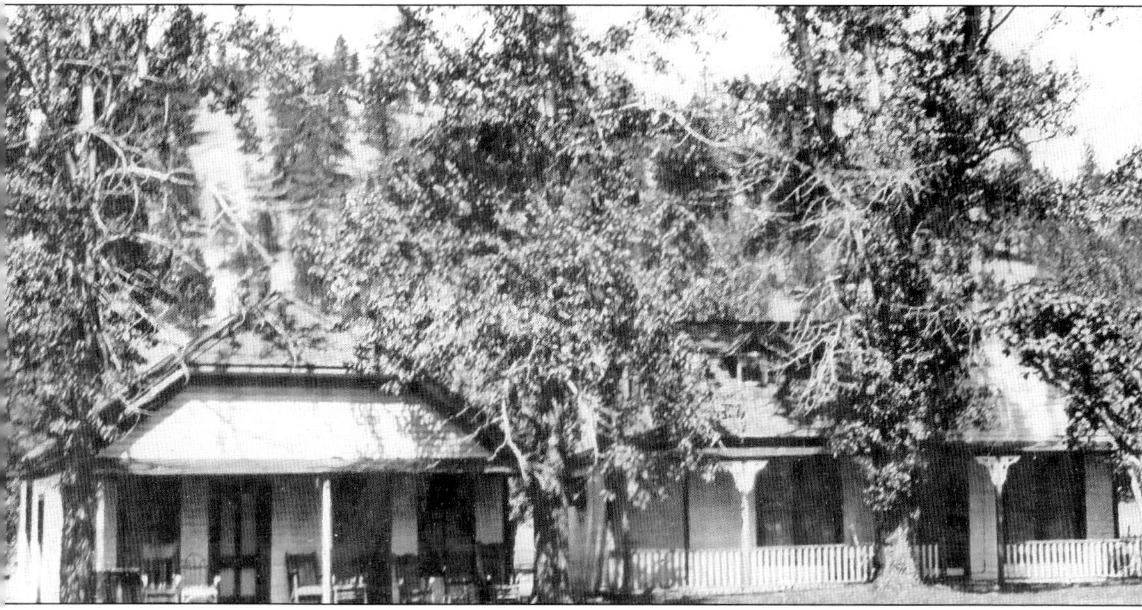

According to the June 22, 1919, *Boulder Monitor*, Wilson Redding, a Confederate officer, bought the land at Alhambra Hot Springs in 1866 from a Mr. Justine for $3,600. He later built the Alhambra Hotel on the property. Wilson Redding sold the property to Mike Sullivan, who built the cottages to accommodate additional guests. (Courtesy of the Jefferson County Genealogy and Heritage Center, Boulder, Montana.)

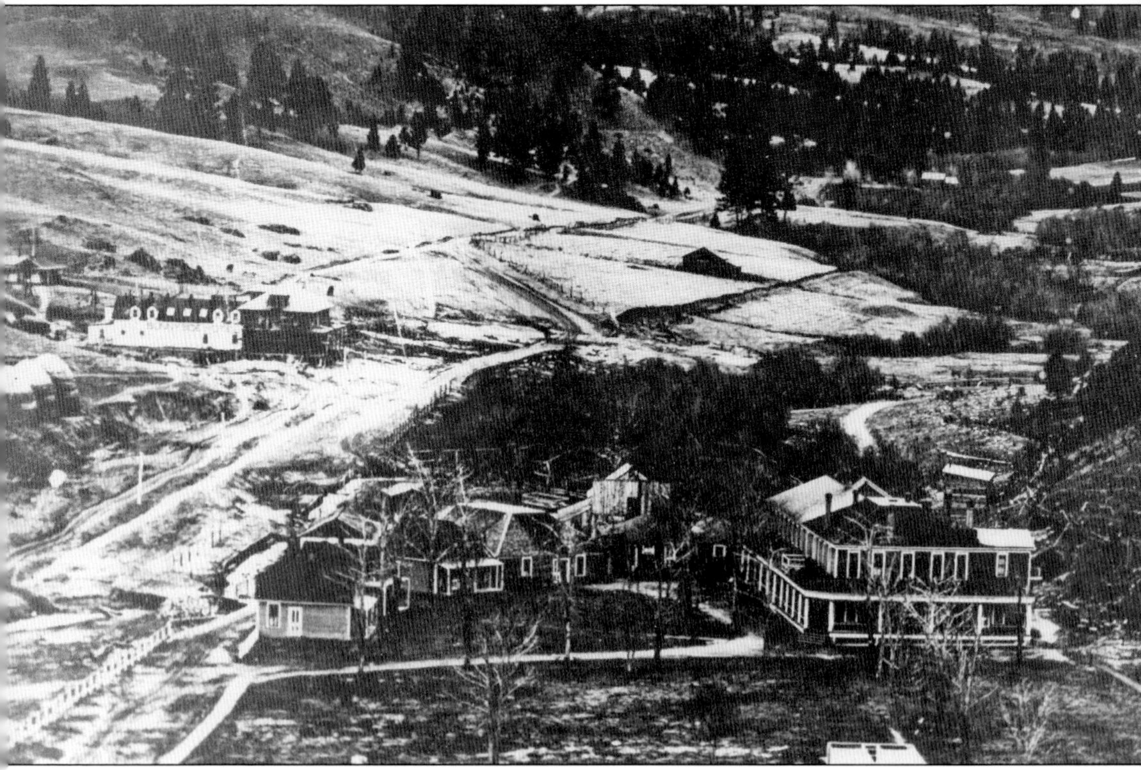

This photograph taken between 1908 and 1916 shows the Alhambra Hot Springs Hotel and its cottages as well as the Sunnyside Hotel, which also offered the opportunity to soak in hot springs. In addition to the hot springs, the residents of Alhambra operated timber and charcoal businesses. The wood products were loaded onto the railroad cars for shipment to area mines, or the wood was placed into brick kilns and heated to manufacture charcoal. The charcoal was then sent to smelters to aid in the mining process. The heavy harvesting of the trees caused the hillsides around the Alhambra Hot Springs to become devoid of vegetation. (Courtesy of the Haab family of Clancy.)

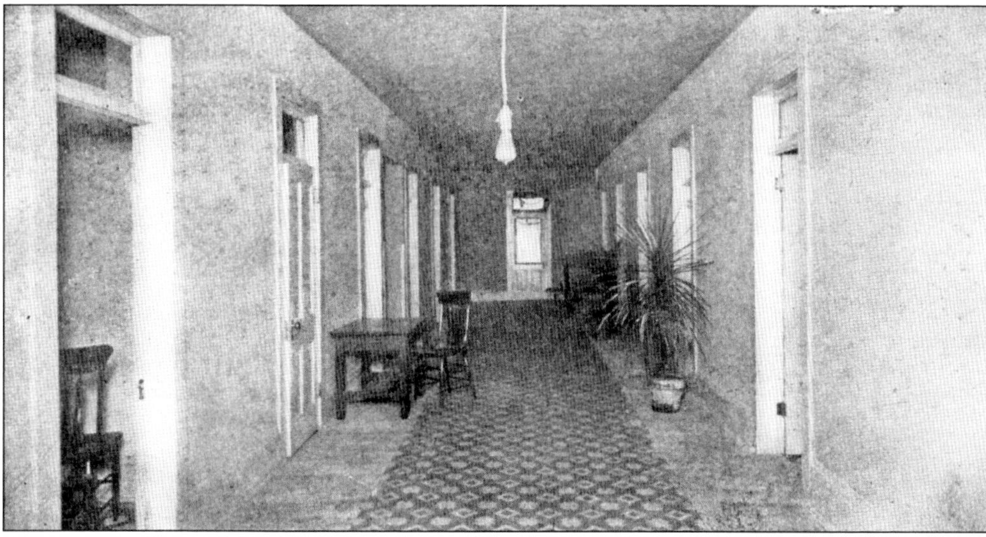

The main hallway of the Alhambra Hot Springs annex building shows a simple yet welcoming design. According to one brochure, the cost to stay in the hotel was $2.50 for the night, $15 for a week, or $55 for an entire month. The hotel provided blankets and fresh towels with each room. (Courtesy of the Jefferson County Museum.)

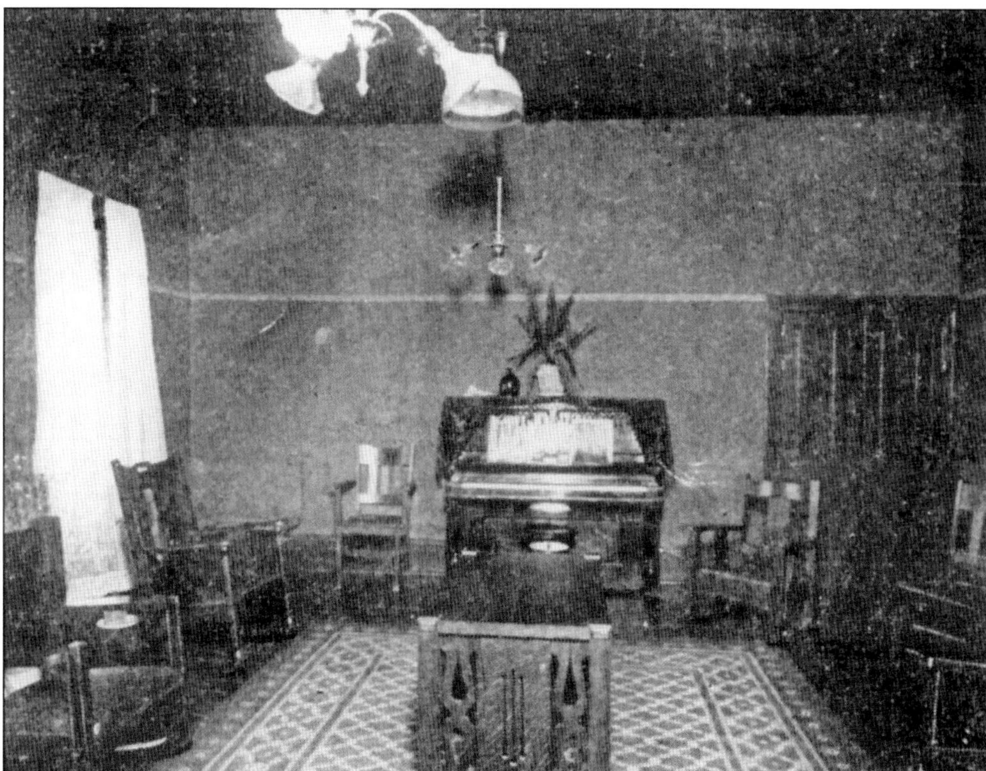

The private guest rooms at the Alhambra Hot Springs Hotel were designed to offer guests a clean and comfortable stay, but this photograph of the parlor illustrates that even common areas were luxurious. (Courtesy of the Jefferson County Museum.)

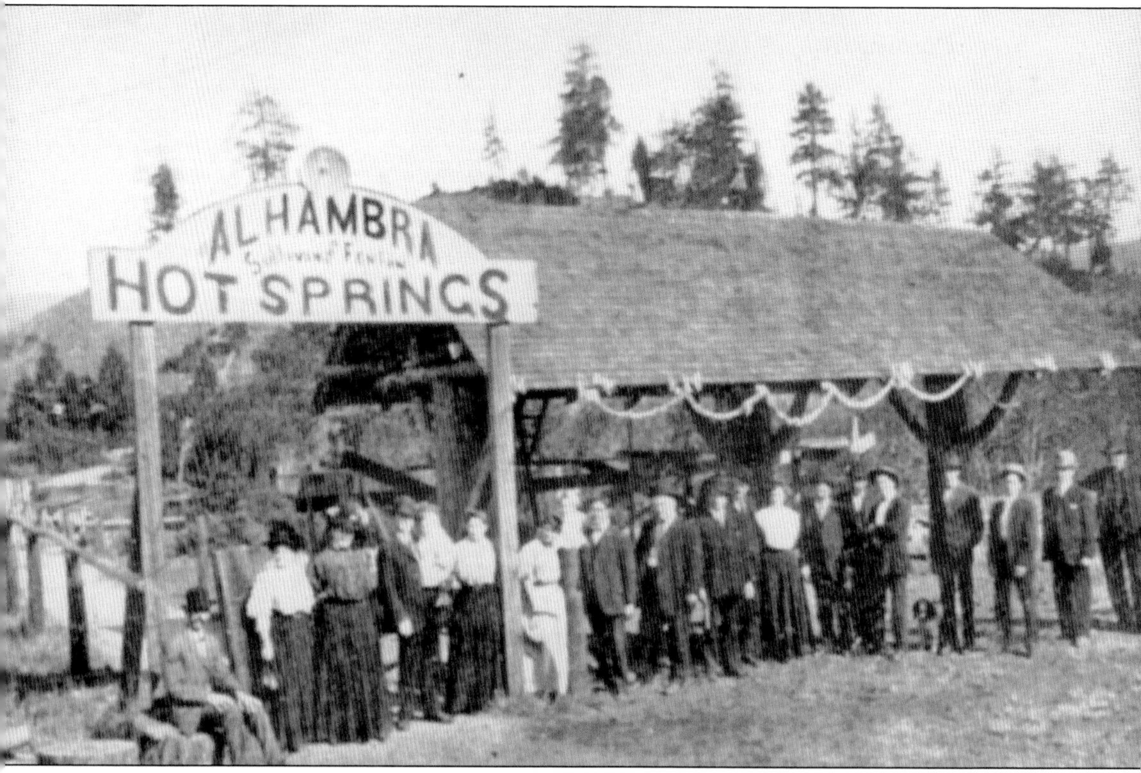

The Alhambra Hot Springs Hotel owners built an elaborate yet rustic depot just 600 feet from the resort for the convenience of their customers. The Northern Pacific Railroad had already provided a stop at Alhambra for early residents to ship mined products and timber. However, the construction of a depot ensured that hotel guests as well as townspeople would benefit from the covered shelter. (Courtesy of the Jefferson County Museum.)

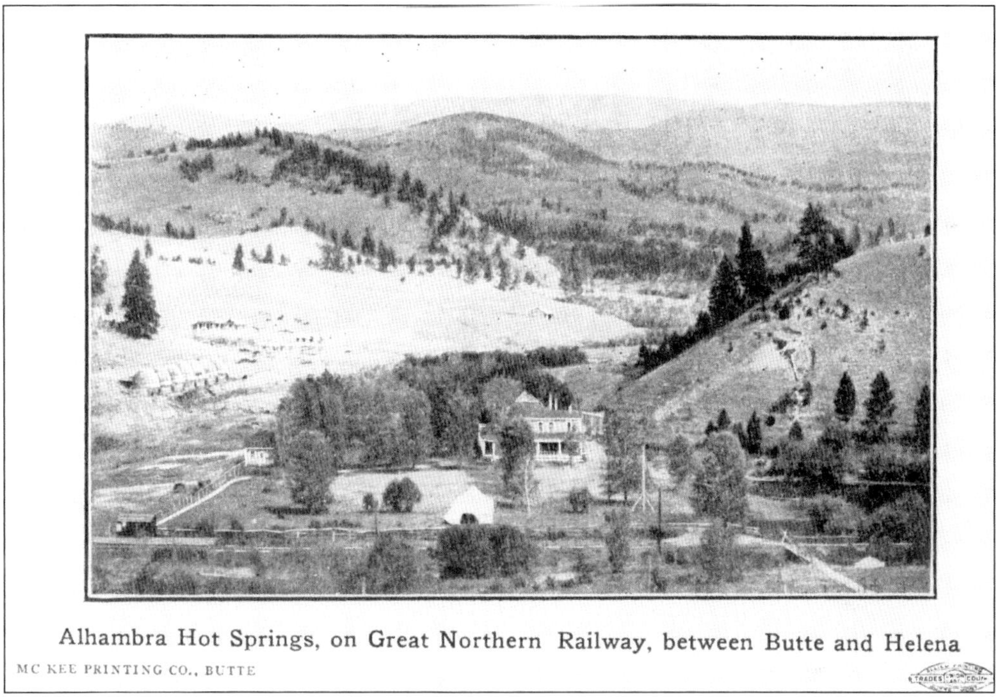

An Alhambra Hot Springs advertisement from 1908 reminds visitors of the convenience of rail travel. (Courtesy of the Jefferson County Museum.)

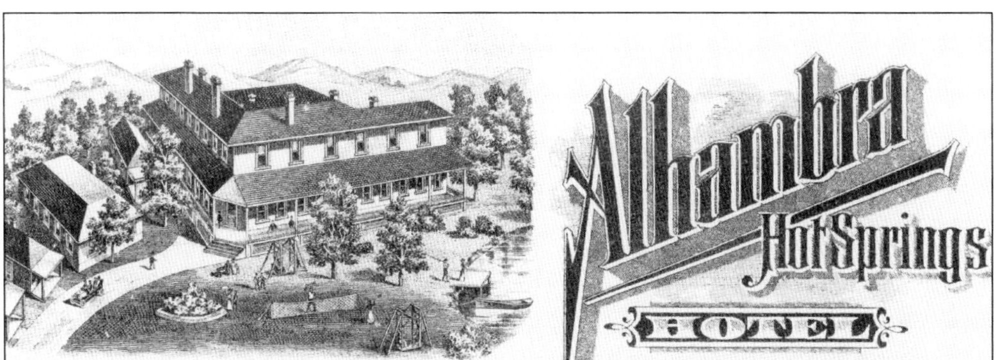

The elaborate letterhead used by the Alhambra Hot Springs depicts a detailed sketch of the resort. (Courtesy of the Jefferson County Museum.)

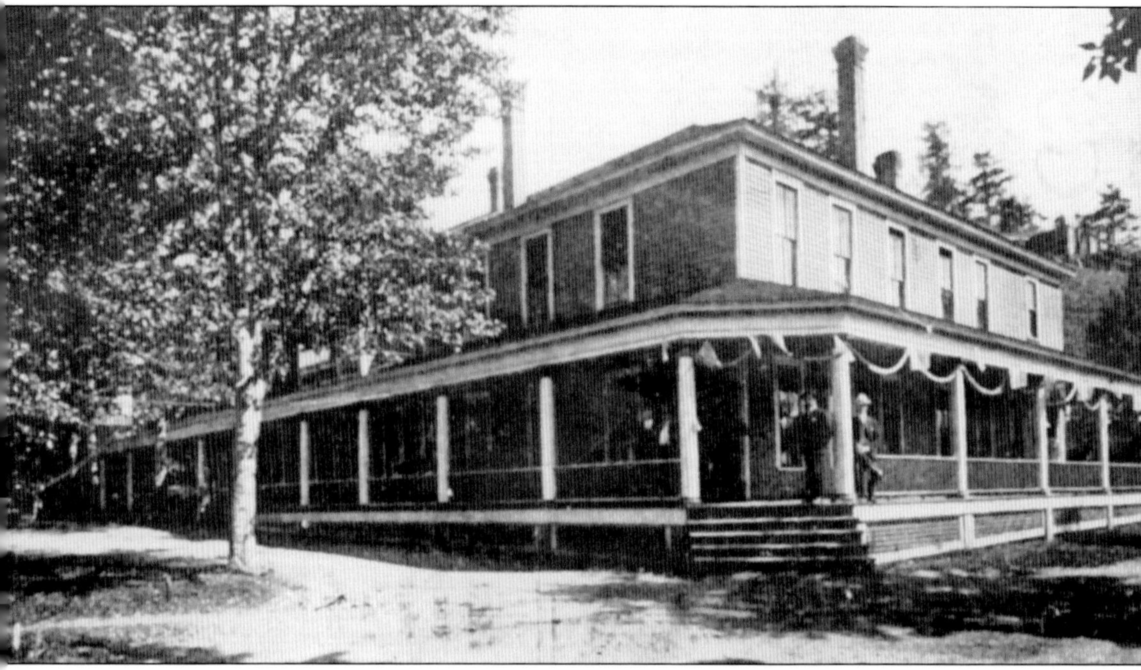

A photograph of the Alhambra Hot Springs Hotel shows a view of its wide front porch. Guests staying at the hotel were encouraged to relax on the porch and enjoy the "Garden Spot of Montana." While visitors sat on the porch admiring the views, hotel attendants offered them glasses of the mineral water. The hotel proprietors asked Emil Starz, a respected Helena chemist, to analyze the water. He claimed that the thermal waters possessed great medicinal virtues. In addition, he stated that the mineral water was beneficial for all types of stomach ailments, the kidney, liver problems, and bladder issues. His analysis showed high concentrations of calcium, magnesium, and potassium in the water. Finally, he instructed the visitors to soak at least twice a day, as the temperature of the water (129 degrees) offered relief from an array of complaints. (Courtesy of the Jefferson County Museum.)

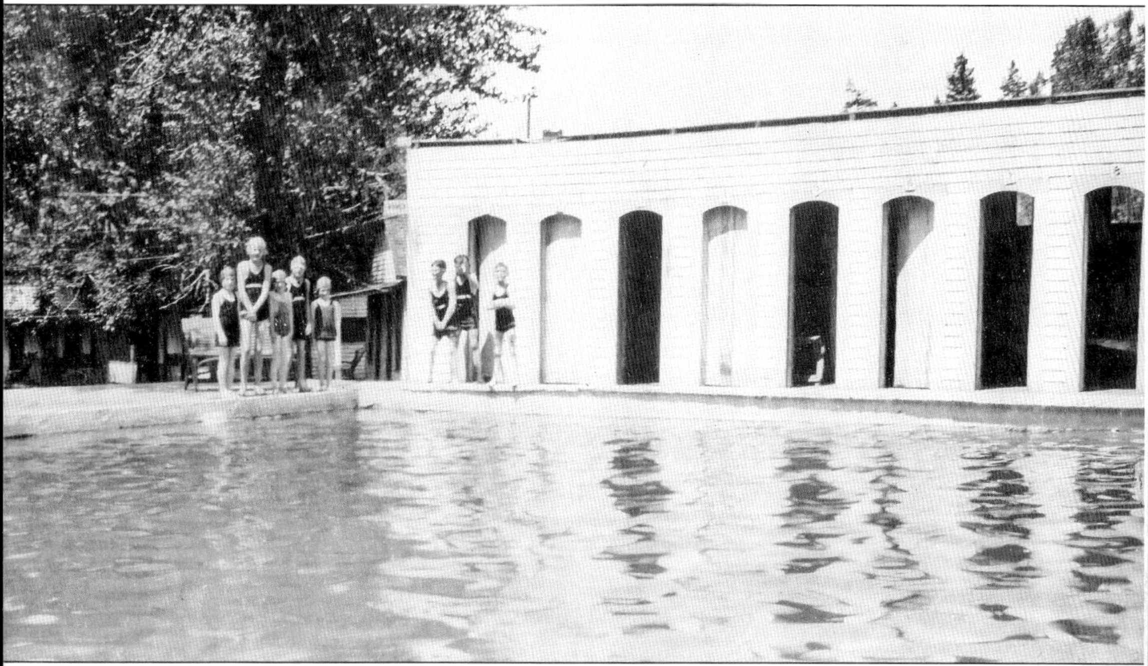

A group of youngsters prepares to take the plunge at the Alhambra Hot Springs Hotel about 1926. Early swimwear fashions dictated that the boys' and girls' modest outfits were similar in design. The girls, however, were the only ones to wear swim hats. (Courtesy of the Jefferson County Genealogy and Heritage Center, Boulder, Montana.)

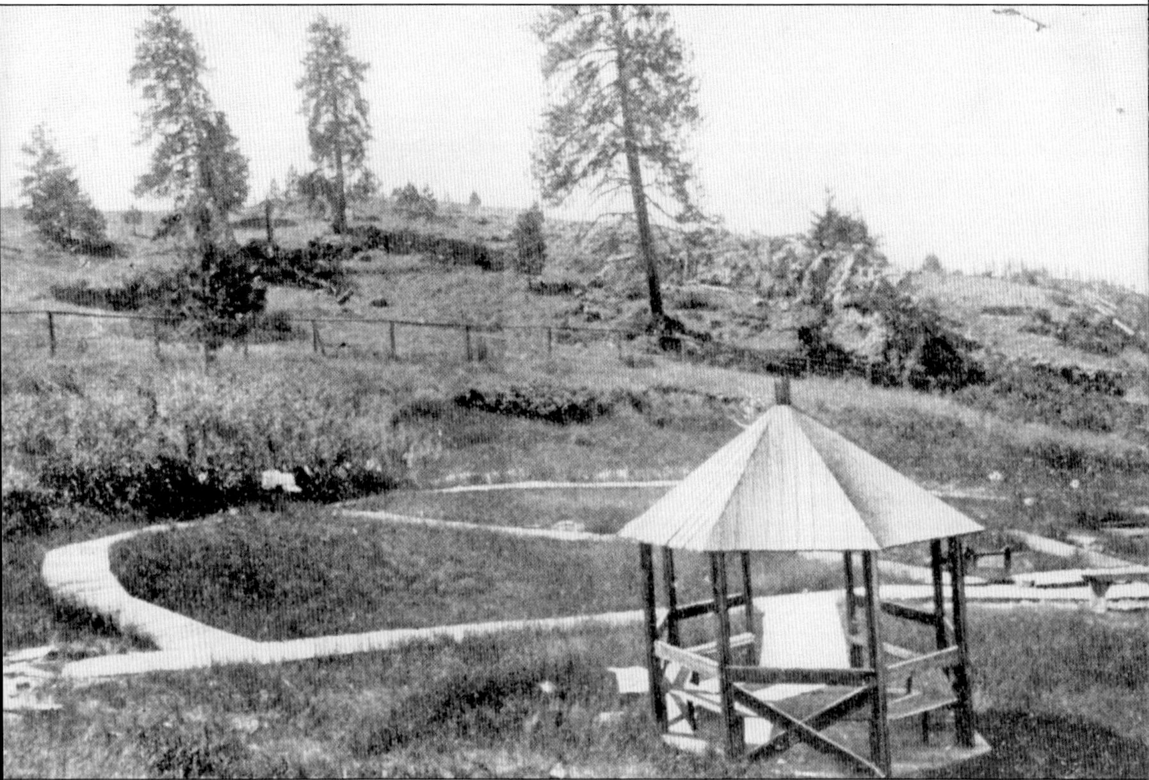

The guests at the Alhambra Hot Springs were offered an array of activities, like walking around the hotel grounds on a wooden boardwalk, sitting under a gazebo, fishing, or renting horses to ride into the surrounding mountains. (Courtesy of the Jefferson County Museum.)

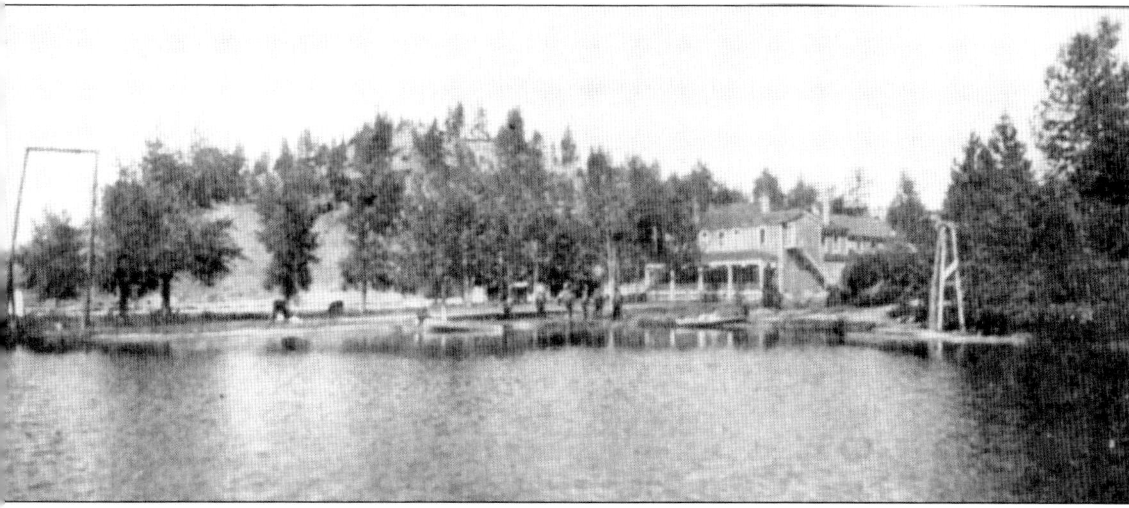

The outdoor pond at the Alhambra Hot Springs was kept well stocked with trout. The hotel also advertised plenty of deer, elk, pheasant, and grouse hunting for the outdoorsman. (Courtesy of the Jefferson County Museum.)

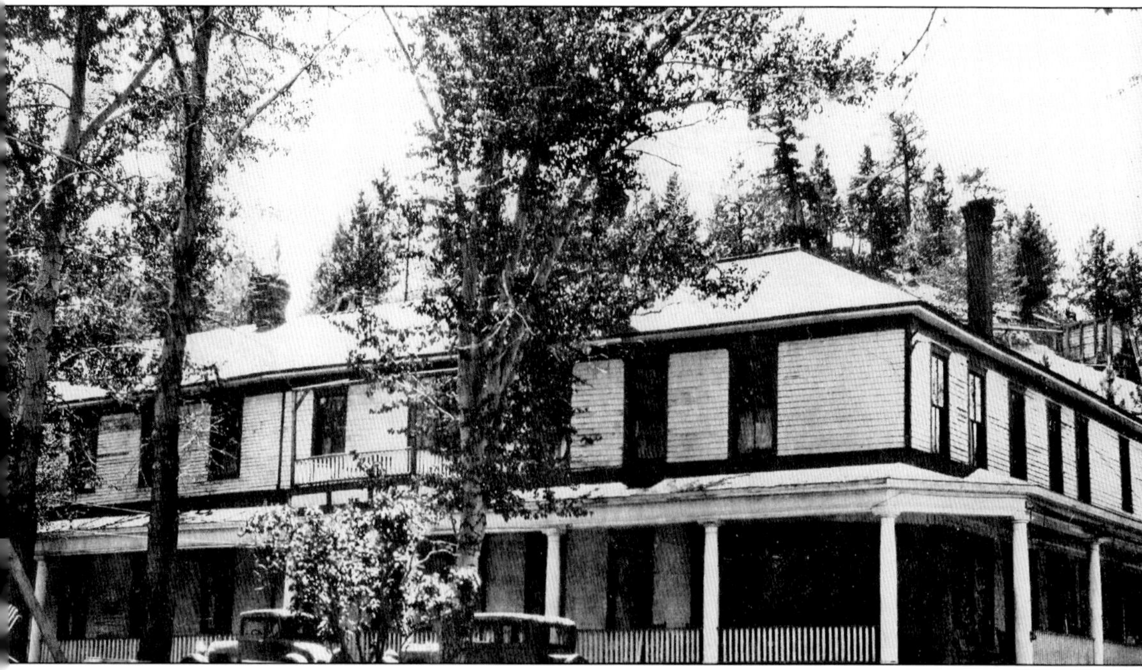

The Alhambra Hot Springs resort is shown in a photograph from about 1926. Guests conveniently parked their early automobiles next to the front porch. One hotel brochure invited visitors to admire "the stately trees and graceful avenues" as they approached the resort. (Courtesy of the Jefferson County Genealogy and Heritage Center, Boulder, Montana.)

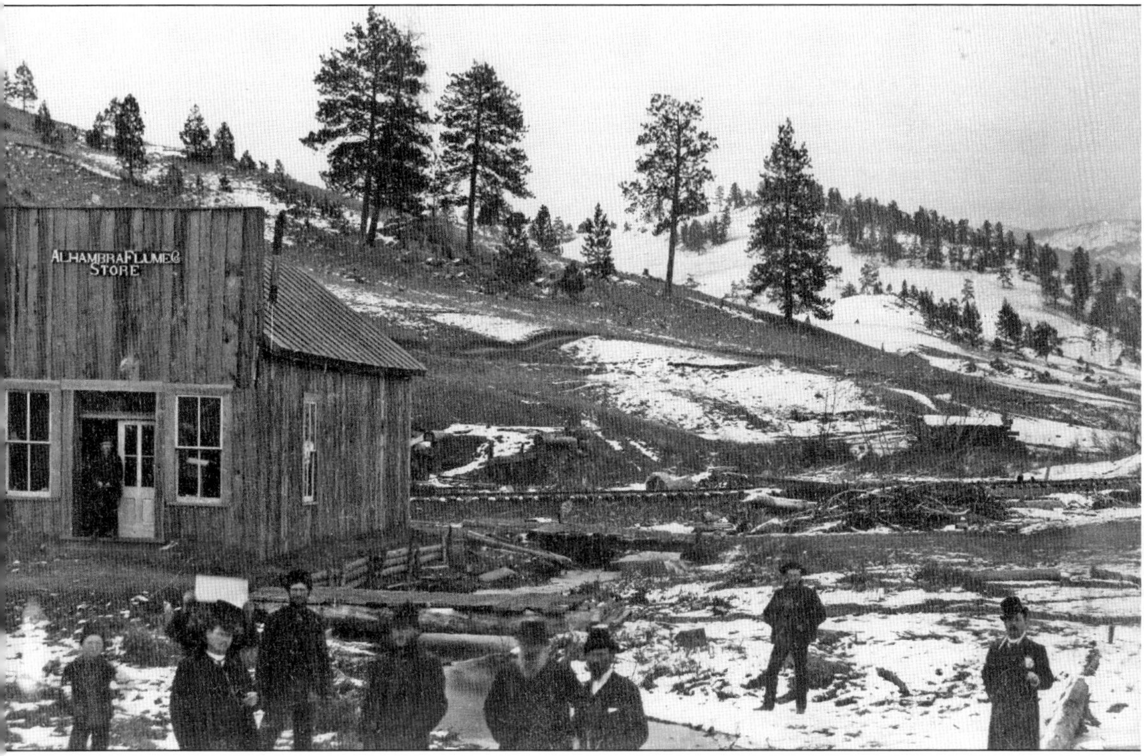

Located next to the Alhambra Hot Springs, the Alhambra Flume and Store used water from Warm Springs Creek to provide services for the mines in the area. (Courtesy of the Jefferson County Museum.)

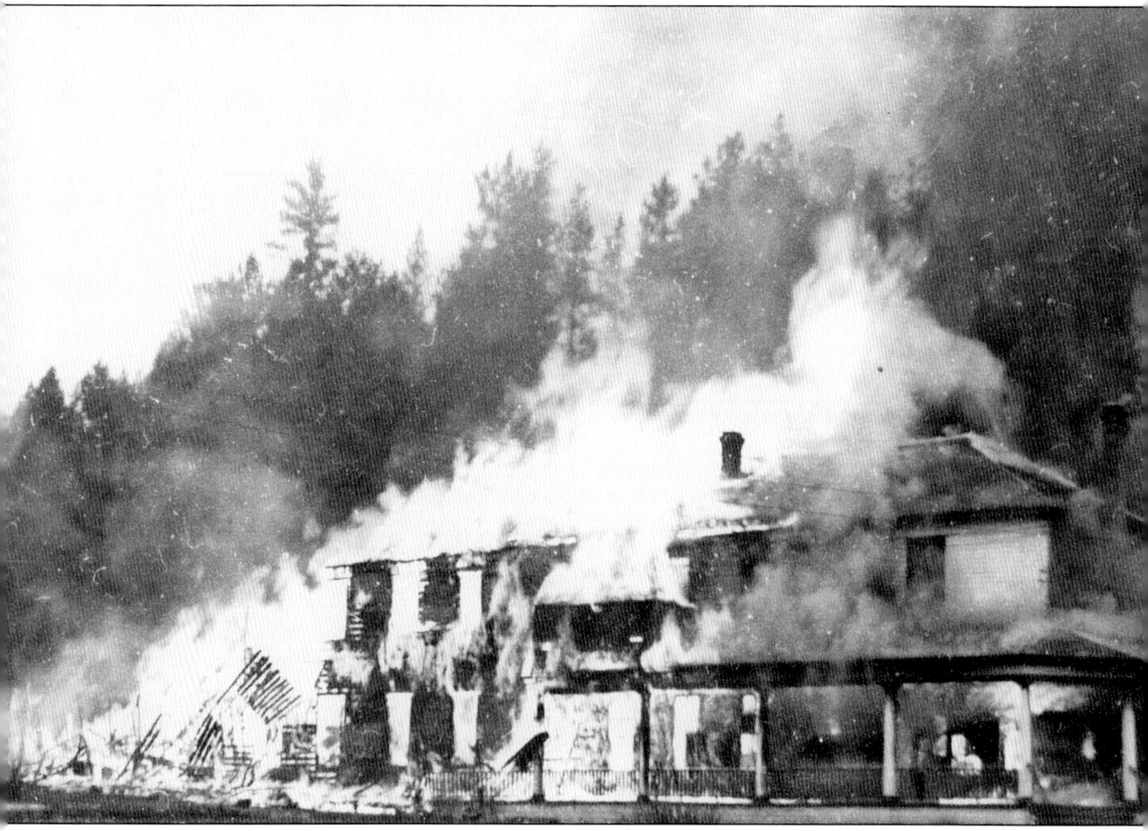

The lovely Alhambra Hot Springs Hotel was consumed by flames on April 24, 1959. According to the May 2, 1959, issue of the *Boulder Monitor*, the fire started at about 5:00 p.m., and by 6:30 p.m., the building was completely destroyed. The owner, W. L. Bompart, told the newspaper that he had just completed a $25,000 remodel that was not insured. The guests staying at the 34-room hotel lost all their possessions. An old player piano was the only piece of furniture to be saved. (Courtesy of the Jefferson County Museum.)

Bibliography

Anderson, Jan. "Last Legal Hanging in Jefferson County." *Whitehall Ledger* (Wednesday, August 5, 1992): 1, 10.

Atwater, Mary Meigs. *Weaving a Life: The Story of Mary Meigs Atwater.* Compiled by Mary Reiter and edited by Veronica Patterson. Loveland, CO: Interweave Press, 1992.

Carlson, Gustaf M. Papers. Montana Historical Society, Helena.

Filpula, Joan. *Woodville—Trask and the Elk Park Valley: Its History and the People.* Butte, MT: Joan Filpula, 2004.

Hagadone, Olive. *Boulder: Its Friends and Neighbors. Boulder Monitor* (April 18, 1985–August 25, 1986), reprinted with permission by the Jefferson County Genealogy Society, 2003.

———. *Surname Index and Small Biographies.* Boulder, MT: The Jefferson County Genealogy Society, 2003.

Hauser, Samuel Thomas. Papers. Montana Historical Society, Helena.

Milligan, Roy. "100 Years Ago, Whitehall—1909." *Tumbleweed Trails* 15 (2008): 2.

"Mining News." *Northwest Magazine*, May 1895.

Peterka, Fr. Dale. "GN's Montana Central Railway." *Great Northern Railway Historical Society* no. 259 (1998): 5, 9, 12, 15.

Ryan, Edward. Papers. Montana Historical Society, Helena.

Society of Montana Pioneers. Society of Montana Pioneers Records. Montana Historical Society, Helena.

Taylor, Bill, and Jan Taylor. *Rails to Gold and Silver: Lines to Montana Mining 1883–1887.* Missoula, MT: Pictorial Histories Publishing, 1999.

Toole, K. Ross. *Montana: An Uncommon Land.* Norman, OK: University of Oklahoma Press, 1959.

Wolle, Muriel Sibell. *Montana Pay Dirt: A Guide to the Mining Camps of the Treasure State.* Denver, CO: Sage Books, 1963; Athens, OH: Swallow Press, 1983.

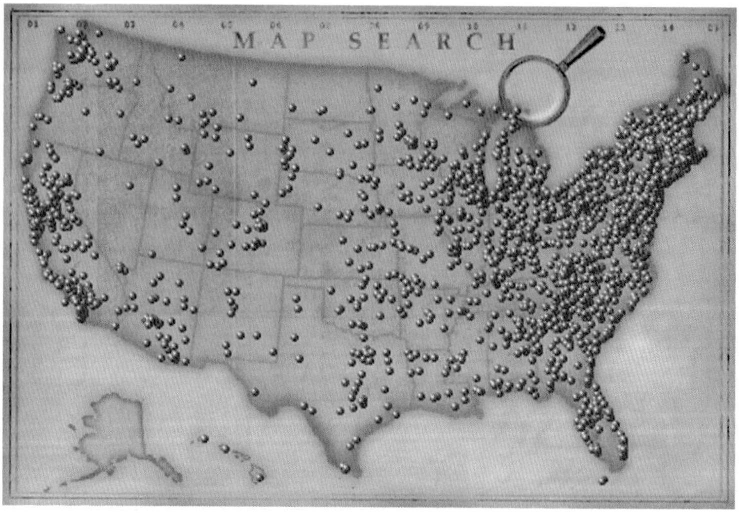
MAP SEARCH